Aoraki Mount Cook

A guide to mountaineering in the Aoraki/Mount Cook region, including the Westland Glaciers and Godley Valley.

Alex Palman

Published by the New Zealand Alpine Club 2001

1

About the author

Alex is originally from Auckland (although, he probably won't admit to it) but is now based in Wellington. Primary school days were spent in Twizel, just down the road from Aoraki/Mount Cook National Park. It was there his parents, Andy and Marie, first introduced him to the magnificent New Zealand outdoors, by dragging him up to Mueller Hut at age six (some say it was the other way around). It was obvious the Copland Pass would follow when he was at high school and since then he hasn't stopped climbing in the region for 19 years. Never short of energy, Alex enjoys all types of climbing; ice, rock, sportclimbing (in which he has represented NZ) and particularly alpine rock, which is evident in parts of this guidebook.

Ensuring he didn't miss a season of climbing he chose Empress Hut to base his fieldwork for a thesis in glaciation. After graduating from Canterbury University with an M.Sc. (Hons), in 1994, he began work at Macpac. He presently works as a Marketing Executive for the Energy Efficiency and Conservation Authority. Although Alex published *Balfour Rock* in 1998 and has written the odd article for mountaineering journals and magazines, he feels much more comfortable on the side of a mountain.

© New Zealand Alpine Club 2001

First Edition: 1982

Second Edition: 1987

Third Printing: 1993

Fourth Printing & Supplement: 1994

Third edition - revised and enlarged from Hugh Logan's second edition.
Published by the New Zealand Alpine Club, 2001
Design and typesetting: CPIT Publishing Unit.
Printed by Saxon PPP

ISBN 0-9597630-1-5

The spirit of the mountains calls one unceasingly and bids one to understand. Those to whose spirit it has spoken can never more be sundered from it though seas and other lands lie between, for they bear the memory of it about in their hearts continually, as if it were a new strength.

Peter Graham New Zealand Mountain Guide (1878-1961)

New Zealand Topographic Maps (260 series, 1:50,000 scale): Mount Cook; H36, Tasman; H37, Whataroa; I35 Godley; I36, Lake Tekapo; I37 and Franz Josef; H34, G35, H35. The Aoraki/Mount Cook Alpine Area map (1:50,000) is also very useful but its future availability is unknown. Also, electronic maps are now available – see the information section at the back of the guide.

The Story of Aoraki – the ancestor of Ngai Tahu

In the beginning there was no Te Wai Pounamu or Aotearoa. The waters of Kiwa rolled over the place now occupied by the South, North and Stewart Islands. No sign of land existed. Raki, the Sky Father, wedded Papa-tua-nuku, the Earth Mother. After the marriage, some of the Sky Children came down to greet their father's new wife.

Among the celestial visitors were four sons of Raki who were named Ao-raki (Cloud in the Sky), Raki-roa (Long Raki), Raki-rua (Raki the Second) and Raraki-roa (the Long Unbroken Line). They came down in a canoe, known as Te Waka o Aoraki. They cruised around Papa-tua-nuku, who lay as one body in a huge continent known as Hawaiiki. Then, keen to explore, the voyagers set out to sea, but no matter how far they traveled, they could not find land. They decided to return to their celestial home, but the karakia (incantation) which should have lifted the waka (canoe) back to the heavens failed and the canoe fell back into the sea and turned over onto its side, turning to stone and earth in the process. The waka listed and settled with the west side much higher out of the water than the east. Thus the whole waka formed the South Island, hence the name: Te Waka o Aoraki.

Aoraki and his brothers clambered onto the high side and were turned to stone also. They are still there today. Aoraki is the mountain known to Europeans as Mount Cook, and his brothers are the next highest peaks near him – Rakiroa (Mount Dampier, the third highest peak), Rakirua (Mount Teichelmann) and Rarakiroa (Mount Tasman, the second highest peak). The form of the island now owes much to the subsequent deeds of Tu Te Rakiwhanoa, who took on the job of shaping the land to make it fit for human habitation.

For Ngai Tahu, the iwi (tribe) of the eastern South Island, traditions such as this represent the links between the cosmological world of the Gods and present generations. These histories reinforce tribal identity and solidarity, and document the events that shaped the environment of Te Wai Pounamu and Ngai Tahu as an iwi.

The meltwaters that flow from Aoraki are sacred. On special occasions of cultural moment, the blessings of Aoraki are sought through taking of small amounts of its 'special' waters back to other parts of the island for use in ceremonial occasions.

The mauri of Aoraki represents the essence that binds the physical and spiritual elements of all things together, generating and upholding all life. All elements of the natural environment possess a life force, and all forms of life are related. Mauri is a critical element of the spiritual relationship of Ngai Tahu Whanui with the mountain.

'He kapua kei runga I Aoraki, whakarewa whakarewa' ('the cloud that floats aloft Aoraki, for every fly, stay aloft'). This saying refers to the cloud that often surrounds Aoraki. Aoraki does not always 'come out' for visitors to see, just as a great chief is not always giving audience, or on 'show'. It is for Aoraki to choose when to emerge from his cloak of mist, a power and influence that is beyond mortals, symbolizing the mana of Aoraki.

To Ngai Tahu, Aoraki represents the most sacred of ancestors, who provides the iwi with its sense of communal identity, solidarity and purpose. It follows that the ancestor embodied in the mountain remains the physical manifestation of Aoraki, the link between the supernatural and the natural world. The tapu associated with Aoraki is a significant dimension of the tribal value, and is the source of the power over life and death which the mountain possesses.

The high mountains inspire fear, awe and respect, for they are the places of the atua and other spirits. Generally, Maori would not climb to the summits of tapu mountains. The bones of high-ranking men and women were laid to rest in burial caves on their tapu mountain. However, the songs, poetry and speeches on the marae of Ngai Tahu are full of references to Aoraki. The high places are the most significant landmarks, tribal associations and relationships.

Ngai Tahu seek to encourage respect for their association with Aoraki by providing education material to climbers and guides, explaining that standing on the very top of this mountain denigrates its tapu status.

Kia tuohu koutou, Me he maunga teitei, Ko Aoraki anake
If you must bow your head, then let it be to the lofty mountain Aoraki.

General information

The coverage of this guide

This guide covers the Aoraki/Mount Cook region of the Southern Alps from Mt Marie, near Barron Saddle in the south, to Cumine Peak, at the head of the Godley Valley in the north. The Liebig Range forms part of the eastern boundary of the guide coverage. Within this area there are five large valley systems, all east of the Main Divide (Ka Tiritiri O Te Moana). It also includes a series of remote high glacier and névés in the west.

All the valleys have long glacier approaches, with extensive moraine at lower altitudes. The routes up the valleys generally involve glacier travel and even the climbs to the huts can be very demanding (sometimes more taxing than the climbs beyond them). It is normally half a day's walk to the main alpine huts in the east, and longer in the west unless air access is used. In some instances four-wheel drive access is necessary, or if you are keen, mountainbikes can be used for access to the Godley and Macaulay valleys and Ball Shelter.

Signing in & useful information

Before beginning any trip to these remote huts and peaks climbers should 'sign-in' at the Aoraki/Mount Cook National Park Visitor Centre, in the village, and check current conditions with park staff. The park and the centre are managed by the Department of Conservation (DoC). The sign-in system involves filling in a card with the names of those in your party and your intentions - and importantly, informing the Visitor Centre of your return. After hours, cards can be filled in and deposited via a mail slot at the front of the Visitor Centre. Also, advise park staff in advance if you plan to arrive in the park from other directions (for example a transalpine trip from the Dobson). This system is not a bureaucratic restraint but a voluntary and essential aid in the case of an accident. Only fools ignore it.

Additional information can be obtained at the Visitor Centre, such as numbers in huts, and access to them, as well as weather forecasts. There is also a notice board for climbers looking for partners. Up to the minute forecasts can be obtained by calling a range of listed pay-per-call weather service phone numbers and/or by visiting websites (see the back section of the guide). Internet access and pay-phones are available at the Hermitage Hotel. At the Franz Josef and Fox Glacier Vistor Centres, similar signing in systems are operated. Weather and other information is also available.

Glacier and avalanche country
Climbing in the Aoraki/Mount Cook region is a serious undertaking by any standards. The climbs almost always require a certain amount of snow, ice and rock equipment, with the former two also being vital for approaches. Glacier approaches typically include white ice and heavily crevassed snow-covered sections. The latter are potentially lethal if a climber falls into a crevasse unroped. As a general rule parties should travel roped up when traversing glaciers beyond the white ice.

Avalanche activity and danger within the region is generally high: icecliff, slabs and wet snow avalanches are the most common. The relatively warm temperatures, steep terrain and high precipitation cause considerable movement in the glaciers, and a large number of ice avalanches result, affecting many routes. As a rule slab avalanches occur between April and December, but beware of these at any time of the year after snowfalls. Slabs tend to form on lee slopes. Wet snow avalanches (especially point-releases) are generally a summer phenomenon, but can occur in winter, especially at low altitudes.

Statistics show that the majority of avalanches, resulting in fatalities, are started by the victim or their party. This suggests that climbers and back-country users need to be more aware of the condition of the terrain they are travelling across. Information about snow and avalanche conditions is available from park staff and Alpine Guides (Aoraki) (web details in the back section of the guidebook).

In 1993 New Zealand adopted the international standard frequency for avalanche transceivers (457 kHz – DIN 32924). Avalanche tranceivers can be hired from Alpine Guides in the village, and from some outdoor shops and clubs.

Red rock
This region is made up of a sequence of metamorphosed sedimentary rock derived from sandstone, siltstone and mudstone, interbedded in varying proportions. It is made up of easily fractured greywackes and argillites. Greywacke, a sandstone, is a hard but brittle rock and is generally grey, however it can be pinkish, orange and red in colour – all indicating good rock. These colourations are due to surface weathering

(called a weathering rind), and this helpfully creates an excellent frictional surface for climbing. The Malte Brun Range, Ben Ohau and Liebig Ranges, Mts Nazomi, Drake and Magellan and a few others all show this character, and offer superb rockclimbing. Argillite on the other hand is the ugly sister. It is a mudstone and typically black (also brown and green), has a slate-like appearance and shatters very easily. Climbers often politely call it 'weetbix'. The alternating strata of the two rock types are tilted to various degrees but reach a maximum angle near the Main Divide. In places, buttresses (greywacke) and gullies (argillite), side by side, have formed as a result of the various resistances of the two rock types. To the west of the Main Divide another rock type is prevalent: schist, which has a layered construction and contains shiny micas and sometimes iron pyrites (Fool's Gold). It can provide good climbing when it forms slabs but can also be friable.

The weather – the bad news and the good news

The weather in the region is highly changeable and difficult to predict – in fact it can be quite volatile. Extremes define the region: winter conditions in summer, rainfalls that wash out roads and nor'west storms that peel roofs off houses as though they were made from cardboard. Understandably, the weather is a major climbing constraint in the Aoraki/Mount Cook region.

So why is the weather so changeable?

New Zealand's mountain weather is dominated by moist westerly winds that flow across the Tasman Sea and are forced to rise and cool as they pass over the Southern Alps. These cooled winds release their water on the western slopes (but commonly spill over into the eastern side) in the form of rain or snow. The drier air then descends to the east, creating warm dry nor'westers over the Canterbury and Otago regions (Europeans will know this type of wind as the Föhn or Mistral and North Americans, as the Chinook). As a result the ranges further east generally have better weather. This pattern follows roughly a 6-10 day cycle. The westerly flow is brought about by depressions (cold fronts) that usually pass to the south of the country. Between these cold fronts, ridges of high pressure (anticyclones) usually bring light winds and generally fine weather. Sometimes a depression will travel directly over the South Island and deliver biblical quantities of rain, on other occasions a slow-moving anticyclone can bring long periods of fine climbing weather.

The free-air freezing level (which influences snow surface condition) is usually about 1650m in winter and 3200m in summer. At Aoraki/Mount Cook Village (764m) the average temperature in winter is 2°C, and 14°C in summer. One of the coldest temperatures, -20°C, was recorded at the airport and at the other end of the scale 32°C has been recorded in the village.

Sunburn is a major problem because of the relatively clean air and the thinner ozone coverage in this part of the world. The problem is exacerbated on glaciers and at altitude. Take and use plenty of suncream and cover up.

On average, in summer, there is about one good day in three, so climbers with only a couple of days on their hands will need to either cross their fingers or invest more time. The good news is that bad weather in the mountains generally means good weather for rockclimbing down the road at Twin Stream or at crags further east.

Winter climbing conditions

Winter conditions usually prevail at Aoraki/Mount Cook from May, and can extend into November or even later. The weather during winter tends to be more stable, and long fine periods are common. Despite the fine weather, temperatures in June and July can plummet, so expect things to get nippy. Also, snow can lie up to half a metre thick around the village and environs, which can limit vehicle access to Ball Road and the camping ground. Climbing during the months of June, July, August and September is a serious undertaking and requires good equipment and a sound understanding of avalanche conditions. Access to climbing huts and routes can be difficult, touring skis or snow shoes are necessary at times.

Despite the additional difficulties, most of the peaks and routes mentioned in the guide have been climbed in winter. During winter there tend to be fewer people in the hills, which can be an added bonus for those looking for a quieter experience.

How to get there

From Christchurch and Queenstown there are Intercity/Newmans and Great Sights bus services. There are also a number of other bus and shuttle services (Atomic Shuttles, Southern Link Shuttles) that travel from Christchurch to Queenstown, stopping at Twizel and Pukaki, then connecting services can take you the remaining 63km to the Aoraki/Mount Cook Village (High Country Shuttles). Mount Cook Airlines offers a daily flight from Christchurch to Mount Cook Airport (~4km from the village). These services may be reduced or not offered during winter. There is also an airport at Glentanner Park, 25km east of the village, which is used by Helicopter Line and Air Safaris for scenic flights. Some huts can be flown to from here. By car it is 335 kilometres from Christchurch, and generally takes between four and five hours. From Fox and Franz Josef townships, the options include flying, driving via Haast Pass and crossing the Copland Pass on foot. If you are not in a rush then hitchhiking is a viable option, but can be particularly slow in winter.

Accommodation

As a general rule there is not much budget accommodation in the Aoraki/Mount Cook Village. Accommodation can be divided roughly into three general price categories: club huts and camping, the Chalets and Youth Hostel and the hotels. There is also accommodation available at Glentanner Park. However, its distance from both the village and climbing makes it less appealing.

Unwin Lodge, owned and operated by the New Zealand Alpine Club, is about three kilometres down the main road from the village, close to the airport. The hut is serviced, with full facilities, and controlled by a resident warden. Club members have preference. Easily confused with the above-mentioned hut is Wyn Irwin Hut, belonging to the Canterbury Mountaineering Club. It is located closer to the village, near the camp ground, en route to the Hooker Valley. Once again, club members have preference, and during summer a warden is usually present (otherwise it is locked). Joining either of these clubs is recommended not just for the accommodation in the village locale but for a range of other benefits including access to other base huts within the park and other alpine regions of New Zealand. For those who wish to camp there are scenic tent sites available at the White Horse Hill camp ground (basic facilities include tap water, toilets and a public shelter). A camping fee is now payable for these sites so it may well be more economic, not to mention more comfortable, to use the club accommodation. This is of particular relevance if you intend to stay in the region for an extended period.

The Youth Hostel, located in the village, is fully serviced with all the usual 'mod cons', but can become full during summer. Again, member and non-member rates apply. The Chalets (closed in winter) are operated by the Hermitage Hotel and can each accommodate four or more people.

The Hermitage Hotel is a landmark identity and focal point of the village and commands premium tourist rates. An imposing six storey wing has recently been added to the Hermitage complex and parts of the original building have also been upgraded. Located down the hill is the Glencoe Lodge, which offers lower rates and is also closed during winter. Some cheaper motel units are also available through the Hermitage.

Glentanner Park, 25 km from the village, offers a broad selection of accommodation services including tent sites, powered sites for campervans and a range of cabins. If you are in any doubt about where to stay ask the park staff in the Visitor Centre.

Services within the village have changed somewhat since the last edition of this guide, and not necessarily for the better. There is no longer a grocery shop as such. Instead, a very limited range of food and basic day-to-day products is available from the Coffee Shop, located in the Hermitage. Many climbers now bring (and send in advance) large supplies of non-perishable foods. Those with a vehicle, staying for longer, can make trips to Twizel, Timaru or Wanaka to stock up.

Petrol and diesel is available from pumps 200m down the road from the Visitor Centre. At the time of printing the payment system for fuel is only partially self-serve and is not convenient if you do not possess the right type of card. EFTPOS and New Zealand credit card payments can be processed at the pump. Cash and other forms of payment require hotel assistance – which incurs a call-out charge! It is not uncommon for the self-serve system to break down, which also incurs a call-out charge. In addition to these dubious arrangements the price of fuel is exorbitant. Best advice: purchase enough fuel at Twizel or Tekapo for the return journey (Tekapo offers a fully functioning 24 hr self-serve system).

Alpine Guides Ltd (Aoraki) has a shop about 150m down the road from the Visitor Centre which sells a range of climbing equipment and clothing, as well as hiring boots, crampons, ice-axes, skis, etc. They also have a bouldering wall outside the rear of their shop.

The public bar is now called the Chamois Bar and is located in the Glencoe Lodge. Although it does not have the character and setting of its predecessor, superb meals are available there. Opening hours seem to vary however. The Alpine Bar in the Hermitage, with its luxurious leather chairs that allow one to view Aoraki on a good day, is an expensive option but certainly worth at least one visit (building developments at the Hermitage may change this).

Postal, phone, internet, transport and associated booking services are all available at the Hermitage Hotel. Buses to the airport also depart from the Hermitage. There are no automatic teller machines (ATMs) in the village, but EFTPOS and other financial services are available at the hotel reception. Both Twizel and Tekapo have ATMs. Twizel also has a bank and a good range of other retail services.

Franz Josef and Fox Glacier Townships

A description of these towns and the activities that can be undertaken from them could easily form the basis of a separate guide. For brevity however, the following is just a snapshot of the basic information. Fox Glacier is probably the better base for those intending to head into the hills because of the NZAC lodge there. Although both towns are tourist magnets during summer, Fox Glacier has an old world charm and character of its own.

From Christchurch there is a daily Atomic Shuttle service to Greymouth and Hokitika. A connecting service continues to Franz and Fox townships en route to Queenstown. This service also operates in the other direction and provides a link to Nelson and Picton. The Tranzalpine train from Christchurch to Greymouth is the most spectacular train ride in the country (costs more than hitching but it's worth trying) and links with an Intercity bus in Greymouth, which continues to Franz and Fox. Both the train and bus offer excellent budget fares if you book and pay early. However, the Shuttle is cheaper overall. An Intercity bus service from Wanaka passes the Copland Valley turnoff at about 3pm en route to Fox. And going the other way, a bus heads south to Wanaka at about 8:30am each day. All the aforementioned services are in summer. You'll need to check the timetables in winter. All the necessary contact details are in the back section of the guidebook. Driving by car takes 5-6 hours and about three hours from Christchurch and Wanaka, respectively. It is also possible to fly from the Aoraki/Mount Cook side to either town and hitching is also an option – but keep your raincoat handy.

In general, all the services found in the Aoraki/Mount Cook Village are available in either Franz or Fox, to a much greater level. Alpine Guides (Westland), based in Fox, have a large café/shop, which also serves as the main booking centre for helicopter flights into the névés. Helicopter and Cessna flights can also be arranged from the Franz township. There is vitually no difference in the cost between flights from Franz or Fox, into the high huts. For those who want to walk in (still a realistic option) a bus service provided by Alpine Guides can be caught to the glacier most days. Conditions on the Franz Josef Glacier seem more variable so check with DoC staff for current information.

Groceries are much more readily available than in the Hermitage Coffee Shop, but prices are not like those in the big centre supermarkets – so stock up in advance in Christchurch, Hokitika or Wanaka. The Fox Hotel is a grand old establishment and is usually open late, has pool tables for when you are waiting for the weather to clear, and offers pretty good pub fare. Across the road is the more modern Cooks Saddle bar and restaurant, which has a more comprehensive menu. There is also a three star pizza café.

There is a good range of accommodation in both townships including backpackers, motels and lodges. The NZAC HEL Porter Lodge, in Fox, is a cosy and well appointed base hut equipped with bunkrooms, drying room, kitchen and shower facilities. Porter Lodge is for members and their guests only and is locked. After verifying membership, the door key code can be obtained from the Nelson-Marlborough Section of the club or the Alpine Guides shop in Fox.

Air access

Mount Cook Skiplanes provide Cessna and Pilatus Porter planes that can carry three and six people with gear, respectively. From Mount Cook Airport, climbers can be flown into 14 approved ski plane landing sites. These include the Murchison Glacier, the Grand Plateau, a number of sites on the Tasman Glacier, the Horace Walker Névé (west of the Douglas Névé), and a number of sites on the Fox and Franz Josef glaciers, when landing conditions allow.

Helicopters that fly from Glentanner Park and elsewhere can be used for access to a limited number of landing sites within the region. They may fly into approved ski plane landing sites only when conditions are not suitable for ski planes. Both helicopter and plane services are available in Westland National Park, but again only to specified landing spots. For more information on where you can and can not fly to, contact the park staff at the Aoraki/Mount Cook or Franz Joseph Visitor Centres. The rockclimbing in Twin Stream can be accessed by helicopter from Glentanner Park.

Aircraft safety

Flying in to the mountains is a great experience but there are some basic do's and don'ts when it comes to flying, particularly when moving to and from planes and helicopters. In all instances the pilot is in charge – do exactly what s/he says or signals. In general planes are somewhat easier to work with because the engine is usually shut down after landing, making unloading safer. Helicopters on the other hand are not turned off and they have extra moving blades, so vigilance is needed. The following points cover the basics. For more information check with the pilot, airport, or staff at the Visitor Centre.

- Fuel for cookers must be available for the pilot to store separately.
- When helping the pilot to load, take care not to snag or tear the upholstery with axes and crampons etc, and ensure that nothing is hanging out of the doors or luggage compartments. When un/loading skis and other long items from a helicopter, be wary of the rotor.
- Ensure that light gear is secured so that it does not get sucked into the rotor or propellor wash (especially foam mats and rubbish bags).
- Shield your eyes when the plane or helicopter departs/arrives.
- Only approach the plane or helicopter when the pilot has signalled you to do so.
- Always approach or leave a helicopter from the downhill side. Never approach from the uphill side. Crouch when you move under the rotor.
- Always approach or leave a helicopter from the front or sides only – visible to the

pilot. Remember there is a tail rotor! If you need to move to the other side of the machine, walk around the front.

- Close the doors GENTLY, after ensuring your seat belt is inside. Fasten your seatbelt.
- Do not rush, and have your camera handy.

Guiding

Qualified guides are available for guided climbs, instruction and skiing. There is a listing of guides who offer services in the Aoraki/Mount Cook and Westland National Parks at the rear of this guidebook. All guides from these companies are internationally qualified, with New Zealand Mountain Guides Association members also being qualified by the International Federation of Mountain Guides Association.

Search & rescue

Search and rescue is the responsibility of the Police, acting in conjunction with the Department of Conservation (DoC). Aoraki/Mount Cook National Park has an agreement with the Police to organise and run alpine search and rescues. The park has a professional search and rescue team, and Westland National Park has search and rescue resources available. The search and rescue team is called out for accidents, medical emergencies and overdue parties. To initiate a search and rescue operation in AMCNP or Westland either contact base using the hut radios, or if you have a cell phone call 111 and ask for the Police. The Police will take brief details and notify local search and rescue personnel. If an accident does occur, climbers should do as much as possible, within reason, before calling on outside help. Search and rescue services are provided free of charge.

The Accident Compensation Corporation Scheme (ACC) automatically covers everyone in New Zealand, whether they are a New Zealand national or an overseas visitor, against accident. It is a 'no fault scheme' which means that compensation is paid regardless of whose fault it was - this removes the ability to sue for damages. If you have an accident climbing, the ACC scheme will pay for your rescue, medical, and rehabilitation expenses. ACC have set maximum limits for each injury. It is no longer possible to claim for clothing or equipment lost or damaged in an accident. ACC will only pay for a helicopter if it is called by the Police as part of an official search and rescue operation. Hence if you order a helicopter, you will have to pay for it.

Personal Locator Beacons (PLB) are now readily available for purchase or hire and are becoming popular with backcountry users. In the event of an emergency the user can activate the beacon, which simultaneously transmits a signal on the two international distress frequencies 121.5 & 243 MHz, which are permanently monitored. The user's location can be determined from the beacon's signal. If you or your party are to carry a PLB whilst climbing in the region, you should indicate this on your intentions card when signing in.

Alpine huts

Since the last edition of this guidebook there have been many changes to the way that high huts are managed and serviced. The New Zealand Alpine Club owns some high huts within the region and in general they are managed and serviced by DoC. In some cases individual servicing arrangements exist. High huts are no longer supplied with cookers or fuel (or matches, for that matter) and so it is the responsibility of each party to carry appropriate cooking equipment. DoC has also indicated that existing pots, cutlery and mugs etc will not be replaced or maintained. Currently there are still good stocks of these items in all huts. Most huts have blankets but to be sure check with park staff. Some huts are now equipped with low wattage electric lights, powered by solar charged batteries.

All alpine huts have radios (recently upgraded). These include Sefton Bivvy, Copland and Ball shelters. They allow communication with the Visitor Centre during normal work hours. Outside these times the radio is monitored by a 'Duty Officer' (DO), to provide help in the case of an emergency. Every night at 7pm there is a scheduled radio call, known as the 'sked', to all huts in the AMCNP. In Westland National Park the sked is at 6pm and 4:30pm in summer and winter respectively. However, it would pay to check this. On the sked a weather forecast is provided and the parties in the hut or camping nearby are recorded – so please have a list of the parties in the hut ready to read out. Flights into and out of AMCNP huts are no longer arranged by park staff. The Mount Cook airport has installed a separate radio in Tasman Saddle Hut with a direct link to the ski plane desk (Kelman Hut users need to relay calls through Tasman Saddle). The private Caroline Hut has an emergency shelter that is equipped with a radio. No hut radio communication is possible between AMCNP and WNP because of the Main Divide.

Beetham Hut was removed after it was hit by a small avalanche in 1995 and has not been replaced. Those wishing to visit this area will need to bivvy or carry a tent. Empress Hut has been replaced and a hut named Centennial (NZAC) has been built at the head of the Franz Josef Glacier. At the time of printing it was established that a new Mueller Hut would replace the existing hut in 2002. This new DoC hut is to be located 200-300m closer to Mt Ollivier. There are also plans to replace Plateau Hut within the next three years. The location of Hooker Hut is also being reviewed because of the continued subsidence of the moraine wall that it sits on. Macaulay Hut, owned and maintained by the Mackenzie Alpine Trust (Tekapo), is situated on the Lower Tindill Stream fan, 19km up the Macaulay Valley (Godley). This new hut is equipped with gas cookers, solar powered lighting and a Mountain Radio, which can be used to communicate with a base in Christchurch.

The Department of Conservation defines high alpine huts as Category One type huts. However, Copland and Ball shelters are charged at a reduced rate and Sefton Bivvy remains free to users. DoC hut tickets can be used for payment (only in AMCNP) but Annual Hut Passes are not valid for Category One huts. Annual Hut Passes can, however, be used for the following: Copland and Ball shelters and Haast and Liebig huts. All other forms of payment for hut fees are made when exiting the park – and if you forget to pay, DoC will invoice you. In some instances hut fee discounts for club members are available – but membership cards must be presented.

Hut etiquette & safety

To ensure that everyone enjoys their stay, here are ten useful tips. These are especially important when a hut is full.

- Dust as much snow and ice off your gear as possible before you enter a hut – and remove your crampons.
- Cook only on the steel bench tops and ensure that there is adequate ventilation – carbon monoxide is an odourless, poisonous combustion by-product and can be lethal in low concentrations. Symptoms are a headache, with possible nausea quickly followed by a coma and death. Open a door or window partially when cooking – even during bad weather.
- Most fuels being used nowadays are highly flammable (as opposed to kerosene) so make a note of where the fire extinguisher is before lighting a cooker. If you are not familiar with lighting the cooker you are using – ask for help before you try.
- Tidy up after cooking, including dishes. As water and fuel may be scarce, organize a communal pot of water for brews/dishes.
- If water becomes scarce (ie late summer, winter) get agreement from all hut users as to where you will source snow for melting – ie avoid yellow snow!!
- Keep your belongings tidied away in one place - this also helps avoid searches at 1am for lost gear.
- Respect those who are trying to sleep – keep the noise down at these times and during the sked.
- Enter your intentions in the hut book – this may be the only way rescuers can find you! And, when you exit the park – sign out at the Visitor Centre or call staff there.
- Don't leave perishable food behind
- Carry out all your rubbish (don't throw it down the toilet!).

Human toilet waste removal

The AMCNP management plan (draft) is proposing a series of policies that require climbers and others using the high alpine regions to carry out their faecal waste. Climbers may be required to use special doggy bags whilst on climbs or when in areas where natural biodegradation is not possible. These bags would then be deposited into toilet facilities at huts or carried out. DoC is recommending these policies for health, aesthetic, recreational appreciation and cultural reasons. This requirement may be included in the final version of the plan – so check with DoC for more up-to-date details.

Skiing

Many of the peaks contained within this guide have received ski descents including Aoraki/Mt Cook (1982, Geoff Wayatt and John Blennerhassett via the Linda; 1986, Mark Whetu via Zurbriggens; 1993, Ardi Reichlin via the East Face), D'Archiac (1999, Mark Seddon and Kane Henderson via the North Face) and Tasman (mid 1990s, French party via Syme Ridge; 1991, Mauro Rumez, via the Stevenson-Dick

Couloir). Although this guide does not address these types of activities specifically the information contained here will be useful for the ski-mountaineer.

The Aoraki/Mount Cook region, including the Godley area and the extensive névés west of the Main Divide offer unsurpassed skiing and ski mountaineering. Vast expanses of virgin snow and big vertical descents (and ascents) await those who are keen to enjoy the people-less winter and spring seasons. Numerous ski touring trips are possible, but the popular areas and link-ups include the Annette Plateau - Barron Saddle - Mueller Glacier circuit, Murchison-Tasman-Rudolf-Graham Saddle, and Franz Josef-Fox Glacier trips. The latter two trips can be linked creating a Kiwi version of the 'Haute route'. The relatively new Centennial Hut at the head of the Franz now provides accommodation for this. The route can begin in the Murchison and involves four days of unparalleled ski touring that concludes in the Fox. Alternative start points could include Rankin Hut in the Godley or the Cass Valley. The upper reaches of the Godley Valley, including the Neish Plateau, also hold unlimited scope for ski touring.

In most of the sections there is a brief list of suggested ski touring routes that can be enjoyed during winter and spring. A simple difficulty system has been used to indicate the suitability for each class of skier, whether they are:

(A) - moderate ,   (B) - intermediate ,   (C) - advanced, or (D) - expert skiers.

Bouldering & crag climbing

Cragging and bouldering can be enjoyed within the region, and, although it is not in the same league as, say, Wanaka or Castle Hill, it has a character and attraction of its own. The rock is deceptively good and the setting and views are superb – seeing is believing. A separate guide: South Island Rock (details in the back of this guide) provides excellent coverage for most of the following areas and much more, but here's a sample. . .

The most significant recent developments in terms of crag climbing in the general area (and it's probably better described as sub-alpine multi-pitch climbing) have occurred on the buttresses of the upper Twin Stream and Fred Stream. These areas offer fantastic routes, over a range of grades. The majority of the climbing at Twin Stream is about four hours walk from the road bridge near Glentanner Park. If you are feeling lazy or have limited time, a helicopter can put you there in about four minutes. The rock is schistose greywacke and is very good to climb on. There are idyllic camping spots and water is readily available. Permission of the runholder at Glentanner Station should be sought for access.

The bluffs on Sebastopol between Unwin Hut and the village are popular and contain a large number of routes. They range from short crag style bolted routes through to longer multi-pitch lines that involve natural gear placements as well as bolts. The rock is greywacke and overall is mostly 'very good', with patches of 'excellent'. But beware: loose rock can be found, as the large scree fans below amply demonstrate. Helmets are recommended. Sebastopol is an excellent half or full day outing if you are waiting for a nor'wester to blow through or just keen to get your money's worth on some longer routes. There is a stream at the base of the bluffs that is worth a dip on a hot day. The Red Arête is an easy multi-pitch Sebastopol classic that is a 'must do'.

There is a small crag called Shaky Town a few minutes beyond the Red Tarns Bridge, up Black Birch Stream. In the same stream there is 'The Pebble' which has half a dozen routes. Poo Pond Crag overlooks the oxidation ponds and has a handful of grade 14-17 bolted routes. The crag was first used 20 years ago by Paul Aubrey and others for top-roping. In 1997 Anton Wopereis and Sam Bosshard rediscovered it and began establishing routes. Poo Pond Crag is apparently more sheltered from nor'west winds than Sebastopol. Check at the Visitor Centre or Alpine Guides for the brochure.

Several boulders near the White Horse Hill camp ground are also popular. These include Zurbriggens boulder, situated in a small valley off the Hooker Valley track about 150m from the campground. There are about 16 or so routes on this boulder. Three boulders, the last of which is clearly visible from the picnic shelter, can be found above and west of the camp ground. To get there, wander past the large pine trees and the toilet. Scramble up a vague track, past the water supply pipe and you will find the first and relatively small boulder on a hidden terrace. Beyond this there is another boulder and finally the third, which has a bolt anchor on top. Worth a look.

Some of the rock on the lower cliffs of Mt Wakefield looks promising, but there are no recorded details. The rock ridge line of Mt Wakefield that starts from the second swing bridge up the Hooker Valley and runs to the summit is a superb easy climb (the 'Guide Route'). The rock is good and the views onto Sefton and the Main Divide are outstanding. There is a large boulder near Husky Flat, up the Ball Road in the Tasman Valley, which has about a dozen routes on it.

The Pukaki Boulders are located on the left side of the Aoraki/Mount Cook road (Route 80) when traveling toward, and about three kilometres before, the junction with the main north-south highway (Route 8). The three main boulders, just visible from the road and about two minutes away, offer 12 or so routes. Another large boulder, overlooking Lake Pukaki a few kilometres north of the Pukaki Dam, is situated about 60m off the main road and offers a range of possibilities.

Further away and rarely visited, the rockclimbing in the Beetham and Reay Valleys, as well as on the Langdale Buttress, is very good. These rockclimbing areas are described in the Upper Tasman Valley section of the guide.

Despite common belief, there is plenty of good quality rockclimbing to be enjoyed. If weather in the village and nearby is not conducive to either alpine or rockclimbing – options further east, such as Twin Stream, the Pukaki Boulders, Beautiful Valley, and options south, such as Aemis Basin (Ohau Ski Area) and Wanaka are likely to be dry.

Bolting
Both Westland and Aoraki/Mount Cook National Park management plans do not specifically limit the use of bolt fixtures on climbs but ask individual climbers and clubs to bolt sensibly, with consideration for the possible visual impact that a bolt(s) may create. The AMCNP management plan (draft) recommends a code of practice for bolting and old sling removal be developed by DoC. The guidebook, South Island Rock provides a brief summary of bolting techniques. However, those intending to

place bolts should consult the New Zealand Alpine Club, the Canterbury Mountaineering Club, or DoC for advice, to ensure that current best practices are used. For example, stainless steel equipment is a must and natural coloured hangers should be considered.

The fine print

The author and the publisher do not accept responsibility for inaccurate or incomplete information, or reliance on fixed protection/bolts, some of which may be unreliable. Fixed protection does not remain in place indefinitely.

First time in the area? – what's needed and where to go

If you are from overseas or if this is your first time in the area, then you should read this section to help make your first season a successful one. The Aoraki/Mount Cook region contains the biggest and possibly the most unforgiving mountains in New Zealand. The following paragraphs recommend some areas to visit, climbs to consider and skills to gain <u>before</u> jumping into the deep end. It is also vital to note that the skills and experience that 'experienced' climbers have, were gained over many seasons. Equally important is getting experience in decision-making. So where to start?

The Copland and Ball passes and the Annette Plateau are good starting points because they allow the climber to become familiar with a range of terrain types and to get a taste of bad weather without being in too deep. In saying this however, no matter where you are in the region, when the weather turns nasty the consequences of being caught out can be very serious. To this end many seasoned climbers always carry basic bivvy equipment. For those climbers from other countries, including those familiar with continental weather systems – keep in mind that the weather here changes from perfect to perfectly life-threatening in a few hours!

The above-mentioned areas also offer the opportunity to climb minor peaks. The Annette Plateau has the added bonus of the Mueller and Barron Saddle Huts that are excellent bases, but tenting can also be a good option. Navigation/route-finding is a key skill for any climber, but particularly so in the Aoraki/Mount Cook region. This is not just because of fickle weather but also due to the glaciated approaches to climbs. The Annette Plateau provides plenty of scope for this. At the same time parties will be able to gauge how long it takes to travel and climb various distances and heights. As highlighted earlier, roped glacier travel is mandatory when crossing snow-covered glaciers. Practising this and crevasse rescue on the Annette Plateau where it is relatively flat and not exposed to icecliffs makes good sense.

Peaks such as Annette, Sealy (via different routes) and the peaks along to Darby, overlooking Barron Saddle, are superb first season objectives and can be climbed from either hut. The views they command are some of the best in the region because there are no major peaks nearby obscuring the view. Watch out for poor rock.

The Main Divide route on Footstool, climbed from Sefton Bivvy, is also worth considering, but it is a significant step up from those peaks in the Annette Plateau region in terms of scale and technical requirement. So, good fitness is required, as is glacier travel and route-finding skills. Because this climb is mostly on eastern and lee slopes, snow conditions can sometimes be hazardous – check conditions with park staff. The views from this peak are similar in grandeur to those from the top of Aoraki and Mt Sefton.

Mt Sefton, when climbed from the west via Scott Creek, is also an excellent option. If approaching from the east, the Copland Pass will need to be crossed first. The height gain from Welcome Flat is one of the biggest in the region (2000m!) and so fitness is very important. Most unsuccessful parties are so, not because of weather but a flawed approach strategy (Hot tip: use two days and a high camp). The terrain covered includes streams, snow basins and slopes, a crevassed névé and a final ice slope. Again navigation skills are vital. The setting and view is amazing – providing a different perspective. And the hot pools aren't too bad either.

If you prefer to begin on a peak that is primarily rock then Aiguilles Rouges, in the Malte Brun Range, could be worth a visit. The Tasman Glacier then the picturesque Beetham Valley need to be accessed first. A large snow slope at the head of this valley leads onto Malte Brun Pass. Although several routes could be considered from the pass, the North East Flank and Ridge routes are the most popular.

The areas and climbs discussed here do not require air access. It is important in your first season to know how to get in <u>and</u> out of an area, without being dependent on a plane or helicopter – it also means you'll save some cash and get fit quicker.

Route grades

Conditions in the Aoraki/Mount Cook region can change in hours, so it is virtually impossible to apply an all-embracing and exact grading system. The grading system used in the previous editions of this guide has been retained because of its general applicability. The 'Mt Cook system' of grading begins at 1 and currently runs through to 7. The system is open-ended, and grades greater than 7 are quite possible. A + or – are also used for further definition. The grading criteria for this system are, in decreasing order of importance, technical difficulty, objective danger, length, and access. The Australasian rock grading system (~8-34) has been used additionally, where appropriate. And, in some cases technical ice climbing grades are quoted in the route description. A grade conversion table can be found in the back of the guidebook.

It is stressed that grades provide only a rough indication of difficulty. The grades assigned to the routes in this guide are for normal conditions. Grades can often be misleading because conditions vary so much.

Climbing is all about using your own judgement and knowing your limits. This guidebook is not a substitute for those important attributes. In the end it comes down to reading the mountain, not the book.

A new name

In 1998 Mount Cook and its namesake national park were officially renamed Aoraki/Mount Cook and Aoraki/Mount Cook National Park, to reflect the Maori heritage of the mountain and the region. Within the following history section 'Mount Cook' is used up to the time of the renaming.

Kat West climbing the Scott Creek waterfall en route to Mt Sefton. Copland Valley below.

27

Aoraki/Mount Cook region

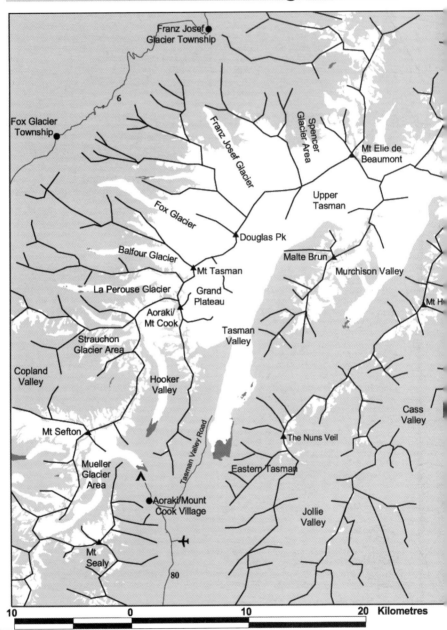

Franz Josef
Glacier Township

Fox Glacier
Township

6

Franz Josef Glacier

Spencer
Glacier Area

Mt Elie de
Beaumont

Upper
Tasman

Fox Glacier

Douglas Pk

Balfour Glacier

Malte Brun

Murchison Valley

Mt Tasman

La Perouse Glacier

Grand
Plateau

Mt H

Aoraki/
Mt Cook

Tasman
Valley

Strauchon
Glacier Area

Copland
Valley

Hooker
Valley

Cass
Valley

Mt Sefton

Tasman Valley Road

The Nuns Veil

Mueller
Glacier
Area

Eastern Tasman

Aoraki/Mount
Cook Village

Jollie
Valley

Mt
Sealy

80

| 10 | 0 | 10 | 20 | Kilometres |

28

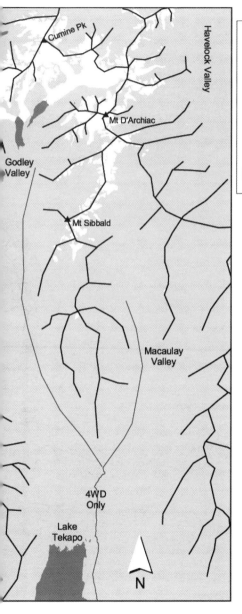

Key

+|- Airport
ʌ White Horse Hill camp ground
● Town
▲ Peak
— Road
— Ridgeline
▮ Lake
☐ Permanent ice/snow

A history of climbing in the Aoraki/Mount Cook region

In the late 1800s the Mt Cook region, as it was known then, became the hub of climbing in New Zealand and has remained so ever since. Mountain exploration was the precursor to this climbing and was undertaken by Europeans independent of all the Maori knowledge of the mountains. But the Maori had for many centuries before this time explored far up some West Coast valleys in search of the treasured pounamu (greenstone). Maori often ventured across the lower passes of the Southern Alps to trade pounamu with tribes in the east. With limited footwear and clothing these excursions were certainly committing adventures, but climbing to the top of mountains was not their objective. Indeed, as for other cultures, many of the mountain summits are sacred to Maori.

The upper reaches of the valleys and snow capped peaks in the Mt Cook and adjoining regions remained untouched until Europeans arrived and began exploring also. In the early 1860s Julius Haast, a German scientist, explored, surveyed and mapped most of the eastern approaches in the Mount Cook region. From 1867-1870 Sealy also visited the region and surveyed extensively. Later Thomas Brodrick continued the surveying work though the 1880s. On the West Coast, at a similar time, gold miners and surveyors were active. Charlie Douglas explored and mapped many of the Westland valleys. Again, however, summits were not the focus and it would take a combination of influences to kick-start mountaineering in New Zealand, not least of which was the fact that Mount Cook was unclimbed.

The ascent of Mount Cook

William Green, an Irish clergyman, arrived in New Zealand in early 1882 with Swiss companion Emile Boss and guide Ulrich Kaufmann, intending to climb Mt Cook. Their expedition was much like a modern day Himalayan adventure. They had travelled 15,000km by ship to New Zealand. After journeys by train and horse and cart they eventually arrived at Birch Hill station (15km down valley from the present-day Hermitage Hotel). Then the trio had to struggle through untracked scrub up beside the Tasman Glacier. Despite a number of false starts they finally struck up the Linda Glacier high onto Mt Cook. On 2 March, with night falling and a nor'westerly storm moving in, the party turned back only 50m from the summit after an epic climb. Green felt that he had as good as climbed the mountain, but to those who followed the issue was still in doubt.

From 1886 a small group of enthusiasts in Christchurch began to turn to the mountains for recreation. It was only natural that the high mountains of the Mt Cook region should become their main focus. In February 1887 George Mannering, Marmaduke Dixon and Charles Inglis climbed to the site of Green's bivouac on Haast Ridge. In December 1890 Mannering and Dixon repeated Green's ascent and like Green they were forced to turn back just short of the summit with darkness coming on. By the mid 1890s, reaching the summit of Mt Cook had become an obsession with Mannering, Dixon and their contemporaries. Tom Fyfe, a mercurial individual, was from Timaru also had his eye on Mt Cook. Self taught, Fyfe was a gifted rock climber. In March 1894, after a string of other ascents, Fyfe showed his remarkable rock climbing ability with his solo first ascent of Mt Malte Brun via the North Face. The note he left under the De La Beche bivouac rock after the ascent read cryptically, "Played a lone hand with Malte and won".

News that an Englishman, Edward FitzGerald, and world famous guide, Mattias Zurbriggen, of Macugnaga, Italy, would arrive late in 1894 to attempt the peak aroused a frenzy of activity amongst local climbers. At least five separate attempts on the Linda Glacier route failed. Finally in mid December 1894 Tom Fyfe and George Graham abandoned the Linda Glacier route and explored the western side of the mountain. The pair had previously made the first ascent of The Footstool, and from that vantage point had seen possibilities for alternative routes up Mt Cook. Fyfe and Graham's first attempt from the west saw them reach the middle peak of Mt Cook, a stunning achievement in itself – but the high peak was too far along the summit ridge, so a second approach was considered.

Mattias Zurbriggen circa 1895

A steep couloir at the head of the Hooker Glacier leads up to a narrow col between Mts Dampier and Cook. Above the col is the North Ridge of Mt Cook, rising in three rock steps. It was this route which Fyfe, Graham and a nineteen year old, Jack Clark (later he used 'Clarke'), set out to climb. On Christmas Day 1894 they reached the summit of Mt Cook, having completed an ascent that even today is regarded as a major undertaking.

FitzGerald was fishing in the Selwyn River, south of Christchurch, the day Mt Cook was climbed. Thwarted of his main objective, he and Zurbriggen turned instead to the other major peaks and climbed Mts Sealy, Haidinger, Silberhorn and New Zealand's second highest peak, Mt Tasman. FitzGerald hired Jack Clark as a porter for these climbs, but in a display of pique over Clark's ascent of Mt Cook blocked him out of the published Haidinger summit photograph. The crowning effort of the visit was FitzGerald and Zurbriggen's ascent of the spectacular and rotten East Ridge of Mt Sefton. Zurbriggen declared he had never encountered such a dangerous mountain before. Zurbriggen did not leave the area without climbing Mt Cook itself. After FitzGerald had returned to Christchurch he tackled the North East Ridge, now known as Zurbriggen's Ridge. Accompanied to about 3000m by Hermitage Hotel caretaker and guide Jack Adamson, Zurbriggen soloed to the summit. FitzGerald later contemptuously dismissed the mountain as too easy.

The golden age
The intense activity of 1894-95 was followed by a lull. The New Zealand Alpine Club, founded in 1891 by Mannering and Dixon, went into recess for many years. While there was an attempt to revive the NZAC in 1914, it didn't get anywhere until after WWI. Although tourism gradually increased, high climbing tended to languish. Nevertheless there were glacier parties to be guided, and the occasional higher ascent.

Adamson managed the Hermitage Hotel through 1896 and did a little guiding. The government, which had taken over the hotel in 1895, employed Tom Fyfe as guide from 1896-97. The following season Fyfe was unable to work due to a leg injury and was replaced by Jack Clark. Glacier parties were his main occupation, but after he had been to Europe in 1900, where he climbed Mont Blanc, Clark returned with more confidence. High climbing soon began again and under him and his successors a strong guiding tradition developed.

On the West Coast, in the early 1900s, mountaineering was developing separately, though it was soon to influence the Mt Cook region. The Hokitika doctor, Ebenezer Teichelmann, and the vicar of the small town of Ross, Henry Newton, a young Englishman who had climbed in Switzerland, had a significant influence on New Zealand mountaineering. They explored at the head of several West Coast valleys and glaciers,

R Low, Peter Graham, Henry Newton, Alex Graham and Dr Teichelmann pose near the old Hermitage, 1905.

and climbed a number of major peaks, including Mts La Perouse, Hicks, Lendenfeld, Haast, Torres, Douglas and Glacier. Newton and Teichelmann also completed the third ascent of Mt Cook, some ten years after the second ascent, when people were beginning to wonder if it would be done again. As well, Newton and Teichelmann encouraged and stimulated two young West Coast brothers, Peter and Alex Graham, to explore the valleys, glaciers and peaks behind Franz Josef, their home town. Alex went on to establish the guiding service which flourished at the Graham family hotel. From late 1903 Peter contributed greatly to the development of New Zealand mountaineering and guiding, on the eastern side of the mountains.

Alex and Peter Graham with Freda Du Faur.

In 1906 Jack Clarke stepped down as Chief Guide at the Hermitage Hotel. His climbing career had already encompassed first ascents of Mts Cook, Tasman, Silberhorn, Haidinger and Sealy, and later, first ascents of Mts Hamilton, D'Archiac and Aspiring. Clarke also established new routes on Mts Cook, Sefton and Malte Brun. More importantly, perhaps, he had established the reputation of Hermitage guides for competent and safe climbing. His successor as Chief Guide, Peter Graham, carried on from where Clarke had left off and lifted guiding to a degree of professionalism and expertise New Zealand had not seen before.

Peter Graham dominated the climbing scene at Mt Cook from 1906 until 1922. Under him both the guide service and climbing activity flourished. Although rather autocratic, his climbing skill and authority was unquestioned. He climbed over 40 new routes in the Mt Cook district, including three new ridge routes and two new traverses on Mt Cook itself. By 1916, Peter and Alex Graham and guides such as Darby Thomson, Jim Murphy and Frank Milne had established technical standards of rock and ice-climbing that were unsurpassed until at least the 1930s.

The "golden age" was a time when mountaineering was a leisure sport for a small sector of the well-off and spanned the years 1900-1915. Clients would hire a guide for long periods at a time and wait for perfect conditions. The amateur New Zealand tradition begun by Mannering and Dixon was temporarily eclipsed. Many of the famous clients of the period such as Laurence Earle, Bernard Head and Freda Du Faur were both well-off and from overseas. Freda Du Faur, a determined Australian lady who initially shocked contemporaries by climbing unchaperoned, ascended Mts Tasman, Dampier, Malte Brun, Nazomi and Sefton. The route she is best known for is the Grand Traverse of Mt Cook, which follows New Zealand's highest mile along a sinuous, corniced and spectacularly beautiful ridge. Freda and her guides Peter Graham and Darby Thomson established what continues to be one of New Zealand's classic climbs on 3 January 1913.

The end of the golden age

The "golden age" culminated in the years from 1910 to 1915. During this period talented local climbers like Hugh Chambers, Hugh Wright and Jim Dennistoun appeared on the scene. Canadian Otto Frind and his guide Conrad Kain climbed a new route on Mt Sefton, traversed Mt Cook and made many first ascents of peaks on the Liebig Range. The tenacious and egocentric Samuel Turner monopolised guides' time and patience but notched up a climbing record second to none, including the first complete solo ascent of Mt Cook in 1919.

While the First World War was being waged in Europe (1914-18) climbing still continued in New Zealand, in fact the numbers of climbers active was strangely greater than before the outbreak of war. Even the 1918-19 period, which was badly affected by the flu epidemic, saw more climbing. However, during the war years there were fewer new or challenging climbs attempted or made. It is thought that the major reason for this was the absence of the top Kiwi climbers along with the reduced numbers of climbers from overseas, who had given considerable impetus to the pre-war "golden age". The war fatalities sustained by New Zealand were colossal and there is no doubt that this impacted on climbing activity during the years after the Great War.

Hocken Library (MS-1164-2/34/12, c/n E614/20)

Otto Frind outside Malte Brun Hut, 1914.

The 1920s and 1930s

In the early 1920s climbing at Mt Cook suffered hard times. New Zealand, like many countries after the First World War, entered a mild economic depression which gradually worsened as the decade went on. Climbing was still a pursuit for those with time and money, and this group showed no signs of expanding. After the war people also desired more independence than before. The guiding tradition, which had raised standards in the pre-war era, now seemed to hinder amateur climbing. In October 1922 the Government Tourist Department leased the Hermitage to the Mt Cook Company. Peter Graham soon left following a disagreement with the new owners. He joined his brother Alex at Franz Josef to bolster the tourist and guiding service there.

Meanwhile at the Hermitage the Mt Cook Company believed that the role of a guide should be one of tourist entertainer and ski tutor, as well as leader of climbs. In this environment Peter Graham's successor, Frank Milne, struggled to retain the high climbing element of the guide service, and was never very comfortable with his social role at the foot of the mountains. Milne himself ran up a string of superb ascents, including the first winter ascent of Mt Cook in August 1923, and a lightning four hour ascent and descent of the East Ridge of Sefton with Harold E Porter. In 1925, however, he was forced to leave the Hermitage, his lungs severely damaged by tuberculosis and his climbing ambitions unfulfilled. He had however succeeded in saving the guiding service, and handed on intact the guiding traditions of Clarke and the Grahams to his successors, Vic Williams, Mick Bowie and others.

Vic Williams, Mark Lysons and Alf Brustad outside the second Hermitage.

Although mountaineering was at a low ebb in the 1920s, one significant development was the widespread introduction of crampons. The adoption of these revolutionary devices from Europe was delayed, by over 30 years, which was surprising as most of the big routes on and around Mt Cook involve ice climbing. FitzGerald and Zurbriggen used full-foot crampons in 1895, and a few people used them and smaller instep crampons occasionally through to 1914. It seems that many climbers at the time considered crampons to be unsporting. Guides, including Peter Graham, found them dangerous with novice climbers, and soon realised the guide's load was heavy enough without crampons:

"Starting out early next morning, we went straight on to the rocks opposite our camp. These were very steep but good. My pack was rather too heavy, containing as it did two pairs of crampons (which we didn't use), water bottles, pineapple…"

(Peter Graham describing the first ascent of the Low Peak of Mt Cook, via the West Ridge, with Henrik Sillem, in March 1906. *Peter Graham: Mountain Guide*)

One can only marvel at the daring and the strength needed to hew a line of steps up routes on Mts Tasman, Sefton, La Perouse and Cook. In 1927 Englishman Harold Porter and Swiss Marcel Kurz convincingly demonstrated the value of crampons by making a traverse of the middle and high peaks of Mt Cook in record time and completing a new traverse of Mt Tasman via the North Shoulder. Porter and Kurz also climbed without a guide on these occasions, and this too was a sign of things to come.

The Godley region

As interest in climbing slowly broadened so to did the areas that climbers visited. The virgin peaks of the Godley region were among the next to attract attention. In 1910 Jim Dennistoun, Laurence M Earle and Jack Clarke climbed Mt D'Archiac, the highest peak in the area. This attention proved to be fleeting however, as seven years intervened before the next wave of first ascents occurred. In 1917 Edgar R Williams, W A Kennedy and T A Fletcher made several first ascents in the area, including Mt Sibbald, seen at the head of Lake Tekapo. The 1920s and 1930s were the busiest decades and saw many new routes pioneered in the Godley region.

Throughout New Zealand in the 1920s there was a growing interest in outdoor recreation which turned into a flood tide during the 1930s. The 1914 attempt to revive the NZAC was restricted by stringent and rather exclusive membership rules. It remained a limited force until regional branches were created in the early 1930s. Greater stimulus to climbing came from such clubs as the Tararua Tramping Club and the Canterbury Mountaineering Club. At a time when transport was limited and expensive, the club system provided the means for large numbers of young, less well-off but strongly motivated climbers to get to the mountains.

Rod Syme and Gordon (Snow) Mace on top of Mt Haidinger, 1930.

During the 1920s there was a considerable gap between the technical ability of the guides and the fledgling group of amateurs climbing (unguided) at Mt Cook, but this gap did close. By the 1930s several amateurs were virtually as good as the guides and their numbers steadily grew through the 1930s. In fact the quality and number of new routes established by amateurs during this period outstripped guided ascents for the first time.

Rod Syme and Dan Bryant were at the forefront of this wave of amateur climbing. Together they effectively relaunched amateur climbing in 1931 with the impressive first ascent of the beautiful right arête on the East Face of Mt Tasman, now known as Syme Ridge. This was the first major new route on any of the high peaks of the Mt Cook district since the Grand Traverse of Mt Cook 20 years earlier. Other amateur climbers established impressive new routes including the East Ridge of Haeckel (1934), South Face of Nazomi and a Syme-Silberhorn traverse of Mt Tasman (both 1936).

Although amateur climbing was taking hold in the 1930s, guided ascents continued. Vic Williams, Katie Gardiner and Harold Porter climbed Mt Teichelmann in 1930. Williams was regarded by many contemporaries as a major force in stimulating amateur climbing, for although Chief Guide, he encouraged new directions for younger climbers. Williams and Porter also climbed the North East Face of Glacier Peak. In 1936 Mick Bowie and Colin Wyatt climbed the West Peak of Elie de Beaumont and in 1938 Bowie, with Harry Ayres and Frank Simmons, climbed the North Ridge of the Minarets. Probably the most dashing of the guides of this period was Jack Cox who led among other ascents, traverses of Elie de Beaumont, Tasman, Dampier and Hicks.

The standout ascent of the decade was the ascent of the East Ridge of Mt Cook in 1938 by Dan Bryant and Lud Mahan. The classic East Ridge is a spectacular arête sweeping 1700m up between the Caroline and East Faces of Mt Cook. In 1933 Bryant and Mahan were turned back after climbing half the route. In 1938 the same pair returned to the attack. Both were now very experienced climbers. Bryant, for example, had been on Mt Everest in 1935 with Eric Shipton. This time the ridge was in good condition. From a bivouac on Cinerama Col, the pair climbed the ridge in twelve hours and traversed over the High Peak. The ascent of the East Ridge of Cook and the earlier climb of Syme Ridge demonstrated that amateur climbers were now a major force in New Zealand climbing.

Guides such as Vic Williams, Mick Bowie, Frank Alack, Jack Cox, Mark Lysons and others continued to display the same high standards of safety established by earlier guides, such as Peter Graham. Bowie's climbs were characterised by fast times despite the length of the routes. Only once was he out for more than eighteen hours. After 1938 however, amateur ascents of bigger routes became the norm. In 1940 Harry Stevenson and Doug Dick, two amateur climbers, ascended Syme Ridge on Mt Tasman and began descending towards the West Ridge. A kilometre along the ridge they turned down the great sweeping slope which borders the western side of the Abel Janzen face of Mt Tasman. This great traverse, like that of Mt Cook in 1913, was a fitting end to a decade of climbing expansion at Mt Cook. But as in 1913, the energies of the period were turned to concerns overseas and a more deadly game.

Post-war developments

The disruptions of World War II (1939-45) took some years to work themselves out but by 1947 a new group of young climbers began to emerge. The late 1940s and early 1950s were characterised by two features, the prominence of guide Harry Ayres and the ascent of a number of the last major ridge routes. In 1948 Ayres and Mick Sullivan led Ed Hillary and Ruth Adams up the South Ridge of Mt Cook. The route marked Ayres' coming-of-age in New Zealand climbing. Trained by the great guides of the 1930s, his skill in ice-climbing and limitless endurance made him the best climber of his day. He went on to guide first ascents of the Dixon-Haast Ridge, the Haidinger-Douglas Ridge, a double

AMCNP Collection

Harry Ayres

Dampier-Hicks traverse, the Divide Ridge of Hicks, the North East Ridge of Malte Brun, the West Peak of Haast, and Mt Magellan. With many of the accessible routes now climbed, mountaineers began to turn to the remoter parts of the Mt Cook district and the New Zealand mountains generally. The early 1950s saw ascents of the Maximilian Ridge of Elie de Beaumont, the South West Ridge of La Perouse and the East Ridge of Malte Brun.

In the early 1950s, climbers began examining the possibility of establishing new routes on faces. In 1952-53 the east faces of Malte Brun and Mt Sefton were climbed. Although not technically difficult, they foreshadowed a surge of new climbs in the mid 1950s. At the same time climber numbers were beginning to swell; post-war prosperity had taken hold, New Zealand successes in the Himalaya gained publicity, and climbing clubs became more active. The increased numbers and a summer of fine weather resulted in a string of harder routes being climbed in 1955-56.

In February 1955 Hamish MacInnes (Scotland), and Peter Robinson (USA), climbed the 1700m MacInnes Ridge on Mt Nazomi. In December 1955 the impressive West Buttress of Tasman fell to Neil Hamilton and Alan Berry. Soon after came ascents of the Hooker Face of Mt Cook, the Bowie Ridge of Mt Cook, and the South Ridge of Mt Green. Part of this impetus came from overseas climbers such as MacInnes and Robinson as well as Dick Irwin (USA). Nevertheless local climbers such as Neil Hamilton, Alan Berry and Graeme McCallum were also in the forefront.

Further significant ascents followed in the next few years. In February 1957 David Elphick and Barry Smith climbed the Left Buttress on the North Face of Hicks. In 1959-60 Mike Gill and various partners put up new routes on the South Ridge of La Perouse and the South Face of Malte Brun. The stage was now set for another move forward.

Climbers had often looked at the 1500m East Face of Mt Cook. It was described as "the Everest of the New Zealand mountaineering world, the most looked at and talked about climb in the Southern Alps". Although not a particularly technical route, it is long, serious and prone to rockfall. During the 1950s, front point cramponing had been introduced and this technique came into its own on routes like the East Face. In November 1961 Don Cowie, Pete Farrell, Lyn Crawford and Vic Walsh put speculation about the climb to an end. They ascended an obvious line on the face up the long bottom snow slopes and into an increasingly steep gully which exited up a 60 degree face just 50m south of the summit.

Julie Crawford/Hedgehog House

Guides in 1965: Peter Schlunegger, Aat Vervoorn, Peter Farrell, Bruce Jenkinson, Lyn Crawford & Herbie Bleuer.

The East Face was such a big break-through in climbing at Mt Cook that it seemed to leave the climbing scene exhausted for a while. In the five years that followed climbers seemed content to consolidate, rather than carry on from the East Face ascent. This was due to many things: bad weather for many summers, an interest in long ridge traverses (such as Derek Winter and Nigel Harrison's Mt Haast to Mt Cook marathon in 1963), and perhaps too, an element of conservatism. More important though was the fact that equipment and techniques were not sufficiently developed to allow the fast, safe climbing which many of the then unclimbed ice and mixed routes at Mt Cook require. Further advances were to wait for improved equipment and a change of attitude.

Murray Jones

A major influence on New Zealand climbing in the late 1960s was the loner Murray Jones who worked away steadily at long hard rock routes in the Darran Mountains. At Mt Cook, Jones and East Face veteran Pete Farrell separately stimulated a group of itinerant climber/guides onto new routes such as the West Face of Mt Haidinger and the South Face of Mt Douglas. The potential that lay in the unclimbed faces of the region was revealed, and these ascents between 1967 and 1968 began to breach a psychological barrier that had built up. In 1968 Jones then took his experience to the big faces in Europe, where he and Graeme Dingle climbed six major north faces in one season in 1968 – a feat that had not been achieved before.

Graeme Dingle

The early 1970s

The breakthrough in the psychological barrier was demonstrated in spectacular fashion in 1970. A summer of stable fine weather saw a whole crop of new routes climbed at Mt Cook. The season started with Peter Gough and John Glasgow climbing the Caroline Face of Mt Cook in November. This 2000m long, icecliff infested route was the last unclimbed face on the mountain. It had seen numerous attempts over the previous ten years. It had also seen four deaths. Although technically not difficult, the route was long and physically demanding. It was also a great headline grabber. "A victory for the hippies" blared the media.

John Glasgow and Peter Gough after climbing the Caroline Face.

Gough and Glasgow descended to the Hermitage to face a massive barrage of reporters, and a sumptuous meal on news media expense accounts. The publicity gave a great boost to climbing and the face itself is now depicted on the New Zealand $5 note.

An interesting epilogue to the ascent of the Caroline Face was the discovery of the remains of John Cousins and Michael Goldsmith on the Hooker Glacier in October 1999. They were last seen in November 1963 departing Ball Hut for an attempt or reconnaissance on the Caroline Face. The fact that they were found on the opposite side of the mountain suggests they may have been the first to climb the face. Film from a camera found with them was unfortunately too damaged to be developed. Other climbers active at the time suggest that although the pair were very capable (Goldsmith having climbed the East Face of Sefton), they probably climbed the South or East Ridge of Mt Cook. This story parallels that of Mallory and Irvine who went missing on Mt Everest in 1924.

Within two months of the Caroline ascent, climbs were made on the East Face of Mt Cook, the East Face of Mt Sefton Direct, and the Whymper Face and Montague Spur of Elie de Beaumont. Meanwhile, up the Hooker Valley, attention was focused on the next "last great problem", the South Face of Mt Hicks.

Mt Hicks is situated close to Mt Cook, dwarfed by its great mass. It is, however, the most demanding peak in the area. Mt Hicks' remote northern rock face drops 800m into the La Perouse Glacier. Its southern face, with its fearsome ice gullies, two prominent ribs and capping icecliff, presents a sunless facade to every tourist who visits the Mt Cook village. In December 1970 Murray Jones and Graeme Dingle ventured onto the Left Buttress and nine hours later reached the summit with an excellent new route to their credit. The intricate linking traverses, delicate mixed climbing, superb position, and good rock have made the Left Buttress on Mt Hicks one of the classics of the Mt Cook district.

The summer of 1970-71 had revealed the potential for new routes in the region. At the same time the climbing scene had enlarged to the extent that serious competition now existed for the next 'last great problem'. Competition and unclimbed routes are a recipe for action. There were two other ingredients, which ensured that the action was fast and furious.

Geoff Gabites Collection

Bill Denz

First came the introduction of curved pick ice-climbing tools. Now it was possible to climb steep to vertical ice with a speed and safety previously impossible. Consequently more and more climbers ventured onto the older classic ice climbs like the East Face of Mt Cook and the South Face of Douglas Peak.

Secondly, Bill Denz made a big impact on the Mt Cook climbing scene. If people were tending toward bigger and better climbing, Bill aimed for longer and harder. He decided early on that only first ascents were worth doing. His direct style and seemingly arrogant attitude rocked the climbing establishment. Nevertheless, Denz's single-minded determination and unwillingness to accept convention put him ten years ahead of his time.

Denz immediately showed what the curved pick revolution meant. Teaming up with Bryan Pooley, he took on the Balfour Face of Mt Tasman. The Balfour Face is a short route of only 600m. However, it involves climbing over a 3000m peak (Silberhorn) just to access the route. The face rises up steep gullies into a series of ice bulges and then merges into steep ice slopes to the summit. It is an ice-climber's test piece. Denz and Pooley made their first attempt with Kevin Carroll in October 1971. In December 1971 Pooley and Denz returned and this time there were no mistakes. Apart from a delicate traverse on vertical ice the climb was executed with little fuss.

After the Balfour, Denz continued to make a major contribution to Mt Cook climbing right through the 1970s and into the 1980s. In November 1972 he soloed the South Face of Mt Cook. His route, a new 950m line, weaves up icecliff threatened slopes. His bold style is reflected in the gear he took: two ice axes, two ice-screws and a jam jar of water! Hard on the heels of this climb was a new route on the Caroline Face, again solo, finishing the last 700m in a storm. According to Denz, the descent into the teeth of a hurricane nor'west wind brought him to despair, and then taught him what his body could withstand. One month later he was in action again, with Peter Gough and Etienne Kummer. Together they succeeded in establishing a route up the long sought-after Central Gullies on the South Face of Mt Hicks. This route was repeated twice in the 1972-73 season, by Bryan Pooley and John Stanton, and by George Harris, Chris Timms, Jim Jolly and Sandy Sandblom, and served to show how active the Mt Cook climbing scene had become.

The winter emphasis

By early 1973 the competition for the obvious new face routes began to trickle away. There was another attraction, however - climbing the routes in winter. Until 1970 winter ascents in the Mt Cook district were few and far between. The winter months at Mt Cook are characterised by comparatively stable weather, by New Zealand standards. However, temperatures are low and the snow conditions notoriously fickle. Severe avalanche danger develops quickly. Aggression and blindness to dangerous snow conditions are useful attributes for winter climbing. There were a few people with these sorts of qualities around in the early 1970s. In August 1971 Mt Tasman was climbed. The same winter Denz and Timms climbed the South Face of Douglas Peak (Timms became a yachting Olympic Gold medallist in 1972). In the winter of 1972 Bryan and Noel Sissons climbed the East Face of Mt Sefton, and soon after Noel Sissons and Graeme Dingle completed the South Ridge of Mt Cook. The following winter saw two further hard routes climbed: the East Face of Mt Cook by Bryan Pooley, Colin Dodge, Robert Rainsbury and John Visser, and the Sheila Face of Mt Cook by Denz and Gough. The latter climb was a major achievement, for it was the first alpine rock route in New Zealand to be done in winter.

The end of the 1973 winter was a minor turning point. Until then there had been a number of climbers competing for first ascents of face routes. For the next two years, until 1976, the New Zealand alpine scene was dominated by Denz and two young Dunedin climbers: Phil Herron and Murray Judge. Denz's drive and flare, coupled with Judge's technical ability and Herron's enthusiasm forged a formidable team. Much of their attention focussed on the dark grey walls of the southern Darran Mountains. At Mt Cook, however, the trio were lured onto Mt Hicks. In the 1974 winter they snatched the beautiful Central Buttress on the North Face of Mt Hicks. This route is one of New Zealand's great classic climbs, following a groove in the buttress for 800m of good rock. The following summer the Right Buttress was climbed by John Fantini, Noel Sissons and Merv English. The Denz, Judge, Herron combination returned to Mt Hicks in the winter of 1975. This time they bagged the fierce Gunbarrels ice route – at the time the hardest ice route in New Zealand.

In June of 1975 Denz and Herron pulled off their greatest coup, a winter ascent of the Balfour Face of Tasman. This climb still stands as one of the most daring winter ascents on account of its isolation, low temperatures, and demanding descent. The pair aimed to do the climb in a weekend but soon realized that they had taken on an ambitious project. After traversing Mt Silberhorn they were forced to bivouac on the face. Their ascent followed the original gully line and then broke left up waves of vertical and near vertical snow ice. Before completing the climb the next day they had broken the picks on both their axes. The descent involved another bivouac in -20ºC temperatures and a slog in heavy snow back over Mt Silberhorn. Phil Herron's death in a crevasse fall under Cerro Torre in Patagonia, five months after the Balfour climb, brought an abrupt end to a successful chapter in New Zealand's climbing history.

The late seventies

The later seventies witnessed a different level of activity from the frenetic pace earlier in the decade. There was as much climbing as before, but climbers were content to repeat established routes. Denz and others had advanced the standards of climbing to a stage where new techniques, new skills and above all, new people were needed. In the five years between 1975 and 1980 climbs such as the Caroline Face of Cook had twenty ascents, and the Balfour Face of Tasman six. New routes were climbed, notably the Abel Jansen face of Tasman by Merv English and Murray Jones. Murray Judge and Dick Price climbed the North Ridge of Cook in winter. Soloing of routes, always a rather rare occasion at Mt Cook because of difficult crevasse-strewn approaches became slightly more prevalent with ascents of the Caroline Face, East Face of Cook and Brian Fish's ascent of the North Face Central Buttress of Mt Hicks.

Colin Monteath/Hedgehog House

Nick Cradock

By 1979 there were signs that the late 1970s lull had come to an end. Fresh from a rock climbing tour in Australia, American climber Tobin Sorenson teamed up with a group of young Christchurch climbers and spent a week in August 1979 at the head of the Hooker Glacier. Tobin and Nick Cradock produced two of the finest hard ice routes in the Mt Cook district, both on the South Face of Mt Hicks. They chose not just the faces themselves, or the obvious features. They chose the good lines. Like Denz earlier in the decade, they showed that it was not climbing the feature or the mountain that gave true satisfaction, but the quality of climbing instead.

Sorenson and Cradock's routes, *The Curver* and the *Yankee-Kiwi Couloir*, were each climbed in the phenomenal time of eight hours. Once again, no detailed account of either climb has been left and like Herron, Sorenson did not live to write one. The harder of the two routes, the *Yankee-Kiwi Couloir*, involves a grade 18 crack climbed in crampons, followed by a succession of steep gully runnels. It is still one of the more technically difficult ice climbs at Mt Cook.

The 1980s – ice then rock

The early 1980s saw a consolidation of the advances of the seventies and a proliferation of difficult ice gully lines. The accomplishments of 1979 were followed by three summers of active climbing. In 1980-81 there were six repeat ascents of major routes such as the *Yankee-Kiwi Couloir*, the first of a series of gully climbs on the left side of the South Face of Mt Cook and a new line on the right side of the same face. This last route took a breathtaking line up a buttress between awesome icecliffs. Called the *Gates of Steel*, it was done by the ubiquitous Denz and Nigel Perry. It was, unfortunately, one of Denz's last great routes at Mt Cook - and the route would not see a winter ascent for fifteen years. Denz died in an avalanche on Makalu's West Pillar in 1983, leaving a void in the New Zealand climbing scene.

Colin Monteath/Hedgehog House

Russell Braddock

In 1981-82 new lines were established on Mt Tasman's Hidden Face and Abel Jansen Face while routes like the Sheila Face of Mt Cook and the Left Buttress on Mt Hicks' South Face were soloed. Guy Halliburton and Alan Woods' direct line on the isolated Hidden Face (also known as the 'Hidden Balfour') was a major new hard route involving very steep ice. This climb defined a new benchmark for difficulty, isolation and commitment. The same season saw a new motivating force appear on the scene. Kim Logan soloed a gully line right of Earle's Route on Mt Cook (without gloves). In 1982-83 Logan and Russell Braddock climbed *Rattus Balfourus* on the Balfour Face of Tasman - originally named by a party who had attempted it in 1979, and beaten a quick retreat to lick their wounds when Nick Cradock took a 20m fall, injuring his ankle. After *Rattus*, Braddock and Logan moved onto the South Face of Hicks, producing *Heaven's Door*, at the start of 1983. This route is now regarded as a Mt Hicks classic. At almost the same time Marty Beare and John Entwisle, looking for some rest and recreation after a guides course, climbed the *Left Buttress* on the Balfour Face. The summer of 1983-84 had been a good season for new ice routes.

In January of 1984, Kim Logan returned to the South Face of Hicks with Pete Sinclair to add the impressive *Logan's Run*. Originally conceived by Denz, *Logan's Run* takes the thin line of ice that runs up the left side of the Right Buttress - it is steep and straight. Because Logan and Sinclair avoided the last pitch by traversing right some felt that the route was not completed. Despite this, *Logan's Run* was the second grade 6+ route on Mt Hicks, and in the region, since 1979. It remains a three-star reference 'hard' technical ice route that climbers look to cut their teeth on today.

With the likes of *Rattus Balfourous, Logan's Run, Heaven's Door* and the *Left Buttress* on the Balfour Face, the quality of lines was very high but the standard of difficulty was only matching what had been achieved in the 1970s.

In the early 1980s major advances in climbing gear such as plastic boots, reverse curve picks, foot fang crampons, titanium ice screws, fast drying synthetic clothing and goretex jackets arrived. These improvements in equipment did not produce the same climbing advances that, say, front points in the 1950s and 1960s, and curved picks in the early 1970s had brought about. The improved comfort and safety afforded by the new gear did however contribute significantly to an increase in the number of active climbers, particularly those repeating "classic hard routes".

As a result the 1983-85 period saw, instead, an energetic phase where many high quality routes and variations were established. Climbers active at this time seemed to be looking for new challenges across all types of terrain and all modes of climbing. Braddock and Sinclair, both involved in prior ice route developments, established new lines on Mt Cook's South Face and Mt Walter. Another motivator, Carol Nash, added the ice line, *Swiss Virgins* to Vampire's unclimbed south-east face, with Rob Blackburne. Opportunities for major new lines were starting to thin out and so some of the less-visited areas received attention.

Guy Halliburton

Carol Nash

The steep and shady South Face of Hicks also received two doses of new route attention and Nazomi had two routes added to its South Face. Over on the Coast, Greg and Deanne Landreth climbed the superb *Moonshine Buttress* at the head of the Fox Glacier in 1984. This buttress offers nine pitches of outstanding alpine rockclimbing and is now regarded as one of the regions 'must do' routes. Despite the wide range of routes climbed in this 1983-85 period, the difficulty levels attained earlier would not be surpassed until 1986.

Off the beaten track
John Nankervis, a dominant figure in the development of new routes off the beaten track, since 1968, established new routes in literally all the distant, and sometimes hidden, corners and fringes of the park. 'Nank', often roped to Dave Bamford, developed routes in the Spencer, Murchison, La Perouse, Balfour, Whataroa and Godley regions. With an encyclopaedic knowledge of the park, and always looking for new areas to explore, Nank did not let many opportunities escape his attention. Routes like the North Ridge and Burton Spur on Elie de Beaumont (1978 & 1984), South Face of Torres (1980) and the Nipple Rib and White Jasmine on Tasman (1982 & 1983) are just a sample of the superb lines that he sought out in the less-visted areas. Having completed more than 20 new routes in the region Nank is in a class of his own – this is more than any other person in the last 30 years.

Also in 1984, the little known Bill McLeod made the first winter solo ascent of the East Ridge of Mt Cook and the first winter ascent of Syme Ridge on Mt Tasman. Again in winter, McLeod returned in 1985 for a month at the head of the Hooker and soloed: Mt La Perouse, Earle's Route on Mt Cook and the Curtain Route on Mt Hicks. It would become obvious later that the quiet tradesman-like McLeod was just warming up.

Winter and solo climbing would continue to be a major frontier through the mid 1980s but added to this would be speed and endurance ascents, as well as 'integrals' – where two or more routes are linked. In 1978 Tim Macartney-Snape and Lincoln Hall set the benchmark for impressive integrals by linking the MacInnes Ridge on

Nazomi with the isolated South Ridge of Mt Cook, the combined ridge lines of which ascend over 2300m from the Hooker Glacier. In the early eighties Cradock and Steve Moon climbed the MacInnes Ridge and the Gledhill Buttress in one day. Not to be outdone, Gavin Tweedie and Athol Whimp climbed the Right Hand Buttress on the North Face of Hicks, continued over Dampier, up the North Ridge of Mt Cook and then finished off with a Grand Traverse.

In 1984 Paul Bayne quietly snatched the impressive and coveted first solo of the Balfour Face of Mt Tasman – taking just two and half hours. This achievement was strangely unheralded at the time, possibly because the psychological difficulties had already been surmounted.

Arrival of competition and the Lycra® influence

In the mid to late 1980s the atmosphere became relatively competitive between climbers – possibly more so for those who were also rockclimbers. It may have been an overflow from the intensely competitive crag scene where new route development was racing ahead with the exploding development of new crags around the country. Available lines for new alpine routes were becoming very scarce too and it would take some Aussies to shake the locals into action.

In 1986 the experienced and intensely competitive John Fantini teamed up with Tony Dignan, both from Australia, and focused on ice. They created a sensational new grade 6 line on the left side of the Balfour face of Tasman – *The Mists of Avalon*, the first of its grade since 1984.

During the mid 1980s the top exponents of crag and big wall climbing became the main motivators for new hard routes. Skills honed on the crags were being transferred to the mountains almost seamlessly. This trend of rockclimbers applying their skills to alpine routes was not new however, as Bill Denz, Murray Judge, Nick Cradock and especially Tobin Sorenson, had all climbed rock separately. Marty Beare, one of New Zealand's strongest rockclimbers in the early 1980s, Cradock, and Kevin Boekholt all added new rock variations to existing routes. The difference in the mid 1980s compared to the 1970s, however, was that rockclimbing had taken hold as a climbing activity in its own right. Because of this, more top rockclimbers became involved in new route activity in the Aoraki/Mt Cook region than ever before.

More ice and new opportunities

The *Mists of Avalon* established by Fantini and Dignan seemed to spark a resurgence in the Kiwi camp. In the winter of 1986, Cradock, ever hungry for ice, joined forces with Guy Cotter and added *Weeping Gash*, a grade 6+ route, to the North Face of Hicks - which does not ice up often. A year later the spring brought good ice conditions of which the mercurial Dave Fearnley and the legendarily strong John McCallum – both at the forefront of New Zealand rockclimbing, took advantage. Together they added *The Tingler* to the Right Hand Buttress on the South Face of Mt Hicks. Although their route is only six pitches long it offers no shortage of entertainment for those looking for steep ice. During the mid 1980s many of the harder routes in the region received repeat ascents. The Caroline Face on Mt Cook and the Balfour Face on Mt Tasman were no exception. Both received first female ascents when Maryann Waters and Lydia Bradey, respectively climbed them in 1986.

During the years 1987-88 the right hand side of the South Face of Cook received four new ice routes. Although the routes didn't push into grade 6 territory they added atmosphere and boldness instead - taking lines directly below a major ice cliff on the right hand side of the face. The names of the routes tell the story: *David and Goliath,* a route of biblical proportions, was the first, established by Paul Aubrey and Pete Axford (who eyed the route from his house in the village). The spine-chilling *Nerve Runner* was added by the ever-lurking Nick Cradock, while *Romeo and Juliet* was put up by Lionel Clay and Anne Palmer. Clay was particularly active in the Cook region during the mid to late 1980s, establishing new ice and rock routes as well as making repeats of hard classics. Brian Alder and Dave Vass also added *Sodom & Gomorrah* under the icecliffs on Cook's South Face.

Going it alone

The mid 1980s are most remembered for solo climbs. The number of climbers taking on the more risky version of the game increased substantially, as did the number and difficulty of routes soloed. Carol McDermott, a super-motivated climber active during the mid-late 1980s, climbed whenever he could, climbing partner or not. McDermott was phenomenally fit and zoomed up the Caroline Face in seven and a half hours, (a day return from Christchurch) his only sustenance – a small bottle of coke and a bag of jelly-beans. He also soloed the isolated Strauchon faces of Dilemma and Unicorn. Steve Elder seized a rare opportunity by soloing the unclimbed North Face of Sefton in late 1988. By the late 1980s the Balfour Face, White Dreams and Central Gullies had all received several solo ascents.

Peter Dickson

Bill McLeod

Despite the impressive achievements of these climbers, one man would quietly emerge as the central soloing force. By the end of the 1980s most of the remaining hard ice routes in the region had been soloed by the dedicated and intensely modest Bill McLeod. McLeod began climbing in the late 1970s and soon developed an appetite for winter climbing – less people, less noise. It did not take long for McLeod to become an antihero for most of the New Zealand climbing scene and his legendary dry wit always produced mirth among followers. Even though he would ski into huts, McLeod was overheard saying, "a ski that slides is a ski that is out of control". After a trip in the hills his companions would typically hit the pub for a few cold ones, but not McLeod - he would return to the campground and do sets of press-ups and pull-ups.

Adept on ice and mixed ground, McLeod, like the newer generation of climbers, worked almost religiously on his rockclimbing skills. He would quietly arrive at a crag and begin at one end not stopping until he had climbed "all the routes". McLeod systematically soloed all the major difficult ice routes in the Aoraki/Mt Cook region

- in winter too - culminating with the Balfour Face and the *Yankee-Kiwi Couloir.* Having run out of objectives for the moment, McLeod shifted his attention to the next area of focus – alpine rock, where again there would be a jump in standards.

The majority of the new ice routes in the mid to late 1980s had been developed in the usual spots. *Far from the Madding Crowd,* conceived and put up by Geoff Gabites with Colin Monteath and Hugh Nicholson in 1988, was an exception. This new route on the rarely visited Vampire, at the head of the Mueller Glacier, along with the earlier established *Swiss Virgins*, helped kick-start a rush of interest to put up new routes in this area in the early 1990s. But more importantly it signalled that rarely visited areas held new opportunities.

In 1988 Carol McDermott joined forces with Peter Dickson and headed into the Balfour for a rock and ice tour. Dickson was shocked to find that the food McDermott brought was mostly Toffee Pops biscuits and Coca Cola. In spite of this, they completed two new routes on Mt Drake, a peak supplying consistently good quality rock, not found on other mountains in the region. Whilst on the superb three star *Astrolabe* Dickson was able to survey the towering and unclimbed neighbouring buttresses of Drake. He couldn't believe his eyes – and made a note to return.

The next grade

Dickson's vision of what was possible became reality when he returned to Mt Drake with Alex Palman in February 1989 for 19 days. In that time they put up six new rock routes. All grade 6+ or harder. The *Pelican* was the break-through route. It was significantly harder than any other rock climb in the region, with a rock crux of grade 22, and earned itself grade 7. *Samurai* was the last of the new routes, with a sting in the tail, and was given grade 7-. Amidst the usual equipment they used rock-shoes, chalkbags and hand-driven bolt drills. What made these routes different was the approach the pair took. They climbed from a nearby camp, carrying a minimum of gear, and put their rockclimbing skills to full use. On return to the village the pair were met with some disbelief. The grades were questioned, as was the use of bolts – it was the first time bolts had been used on a high alpine route in the Mt Cook-Westland region (excluding Mt Sebastopol and the 'Lost Bolt Buttress' route). It was not until 1992 when Pete Smale and Paul Jenkins (UK) climbed the *Pelican* and confirmed the grade and quality, that New Zealand had its first grade 7 route.

The 1980s was seen out in style by Gottlieb Braun-Elwert and Erica Beuzenberg. They became the first to climb all of New Zealand's 3000m peaks in a winter season. Beuzenberg also became the first woman to summit Mt Cook in winter. The last act of the decade however, was a new ice route on the rarely visited Hidden Balfour Face of Mt Tasman. *Hippo Takes A Holiday* (grade 6) was created by Brian Alder and Dave Vass in October 1989.

The 1990s – more new rock, harder ice and Bill McLeod

The new decade was heralded mainly by a focus on new routes on more isolated and previously overlooked peaks. Standards remained relatively static during this time as the number of climbers getting onto harder routes declined.

Winter ascents increased in popularity and traverses also featured. Phil Penney and Al Uren, following Braun-Elwert and Beuzenberg's example, traversed from Elie de Beaumont to Mt Cook in winter. Beuzenberg also climbed the Balfour Face in winter – becoming the first woman to do so.

Alpine rock climbs, however, continued to grow in popularity, fuelled not just by developments within the district, but also by those outside. Both Cloudy Peak, of inland Canterbury, and Twin Stream received significant attention, with the latter still experiencing ongoing new route development. Activity in the Darran Mountains also remained high, contributing to an increase in alpine rock routes.

Peter Dickson, also a keen soloist, added *For Whom The Bell Tolls* to Sefton's daunting east face and the Slovakian, Slavko Miroslav, made a bold new line to the right side of the Caroline Face in 1990. Boosted by the success of the Drake trip, Dickson launched into the Strauchon Valley to attack the 1200m rock slabs of Mts Unicorn and Dilemma. Initially he soloed a new route on Unicorn, producing a sustained grade 6- line with cruxes of grade 15. The following year Dickson completed the futuristic *Direttissima* route on Dilemma. It was an ambitious project with the preparation paralleling Maestri's efforts on Cerro Torre in Argentina, where in place of a petrol driven compressor, Dickson hauled a small generator to the top of the peak to re-charge his drill. With Jo Kippax he then abseiled down the entire face placing bolts on the way. All was going well until the drill-bit broke and they had to make a desperate descent rappelling off wafer size flakes to the valley floor. The route gained plenty of critics but not many got out of their armchairs to make a second ascent. Many did sit up, however, when Peter Taw later guided Len Harvey up the route and spoke highly of the line. This was also the first guided ascent of the Strauchon Face of Dilemma. With Bill McLeod, Dickson later added *Classical Gas* to Unicorn in 1992.

In July 1991 McLeod and Dickson met up at Plateau hut and began a blitzkrieg on Mt Cook including the first winter ascent of the Bowie Ridge and a major new route on the East Face - *Rumblestiltzskin* (grade 6-). Two years later the same pair travelled to the rarely visited South Face of Sealy to snatch its first ascent (grade 5). McLeod later returned alone to Sealy's south side to add *Hello Darkness* in 1993.

The new-look cloud-piercer

On 14 December 1991, at about midnight, Mt Cook let go of more than six million cubic metres of rock and ice debris. The summit that Jack Clarke, George Graham and Tom Fyfe had gained in 1894, and hundreds of climbers since, fell some 2700m to the floor of the Tasman Valley, in a matter of minutes. The new razor-sharp ice shard summit is ten metres lower than its predecessor. After the dust settled Bryan Moore was the first to look over the abyss, showing that it was relatively safe to summit the new-look cloud-piercer.

As a result of the changes to Mt Cook, climbers flocked to the other side of the massif, packing the Hooker Valley like never before. However the amount of climbing in the region began to wane from 1991. Fewer climbers visited the park and fewer still attempted new routes. The exact reasons for this were unclear, but poor ice conditions for a series of seasons, both winter and summer, combined with a general increase in crag-climbing and interest in other areas (e.g. Darrans and Aspiring regions) was certainly partially responsible.

With a relatively quiet park to themselves, the unstoppable McLeod and Brian Alder added the ice route *Nosferatu* (grade 6-) to Mt Vampire's South East Face in July 1993. This route helped refocus attention on the Mueller area and as a result several other new routes were established. McLeod then returned to the North Face of Hicks to add *Book of Days* (grade 5) with Mark Taylor.

Possibly the most looked at and most revered new route opportunity in the park was the South Face of La Perouse. In the late 1980s several parties had eyed up the route thinking that it might be harder than any ice route that had gone before it. The face during winter is usually dominated with an intimidating weeping wall of ice and is completely shaded. A month after *Nosferatu*, Alder joined forces with, guess who, McLeod, to complete the impressive *Bill and Ted's Excellent Adventure*, grading it 6+. Many think that it may be harder. At the time of printing a second ascent had not been recorded.

After the creation of *Bill and Ted's* the interest in ice elsewhere began to increase. Nick Cradock, who first established a new ice line on the south face of Mt Mallory in 1990, returned several times during the following years to develop more ice routes. This in turn stimulated others into action and Mallory's south face now sports six routes. The neighbouring Mt Barnicoat received attention later in the decade and currently hosts four south face routes. These routes, along with Vanya Furlen's (Slovenia) route on the South Face of Aoraki/Mt Cook in 1994, were the last major ice developments before the focus swung back to alpine rock again.

Red rock west

In January 1995 Alex Palman and a talented young rockclimber, Nick Flyvbjerg, headed into the Balfour to tackle the unclimbed West Face of Mt Magellan. They produced *Anyone Can Play Guitar* (6-), a straight line made of the same high quality rock found on Mt Drake. Palman knew from his time on Drake that Magellan held more new route potential. In early 1996 Peter Dickson joined the pair to help add two more lines to Magellan. Both *Pooh Corner* (6-) and *Menage a trois* (6+) provided superb quality climbing with *Menage* offering a crux of grade 20. Back on Drake the team added *Superconnected,* a grade 27 direct start to the *Pelican* route. This latter route showed just how hard alpine rock routes could be pushed and where the future routes might be.

Over to the east others were putting rock-shoes on too. Sean Waters and Tim Balla added *Unveiled* (crux 20) in 1996 to the West Face of Nun's Veil. Dave Crow and Kiersten Price ventured onto the previously unclimbed East Face of Nun's Veil in 1995 creating *The Far Side* (5) - a committing and classic mixed climb. Throughout this intense period of alpine rock route development a few new ice lines were established during the winter months. *'Notforustwo'* (5-) put up on Mt Vampire, in 1996, by Al Uren and Davie Robinson, was the most significant of these new lines.

In 1999, at the head of the Hooker Valley new route development of another type was taking place. When the *'Original Gunbarrels'* was first established on the South

Face of Mt Hicks in 1975 the now famous crux (a 50m ice pillar on the second pitch) had been aided. All attempts to free this section were repelled, and these included several monster falls taken by Uren and Paul Rogers. It was not until November 1998 that the first two pitches were freed by Uren and Julian White. Uren later commented that if the whole route was climbed free it would probably be grade seven. Alas this was not to be: a large rock avalanche in June 1999 spelt the end of the first two pitches and the first ascent of the new Gunbarrels start was quickly snatched by Jono Clarke and others.

Others were also looking to push the grades. The old firm of Palman and Dickson teamed up once again to look at Mt Drake in the new millennium. A line of unbroken red rock straight up the Right Hand Buttress had been earlier overlooked but now captured Palman's imagination. Their efforts produced *Red Scorpion* a sustained route with a demanding finish.

New possibilities

Compared to the 1980s, which saw large numbers of climbers in the hills completing new routes, the 1990s seemed somewhat quieter. The large numbers of "long term" summer student climbers were also notably absent from the latter part of the decade – possibly a sign of the student-debt times. Those climbing new routes tended to be quite focused on alpine rock or ice – when it was there, and that was generally in winter. Others were busy too, but not in the usual places - they were searching out more remote virgin country.

From the grade six ice route developments of the 1970s, through to the 1980s when rockclimbers brought new skills aplenty to solve ice and alpine rock problems, to the 1990s and beyond where new boundaries in alpine ice and rock have begun to be pushed, the Aoraki/Mount Cook region seems always to have new possibilities. During the mid 1980s it was said that the region was climbed-out, but the activity of the last 15 years has shown that the opportunities are endless for climbing, in what is one of the world's most spectacular and challenging alpine regions.

Mueller Glacier Area

Mueller Glacier Area

This area is easily accessible from the village, with the peaks on the Sealy Range being especially popular. They provide short, relatively easy climbs for the beginner or the climber seeking a gentle introduction to the region. In saying this, however, peaks on the Main Divide and the south faces of the Sealy Range, such as Vampire and Jean, offer excellent routes that are technically more difficult, longer and more committing, due to remoteness.

Access

There are two huts in the area. The first, **Mueller Hut,** is gained from the village via the Kea Point and Sealy Tarns tracks. Beyond the tarns, slopes lead to a ridge, which flattens out to reveal the hut close under Mt Ollivier. During winter the slopes above the tarns can pose an avalanche risk.

Barron Saddle Hut can be reached via the upper Mueller Glacier from Mueller Hut, head south and drop over the ridge down tussock and scree slopes, past the original Mueller Hut site and finally down the rubbly moraine wall onto the moraine covered glacier. Once on the upper Mueller Glacier, it is a relatively straightforward trip up the centre of the glacier and up final scree and rock slopes under Scissors to the hut on Barron Saddle. The 'high' route to Barron Saddle starts from the Mueller Hut and crosses the scree shelf on the southern slopes under Mt Kitchener (beware of avalanches in winter) and so up onto the Annette Plateau. From the plateau cross onto the Metelille Glacier and through Sladden Saddle, then cross a névé and either ascend over the North West Ridge of Mt Darby or descend around the bottom of the ridge via a shelf 250m above the Mueller Glacier to Barron Saddle Hut.

An alternative route to Barron Saddle, particularly during winter, is to descend the moraine wall from the western end of the White Horse Hill (this route has become more difficult). Once on the Mueller Glacier you can walk (or skin) up the moraine until you reach the white ice, where the travel becomes easier. This is also the best way to reach the direct routes on the East Face of Sefton and other mountains further up the Mueller Glacier.

Another option to access the Mueller Glacier is to follow the Mueller Lake edge from the first swing bridge on the Hooker Valley track. Glacial recession and the enlargement of the lake continue to make access difficult so check locally for up to date conditions.

The Sealy Range can also be reached via the ridges behind the village, the most popular route being via Sebastopol up the ridge to Mt Annette.

Shelter

Mueller Hut. Owned and operated by AMCNP, the hut has 12 bunks, some cooking utensils, blankets and a radio. This hut is scheduled to be replaced in 2002, 200-300m closer to Mt Ollivier new hut ~1800m, cell phone coverage (025). A warden is resident during summer.

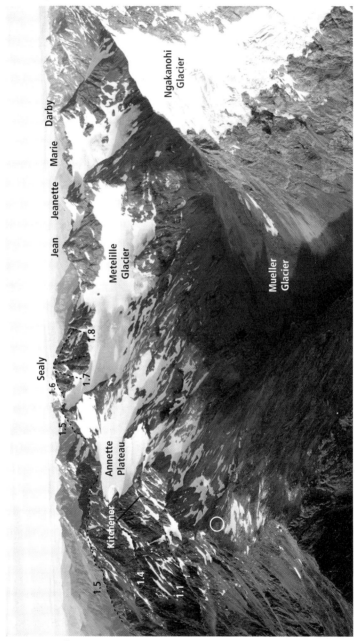

Fig. 1 Sealy Range from the north. Circle denotes possible new Mueller Hut location.

Barron Saddle Hut. Owned and operated by AMCNP. The hut is barrel-shaped with two large bench bunks that sleep four or more each. Services include some cooking utensils, blankets, solar powered lights and a radio (~1990m, grid ref: 685-122).

Times
Mt Cook Village to Mueller Hut 3-4 hours.
Mt Cook Village to Barron Saddle Hut via the upper Mueller Glacier 7 hours.
Mueller Hut to Barron Saddle Hut via the 'high' route 5-7 hours.

Ski Touring Routes
• Annette Plateau from Mueller Hut. Care to be taken on the very exposed traverse west of Kitchener (B).

Route Access
Routes on the south faces of Mts Sealy, Jean, Jeanette, Marie and Darby are included here, but access to the first three is best gained from the Upper Dobson Valley, using Jamieson Saddle. The south side of Mts Darby and Marie however are easily accessed from Barron Saddle.

Mt Ollivier 1933m

1.0   Grade 1-
>   A short walk from Mueller Hut. There are numerous variations.

Mt Kitchener 2042m

1.1   Watertank Ridge   Grade 1
>   Starts directly behind the Hermitage. A pleasant day trip.

1.2   Grade 1-
>   Up easy rock from the slopes beyond Mueller Hut.

Mt Annette 2235m

1.3   Grade 1-
>   From Mueller Hut traverse 200m below the ridge above the Mueller Glacier before ascending to reach the Annette Plateau. Cross the plateau to the small bump to the east.
>   Arthur Harper, Percy Johnson, Jan 1891.

1.4   Sebastopol Ridge   Grade 1
>   Traverse or sidle Sebastopol and follow the ridge, at the top using either the steep rock or the snowslope on the right (beware cornice). It is thought that Glenthorne shepherds may have climbed Mt Sebastopol (1468m) early in the 1800s.
>   Freda du Faur, Peter Graham, Nov 1910.

Fig. 2 *The Mueller Glacier and Barron Saddle. Circle denotes Barron Saddle Hut.*

Lloyd Homer/IGNS

Mt Sealy 2627m

1.5   **Low Peak**   Grade 2 +
Just a small bump when ascended from the Mueller Glacier side but the
Hoophorn Ridge which connects with Mt Edgar Thomson provides good
rockclimbing when climbed from the lower Tasman Valley.
Hugh Logan, D Pluth, Dec 1973.

1.6   **East Ridge**   Grade 2
The ridge rises from Barrow Col between the Low and High Peaks in a
series of steep rotten steps.
Jack Clarke, C L Barrow, Edward FitzGerald, Mattias Zurbriggen, Jan 1895.

1.7   **North Face**   Grade 2
A number of routes exist from the Metelille Névé. A steep couloir leads
almost directly to the summit, the rock face to the couloir's right gives more
technical climbing, and further right there is a short couloir leading onto
the North West Ridge.
Freda Du Faur, Peter Graham, Dec 1909.
(The couloir route was climbed by Peter Graham and Claude Macdonald, Feb 1909,
while a couloir and chimney were climbed by O Bainbridge, Jack Clarke, W Tennant,
Mar 1903.)

1.8   **North West Ridge**   Grade 1+
Although sometimes gained from Sladden Saddle, the ridge is usually gained
via the couloirs on the North or South West Faces.
Otto Frind, Conrad Kain, Feb 1914.

1.9   **South West Face**   Grade 1
Ascend to Sladden Saddle, circle round the back of the peak and head up
the 150m snow slope (beware of slab avalanches in winter or early summer).
Then follow the ridge over a short step to the summit. This is the usual
descent route.
Descended: Peter Graham, Mr & Mrs L H Lindon, B Spencer, W Fisher, Jan 1911.

South Face

★ **1.10**   **Prime Time**   Grade 5
Climb the 800m rock buttress in the centre of the face, passing right of the
snowfield to finish 50m right of the summit. Involves good climbing on
sound rock (crux 15/16). The most difficult section is a smooth snow covered
slab near the top.
Bill McLeod, Peter Dickson, Feb 1993.

1.11   **Hello Darkness**   Grade 4+
On the right side of the south face, the route follows a snow/ice gully system
directly to a low point between Sealy's summit and east peak. Some mixed
ground near the top. Crux is at the 3/4 point. 650m.
Bill McLeod, Nov 1994.

Sladden Saddle 2344m

1.12

This saddle is situated between Mts Sealy and Massey and allows easy passage between the Metelille and Sladden Glaciers. Sladden Saddle is commonly used as part of the 'high route' to Barron Saddle Hut. It should be noted that after a southerly storm significant slab avalanche risk exists on the lee side. Several parties have been caught out in the past.

Mt Massey 2436m

1.13 Grade 1

Routes may be found almost anywhere up either the North Face from the Metelille Glacier or the short South Face from the Sladden Glacier. Rock buttresses further down the South Face should give good rock climbing.
Hugh Wright, J Robertson, Feb 1915.

Mt Jean 2519m

1.14 Grade 1

Short easy routes exist from the Sladden Névé up the northern rock and snow slopes of Mts Jean, Jeanette and Marie.
W Fisher, Maughan, M Sloman, Conrad Kain, Dec 1914.

South Face

1.15   Vanity Fare Grade 5-

Start at the centre of the face and progress up through bulges to the main gully. This gully exits 70m left of the summit; but when well up, a gully/ramp leads right and finishes on summit. A 1000m route with 500m of that being quite steep.
Bill McLeod, Oct 1993.

Mt Jeanette 2485m

1.16 Grade 1

See Route 1.14
Conrad Kain, J Thomson, Feb 1916.

South Face

1.17   Keep Your Seats Please Grade 5

Approach the climb from the right hand side by angling up the face to gain the rock. About 10 pitches of steady climbing on fractured rock with a crux (15) on the last pitch. A central line finishing 100m west of the summit.
Bill McLeod, Feb 1994.

Mt Marie 2504m

1.18   Grade 1
See Route 1.14
Conrad Kain, M Sloman, Jan 1916.

Dobson Face

1.19   Birdland   Grade 4
Follow the south spur by an excellent rock rib. Gain height on the snow,
then climb two challenging rock pitches. Easy snow slopes lead to the summit
tower and five zig zag pitches up snow and ice to the summit. Descend via
Sladden Saddle.
Bill McLeod, Ross Cullen, Nov 1993.

Mt Darby 2531m

1.20   East Flank   Grade 1
Follow the snow slope to the ridge east of the summit.
First ascent party unknown.

1.21   North West Ridge   Grade 1
This ridge can be reached at almost any point. A route to Barron Saddle
exists round the foot of the ridge via a shingle ledge 250m above the Mueller
Glacier. (Be careful in winter though!)
Freda Du Faur, Peter Graham, Nov 1910.

1.22   From Barron Saddle   Grade 1+
Via the Williams Glacier ascend the North West or West Ridges, or a rib up
the middle of the West Flank.
Tom Fyfe, George Graham, 1894.

1.23   North West Ridge   Grade 1
Conrad Kain, Otto Frind, Feb 1914.

1.24   West Rib   Grade 2
Mike Andrews, Kevin Conaglen, Jan 1977.

South Face

1.25   Bengal   Grade 4-
Access to the face is easy, descend from Barron Saddle, then follow a gully to
the snow slopes to beneath the face. This is a 300m rock route which begins
in the centre of the face, on the right side of the black gully. Cross left
through the gully to gain the left trending corner. Follow this corner to a
broad ramp which leads to the summit. (crux 12).
Bill McLeod, Mar 1995.

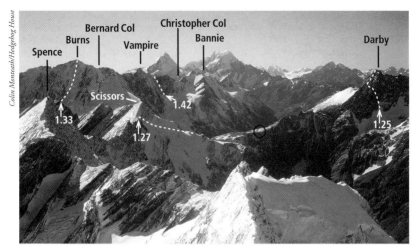

Fig. 3 Barron Saddle from the south. Circle denotes Barron Saddle Hut.

Barron Saddle 1992m

1.26   Grade 1-

Via Mueller Hut. The saddle is reached via the upper Mueller Glacier route to Barron Saddle Hut or the 'high route' via the Annette Plateau, Sladden Saddle and either across or beneath the North West Ridge of Darby. On the Dobson side either follow a rotten rock rib directly below the saddle or diagonally down snowslopes under Scissors.

Thomas Brodrick, Louis Sladden, 1890.

Access to the Landsborough Valley and Scissors 2339m

1.27   Grade 1+

The saddle (spot height 2240m) between Scissors and Mt Spence provides the best access to the route down the rock slabs/snow slopes, onto the Spence Glacier thence Rubicon Torrent and Landsborough Valley. Either climb the easy ridge onto Scissors from Barron Saddle and traverse toward Mt Spence or sidle beneath Scissors on the Dobson Valley face to gain the saddle - the traverse is exposed but relatively straightforward. On the western side, descend the slabs generally on the true right where the strata allows, taking care in icy conditions. A good bivvy rock can be found on the grassy terraces on the true right of the Rubicon where it meets the Landsborough (~1180m, map 260-H36, grid ref: 634-131).

Scissors: Otto Frind, Conrad Kain, Feb 1914

58

Scissors

1.28 Crew Cut   Grade 4+

North East Face. About the centre of the wall between Scissors and Mt Montgomery there is a broad gully that forms ice in the cooler months. A steep headwall caps the gully and is bypassed on the right, then straight up slopes to ridge.

Andy MacFarlane, Bill McLeod, Sep 1993.

1.29 Direct from the Mueller Glacier   Grade 2

Ascend sound rock which gradually eases back.

Faye Kerr, M Clarborough, early 1970s.

1.30 From Fyfe Pass   Grade 1

An easy scramble. It is possible to ascend up under Mt Montgomery from the Upper Mueller Glacier and so onto Scissors.

Tom Fyfe, George Graham, Feb 1894.

Mt Montgomery 2340m

1.30i   Grade 1

From the top of Scissors traverse to Hardies Gut and then continue up to Mt Montgomery.

Otto Frind, Conrad Kain, Feb 1914.

Fyfe Pass 2266m

1.31   Grade 1+

This used to be the traditional route to the Landsborough Valley, but it is not recommended unless the western rock slabs are free from avalanche danger, which is rare. A slightly slower but safer route exists via Barron Saddle and traversing Scissors towards Mt Spence, described under Route 1.27.

Tom Fyfe, George Graham, Feb 1894.

Mt Burns 2746m

1.32 Watchtower (SW) Ridge   Grade 3+

Gain the ridge from the upper Mueller Glacier north of the Watchtower (a prominent knob near Fyfe Pass was first climbed by Otto Frind and Conrad Kain in Feb 1914) via a short face climb. The upper ridge is complicated by awkward slanting rock. The rock steps can be best turned on the slabby western face. The eastern side tends to be rotten.

H T Barcham, Ash Cunningham, A Witten-Hannah, Dec 1952.

1.33 South Face   Grade 3+

From the Welchman Glacier ascend the obvious ramp which angles from left to right directly under the summit. Finish up the rock rib to the summit.

Brian Weedon, Richard Schmidt, Apr 1980.

Mike Smith, Gary Dickson, Jun 1985 (followed 1.33 half-way then up a rock rib to the right).

1.34   Welchman Glacier Route   Grade 2

Ascend the glacier and up a couloir (sometimes cornice threatened) to an unnamed col. Then either follow the Main Divide to the summit or drop down onto the western slopes and ascend from there. It is also possible to cross to Bernard Col from the Welchman Glacier, but it is a longer climb. The Welchman Glacier route is the best means of descent from Mt Burns. Three or more abseils may be necessary to descend over a cornice at the top. (Bernard Col may present similar problems.)

Peter Graham, Samuel Turner, Mar 1914.

Bernard Col 2653m

1.35

Can be used to ascend Burns but is not a good route to the McKerrow Glacier.

Jack Clarke, Laurence Earle, Alex Graham, Peter Graham, Bernard Head, Darby Thomson, 1909.

Vampire Peak 2645m

1.36   Grade 2+

Via the Welchman Glacier and Bernard Col, follow north along rotten rock on the Main Divide. It is also possible to drop down to the west and use the North West Ridge.

Peter Graham, Samuel Turner, Mar 1914.

1.37   Grade 2+

Via the Bannie Glacier and Christopher Col, then south over and around rotten rock towers on the Main Divide.

Harold Porter, Vic Williams, Jan 1936.

South East Face

★1.38   Notforustwo   Grade 5

Vampire's left fang. This is the line left of Route 1.39. It starts beside a big block, then weaves through to a prominent pillar in a gully, then straight up to the top of the South Peak.

Allan Uren, Davie Robinson, Nov 1995.

1.39   Far From The Madding Crowd   Grade 5-

Ascend the obvious deep, broad gully to the left of the summit for 12 rope lengths.

Geoff Gabites, Colin Monteath, Hugh Nicholson, Jun 1988.

1.40   Nosferatu   Grade 6-

Follow the gully which starts on the left side of the lowest rock buttress beneath the summit. The climb eases back after five rope lengths. Further up an obvious snow ramp leads left to gain the main summit gully. Follow this up to exit 30 metres left of the summit. Fifteen rope lengths in all.

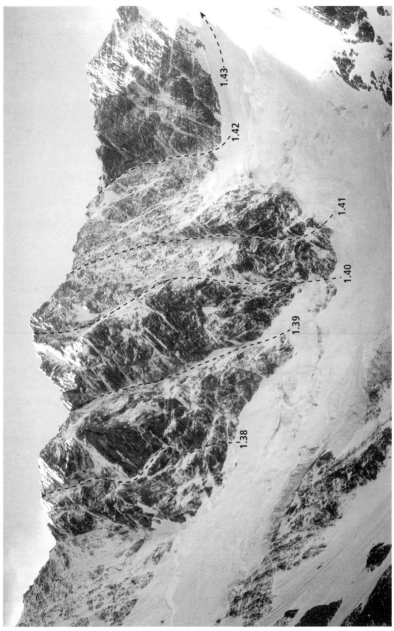

Alex Palman

Fig. 4 South East Face of Vampire Peak as seen from Barron Saddle

Descend via the snow ramp NE of Burns.
Brian Alder, Bill McLeod, Jul 1993.

1.41   **Bram Stoker**   Grade 5-

An obvious deep cut gully that starts just right of the lowest point of rock beneath Vampire. Well up the face the gully ends, but the route continues tending left. Exit on the ridge just beneath summit tower. Eleven rope lengths.
Andy MacFarlane, Bill McLeod, Sep 1993.

1.42   **Swiss Virgins**   Grade 4+

Ascend a couloir right of Bram Stoker for six rope lengths to reach the Divide north of the summit.
Carol Nash, Rob Blackburne, Oct 1983.

Christopher Col 2452m

1.43

Reached by an all snow route up the Bannie Glacier, complicated by heavy crevassing later in the summer. Not a good crossing route.

Mt Bannie 2560m

1.44   Grade 2

Via the Bannier Glacier to either (1) the West Ridge and the summit or (2) the South Ridge and summit.
Otto Frind, Conrad Kain, Mar 1914.
Anne Palmer, Ian Carlisle, Hugh Nicholson, Chris Wyatt, Alan Hooker, Aug 1983.

1.45   **East Face**   Grade 3

Start south of the face, traverse up the full length of a snow ramp, then head up mixed snow and rock past a prominent large block.
Peter Dickson, Sep 1993.

Mt Isabel 2598m

1.46   Grade 2+

Via Twain Col, climb south along the Main Divide over Mt Eric. The rock on the ridge is rather rotten. See Route 1.48.
Peter Graham, Samuel Turner, Mar 1914.

Mt Eric 2466m

1.47   Grade 2+

Via Twain Col and south along the Main Divide. See Route 1.48.
Peter Graham, Samuel Turner, Mar 1914.

Twain Col 2375m

1.48   Grade 2+

Access directly from the Mueller Glacier is not recommended as it is generally steep, loose and subject to rockfall until the Ngakanohi Glacier is reached. Above here the last slope to the Col is steep. An easier approach to the Ngakanohi lies via the slopes diagonally below Maunga Ma, as described in Route 1.50.

Peter Graham, Samuel Turner, Mar 1914.

Mt Maunga Ma 2503m

1.49   Grade 2+

Direct from the Mueller Glacier to the Ngakanohi Glacier and continue up the East Rib to the summit. Glacial retreat since the first ascent has made the lower part of this climb loose, unpleasant and quite dangerous.

Otto Frind, Konrad Kain, Peter Graham, Feb 1914

1.50   Grade 2

From the Frind Glacier, use the rocks or avalanche cones near the Ngaroimata Falls, gain the glacier and traverse diagonally up the Ngakanohi Glacier to the East Rib which is followed direct to the summit up rotten rock (covered by snow early in the season).

Otto Frind, Peter Graham, Conrad Kain, Feb 1914.

Eagle Peak 2548m

1.51   Grade 2+

Climb via the Main Divide from Maunga Ma.

Conrad Kain, Hugh Wright, Jan 1915.

1.52   Grade 3

From the Mueller Glacier ascend via the Ngakanohi Glacier and then up mixed rock and snow directly to the summit.

Aat Vervoorn, Jan 1984.

(An ascent from the west: D J S Cook, R W Gudgeon, M J Davie, Jan 1953.)

Mt Thompson 2642m

1.53   Original Route   Grade 2+

From the Frind Glacier, head up a gully onto a rock rib north of the Ngaroimata Falls gaining height to reach the Donne Glacier. Ascend left towards the col between Thompson and Eagle Peak, but well before the col head up a rock rib onto the South (Main Divide) Ridge.

Otto Frind, Conrad Kain, Feb 1914.

1.54   Grade 3

From the Donne Glacier head up the face on Thompson via a rib left of the prominent overhang on the face.

A Vervoorn, Dave White, Feb 1973.

1.55 Grade 3+

From the Donne Glacier ascend the face and turn the overhang on its northern extremity.

Otto Von Allmen, Paul Von Kanel, Jan 1973.

Sharks Teeth 2518m

1.56 Grade 2

Ascend to Brunner Col via the route described under Route 1.60. Then follow the Main Divide.

Otto Frind, Conrad Kain, Dick Young, Mar 1914.

Brunner Col 2464m

1.57 Cave Route Grade 4+

A direct, but hard, way onto the upper Frind Route (see Route 1.60) from the Frind Glacier. Ascend five rope lengths tending left to a cave in an obvious gully and up this for four rope lengths to easier ground and then to the upper Donne Glacier. The cave is good for a bivvy.

Sam Bosshard, Andy MacFarlane, Sep 1993.

Mt Stephen 2546m

1.58

Ascend to Brunner Col. Access to the Shelf Glacier below Sefton is possible, but has not been used.

Mt Brunner 2643m

1.59 Grade 2

Traverse from Brunner Col

Earle Riddiford, D Beaven, Bill Beaven, J Gummer, M Spencer, Dec 1946.
R E Cook, Aug 1987.

Mt Sefton 3151m

1.60 Frind Route Grade 3+

From the Frind Glacier, head up a gully onto a rock rib north of the Ngaroimata Falls, gaining height to reach the Donne Glacier. From here ascend northwards across the glacier under Sharks Teeth to reach Brunner Col. Cross the Col and drop onto the west side. Exposed and avalanche prone slopes under Brunner then give access to the Douglas Névé. From here ascend either the upper South Ridge or cross the névé to the West Ridge.

Otto Frind, Conrad Kain, Dick Young, Mar 1914.

1.61   South Ridge   Grade 4

From Brunner Col traverse Mt Brunner onto the ridge. Ascend a prominent step and head on up a blocky rock ridge to a snow peak. Descend to a small col, then climb a steep rock buttress (traversable on the west), follow a snow arête and up a final step to the South Summit.

Stu Allan, Olly McCahon, Rob Rowlands, Brin Williman, Jan 1971.

East Face

This can be climbed in number of ways: either by the Direct Route or For Whom the Bell Tolls, from the Mueller Glacier, or via Sefton Bivvy and across the slopes under the Footstool Ridge, which gives access to the lower and upper Shelf Glacier.

1.62   Direct Route   Grade 4+

Scale scree and bluffs above the Mueller Glacier, to reach the lower Shelf Glacier, beneath and just north of the prominent cliffs of the upper Shelf Glacier. Ascend the lower Shelf Glacier onto a snow face below and to the right of the icecliffs. Use the snow face to reach an arête on the right hand edge of the upper Shelf. At this point the two access routes from Sefton Bivvy join.

Ross Gooder, Murray Jones, John Stanton, Jan 1971.

1.63   For Whom The Bell Tolls   Grade 5

From the lower Shelf Glacier head up the right side of a buttress which is in the centre of the serac wall (crux 14). There is an exhilarating bivouac site at the top of the buttress. Negotiate the icecliff, cross the upper shelf and finish up sustained 65° ice to the subsidiary southern peak, or consider the options below.

Peter Dickson, Jan 1990.

Above here there are a number of alternatives:

i   The Ramp   Grade 4+

Drop onto the upper Shelf and head out on the prominent ramp angling onto the upper South Ridge.

Bert Barley, Fred Edwards, Geoff Harrow, Jan 1953.
Bryan & Noel Sissons, Jul 1971.

ii   Goldsmith Route   Grade 4+

Up a short couloir onto snowslopes leading onto the South Summit.

Kobi Bosshard, Mike Goldsmith, Fritz Schaumberg, Jan 1963.

iii   Direct   Grade 5-

Straight up the couloir dropping beneath the two summits. A number of leaders have experienced falls here!

Peter Gough, George Harris, Dec 1967.

Lloyd Homer/IGNS

Sefton

Tuckett Col

The Footstool

ii

1.64

iii

Upper Shelf
Glacier

1.63

2.5

L. Shelf Glacier

2.0 2.1

1.62

Tewaewae
Glacier

Eugenie
Glacier

Stocking
Stream

Mueller Glacier

Hooker
Valley

Fig. 5 Mt Sefton and the Footstool from the east, with the Mueller Glacier terminus below. Circle denotes Sefton Bivvy.

1.64 East Ridge   Grade 4

From Sefton Bivvy climb up and along under the Footstool Ridge. Crevasses may give trouble here. Then either climb directly or up the arête to Tuckett Col. From the Col ascend three prominent steps in the ridge to the summit. The rock is appallingly loose in the lower sections, but improves towards the top. Used on the first ascent of Sefton. In 1924 Frank Milne and Harold Porter ascended and descended the ridge in four hours. Now rarely climbed because of the poor rock.

Edward FitzGerald, Mattias Zurbriggen, Feb 1895.

1.65 North Face   Grade 4+

Access to this face is probably best from the east, crossing Tuckett Col (see Route 1.64). Ascend a snow ramp right towards the centre of the face, then straight up on left towards the East Ridge and break out onto a shelf some 180 metres from the summit.

Steve Elder, Nov 1987.

Routes from the Copland Valley

1.66 North Ridge   Grade 3+

Starting 15 minutes up the Copland Track from Douglas Rock Hut, this magnificent 2000m climb leads directly to the summit. Climb slabs on northern side of the Jasper Glacier Stream. The ridge then rises up a number of rock buttresses before flattening out and merging into a glacial bulge. Then ascend a vague snow rib to reach a shelf just below the summit. Above this either climb direct to the summit, or traverse south onto the West Ridge.

Bruce Harrison, Nick Von Tunzelmann, Aat Vervoorn, Dec 1964.
Nick Cradock, 1991.

1.67 Scott Creek/West Ridge   Grade 2+

The West Ridge of Mt Sefton from the Douglas Névé is a relatively straight forward 500m climb and is commonly used as a descent route. To reach the névé from the Copland Valley, the best route lies up Scott Creek. Surmount the waterfall on the western side (true L) using vegetated ledges and follow the creek, up and up, trending left. Beyond the bushline a rounded spur on the left can be gained (there are cairn-marked bivvy rocks and a stream in a small vegetated valley just north of the rounded spur) which ascends to a steeper craggy section followed by snowbasins. These in turn lead onto the ridge separating the Scott and Tekano Glaciers. Cross the Tekano Névé (watch for wet snow!) and ascend to Welcome Pass (2390m). From here follow the Sierra Range to where the West Ridge begins. Alternatively, from Welcome Pass use the Douglas Névé to access the West Ridge where it steepens. Beware of mist. Bivvying on Welcome Pass makes the summit day easier.

Jack Clarke, Laurence Earle, Alex Graham, Bernard Head, Mar 1912.
Roland & N Rodda, Aug 1963.

Fig. 6 The North Ridge of Mt Sefton.

1.68   Footstool-Sefton Traverse   Grade 4

Routes onto Footstool are described under the Hooker Valley Section. The
ridge to Tuckett Col (2662m) is best climbed on the western side and presents
few difficulties though the rock is rotten. The East Ridge of Sefton is the
crux. Also see Route 1.64.

P Miller, J Sheffield, Jan 1963.

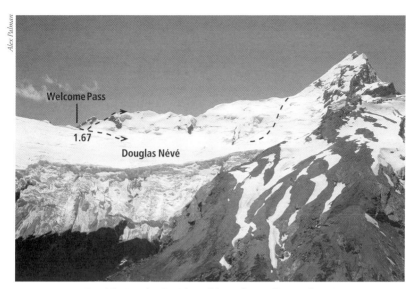

Alex Palman

Welcome Pass

1.67

Douglas Névé

Fig. 7 The West Ridge of Mt Sefton and the Douglas Névé (from Douglas Pass).

Hooker Valley

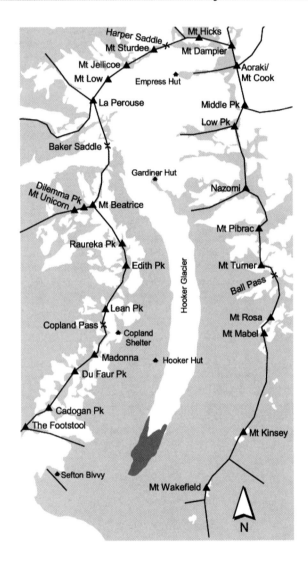

Hooker Valley

The climbs in the upper Hooker are generally serious and demanding, while the lower valley routes are easier, with peaks of the Mt Cook Range especially providing enjoyable climbing. The Hooker Valley is one of the more spectacular in the Aoraki/ Mt Cook region but access to the upper valley involves technical difficulty and some objective danger. There is no air access or flying permitted in the Hooker Valley and for some, this adds to its appeal.

Sefton Bivvy is reached by following the Stocking Stream from the shelter on the west Hooker track, until below the Stocking Glacier. Then head up screes into a large rubble gully (some snow) that leads onto a rocky slope to the north of the main ridge. Above this slope follow a steep tussock gully onto vegetated rock ledges that ramp back to the ridge proper. Follow the ridge mostly on the south side to the bivvy. An alternative route lies up the tussocky crest of the main ridge, starting from the lower scree slopes. Although getting to Sefton Bivvy in summer is relatively straightforward, a number of falls have occurred on this route (2-4hrs).

Getting to Hooker Hut and beyond

The access route to Hooker Hut has changed significantly and no longer uses the vegetated moraine terraces to the west of the Hooker Lake. Avalanches and storms have damaged this route beyond repair. Alternative routes are described below. Hooker Hut has been moved approximately 70m west of its previous position due to the on-going collapse of the moraine wall. At the time of printing this guide the location of the hut was being reviewed. Access to the Copland Ridge, near Hooker Hut, has also been badly affected. Alternative route options are described in the Copland Pass description in this section.

From the White Horse Hill camp ground follow the Hooker Valley track over the swingbridges to the Hooker Lake. Traverse around the western side of the lake at the waterline. Beware of rockfall. At the lakehead continue up the trough between the Hooker Glacier and the moraine wall to a point about 150m south of Hooker Hut (not visible). This point is currently marked by a large (3m high) square shaped rock, with two painted arrows: one indicating the direction of the hut and the other the track to the Copland Ridge. Climb up a loose gully in the moraine wall, adjacent to this rock, to **Hooker Hut**. Check with park staff for current access information.

If travelling further up valley, to **Gardiner Hut** or beyond, continue up the Hooker Glacier, possibly using the ridges in the centre (although on moraine there is no perfect route) until the white ice, where the travel becomes easier. Then proceed to the Hooker Icefall. Access to Gardiner Hut is described later in this section.

An alternative to the glacier route lies up the east side of the Hooker Valley, commencing just after the second swingbridge. This route provides access to the upper valley and Ball Pass. A vague track, marked occasionally with cairns, follows vegetated terraces. At roughly the same latitude as Hooker Hut there is a large tussock shelf, continue past this, scramble up around a slip scar and descend back down onto another shelf with a rocky basin. At the end of this, descend down a stream to gain Hooker Glacier.

Labels on figure: Aoraki, Hicks, Harper Saddle, Pudding Rock, La Perouse, Copland Pass, Du Faur, Cadogan, 2.11, 2.9, 2.7

Fig. 8 The Hooker Valley and the Main Divide.

Nick Groves/Hedgehog House

The eastern Hooker Valley route is about an hour longer than the glacier route, quite beautiful and a good way to avoid the bulk of the moraine.

From Gardiner to **Empress Hut,** either head up the main glacier from Gardiner to beneath Harper Saddle before swinging around to Empress Hut (2-3 hours), or else ascend from Gardiner towards the West Ridge of Mt Cook and around the lower Empress Shelf (3-4 hours).

Shelter

Sefton Bivvy. This bivvy was lovingly rebuilt by DoC staff in 1999 retaining its original character. There are no amenities, except a radio. It will sleep about four people on its wooden floor. The bivvy may be buried by snow in winter or spring. A large rock just beyond the hut can accommodate three people and also provides some good bouldering and top-roping (take a piton or two). Water: if the puddle behind the bivvy is dry, try the basin to the south (~1617m, cell coverage (025), grid ref: 743-203).

Hooker Hut. Managed by AMCNP, with 12 bunks. This hut was the busiest in the park but, due to the problems with access to it and the Copland Pass, it is now one of the quietest. The hut has a radio (and possibly a ghost) (~1140m, grid ref: 770-233).

Copland Shelter. A small barrel-shaped shelter with water (at the rear), a radio and mattresses for four. The shelter may be covered by snow in winter (~1960m, cell coverage (025), grid ref: 760-240).

Gardiner Hut. Managed by AMCNP, a grey barrel-shaped hut with two bench bunks sleeping four or more each. Also has a radio (~1755m, grid ref: 770-279).

Empress Hut. A state-of-the-art DoC hut built in 1994 on the original site with significant help and funds from the CMC. Also managed by the AMCNP. It can accommodate 10-12 people, has a radio and a superb deck for viewing and g & ts after climbs (~2516m, cell coverage (025), grid ref: 776-307).

Times

Village to Sefton Bivvy ~3 hours.
Village to Hooker Hut 3-4 hours.
Village to Gardiner Hut 6-8 hours (depending on access onto Pudding Rock).
Village to Empress Hut 9-11 hours.

Ski touring routes

Although the Hooker Valley is not a touring area per se, skis can be useful during winter for access. Snow coverage is variable and in general skis tend to be used from the white ice of the Hooker Glacier. The downhill section (~900m) from Empress Hut to Gardiner Hut (and beyond) is certainly worth checking out.

The Footstool 2764m

East Face

2.0   **Wombats on Heat**   Grade 3-
Ascend the snow slopes left of Route 2.1, crossing an easy rock section that
links to a broad snow face, then onto the Divide south of Footstool. A good
alternative to Route 2.1 if the schrund conditions are not favourable (options
to the south also exist).
Michael Batchelor, Gordon Poultney, Jan 1988.

★ **2.1**   **Couloir Route**   Grade 3-
From the Stocking Glacier ascend the prominent couloir either to the ridge,
or near the summit move right up an offshoot couloir. The schrund at the
base of the couloir may prove troublesome late in the season.
Graeme Dingle, Jill Tremain, Jan 1967.

2.2   **Direct**   Grade 4-
Follow the face to the right of Route 2.1 via a shallow gully.
Ray Button, Graeme Dingle, Jul 1979.

2.3

Three short ice routes have been climbed to the right of the Direct route
joining the East Ridge: i) *Footstolen* (3+), ii) *Infoleak* (3+), iii) *Smash n grab*
(4-).
Jo Kippax, 1990.

2.4   **East Ridge**   Grade 3-
From Sefton Bivvy ascend the Stocking Glacier and cross northwards to
gain the ridge where it rises from a level section. Follow the ridge directly to
the summit. The rock is complete choss – avoid like the plague, unless snow
covered.
Jack Clarke, Peter Graham, Henrik Sillem, Mar 1906.

★ **2.5**   **Main Divide**   Grade 2+
Cross the East Ridge and work up the slopes of the Eugenie Glacier to reach
the Main Divide, then follow up the north-east snowslopes to the summit.
This is the regular descent route.
Tom Fyfe, George Graham, Jan 1894.

2.6   Grade 2
A route exists from the névé south of the Copland Pass and connects
snowslopes on the west to reach the col north of the peak, then as for Route
2.5. The ridge from the Copland Pass has also been traversed.
M R Barwell, A F Reid, Feb 1953.

Cadogan Peak 2449m

2.7   Grade 2

Via the rock ridge between the Eugenie and Hayter Glaciers and a rib right
of centre on the East Face. A bad area for slab avalanches early in the summer.
Freda Du Faur, Peter Graham, Mar 1913.
(Possibly) Nick Groves, Grant Prattley, Jun 1992.

2.8   Grade 2-

From the Copland Pass
Franz & Julius Malcher, E Ranft, Feb 1914.

Du Faur Peak 2330m

2.9   Grade 2

Via the ridge between the Stewart and Hayter Glaciers and then via rock
buttress to the summit. A descent can be made directly down the Eugenie
Glacier.
Freda Du Faur, Peter Graham, Mar 1912.
(Possibly) Nick Groves, Grant Prattley, Jun 1992.

Madonna Peak 2265m

2.10   Grade 2-

Via the ridge behind the Hooker Hut or traverse from the Copland Pass.
Jack Clarke, J E Walker, Hugh Wright, Jan 1911.
(Possibly) Nick Groves, Grant Prattley, Jun 1992.

★ Copland Pass 2150m

2.11   Grade 1+

The route immediately beyond Hooker Hut has deteriorated markedly. For
current route information consult park staff at the visitor centre. *Despite the
problems near Hooker Hut, the Copland Pass still remains one of the most stunning
alpine crossings in New Zealand, affording breathtaking views of Aoraki/Mount
Cook and the peaks of the same range. The hot pools at Welcome Flat are an
added bonus.*

Getting on to the Copland Ridge

Don't go to Hooker Hut. A safer and more enjoyable route is to continue
along the Hooker Glacier past the Copland Gully to the next moraine terrace.
Use the gully beyond this terrace to access the slumped vegetated section of
terrace and then the terrace itself. Climb onto the Copland Ridge directly,
through pleasant vegetation. The original Copland track started with a zig
zag at the base of the ridge before the gut became impassable. That track is
still evident and usable in places.

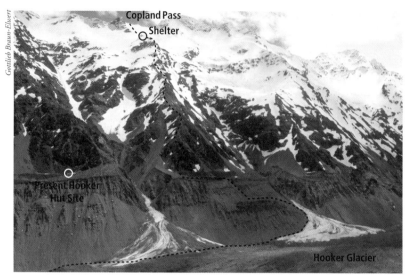

Fig. 9 Copland Ridge and Pass.

Copland Ridge

Once on the ridge follow it to where it narrows, and tends left across scree slopes (may involve snow in early summer). Above here negotiate some bluffs keeping just left of the crest of the ridge. The route alternates from left to right, before the ridge then narrows again and flattens before it reaches the **Copland Shelter** (1960m). [When descending it is possible to drop into the Copland Gully from the lower reaches of the ridge and follow it down to the Hooker Glacier – but keep in mind that this is an *avalanche* gully. Access into the gully from all directions has deteriorated significantly and so this route is not recommended.]

Copland Shelter → Westland

Above the shelter climb to the right of the rock ridge, tending right on a steep diagonal until flat snow is reached. The Copland Pass is any one of a number of rock notches, but the best one to use is the leftmost notch. Late in the summer schrunds on the eastern slopes and adjacent to the rock can present difficulties. On the western side, descend a steep rock gully (50m) and follow a series of easy snow basins (marked occasionally with cairns) into a stream that gradually steepens. Keep to the left of the stream/gully until a zigzag track can be picked up.

The Copland Pass is an alpine crossing requiring some alpine experience and the necessary equipment. It should not be taken lightly. At least some members of the party should be familiar with the use of ice axes, crampons and ropes. A good tactic is to travel from the village to Copland Shelter on the first day. This allows an early (and rested) start to the pass itself and it gets most of the uphill done on the first day.

Edward FitzGerald and Mattias Zurbriggen used the pass to the south ('FitzGerald') of the Copland Pass in February 1895, whereas Arthur Harper crossed the Copland Pass in March 1895.

Times

Village to Copland Shelter 6-8hrs.
Copland Shelter to Pass ~1hr.
Copland Shelter to Douglas Rock Hut 6-8hrs.

Lean Peak 2360m

2.12   Grade 2

A short ascent up steepish rock from Copland Pass
Peter Graham, Freda Du Faur, 1912.

Edith Peak 2248m

2.13   Grade 2

Reached either via the ridge over Lean Peak or by traversing snowslopes below the Copland Pass, or via a steep rotten ridge from the Hooker Valley.
Conrad Kain, E Hamlyn, E Day, Mar 1914.

Mt Raureka 2333m

2.14

Via the Divide ridges.

2.15   Grade 2

Via a prominent ridge leading up from the Hooker Valley.
Tom Fyfe, Conrad Kain, Mar 1914.

Pudding Rock and Gardiner Hut

The Hooker Icefall flows around a 100m high and rounded protrusion, on the eastern side of the valley, known as Pudding Rock. Although not visible from the icefall, Gardiner Hut is situated on top of this rock. Accessing this hut is not easy – some parties have been forced to bivvy and/or return because of conditions.

Before about mid-December the hut can be gained via the icefall directly. Continue up the centre of the glacier past the hut until the glacier flattens out and then loop back to approach the hut from up-valley. Once the glacier becomes too broken alternative options need to be considered.

i)   Pudding Rock - using the fixed wires
This is the most regularly used option during summer. Keep towards the middle of the glacier until roughly opposite a waterfall coming down a gully (with an avalanche cone at its base) to the right of Pudding Rock. From near the centre of the glacier there is usually an obvious shallow trough (approximately 150m long) running diagonally towards Pudding Rock, and

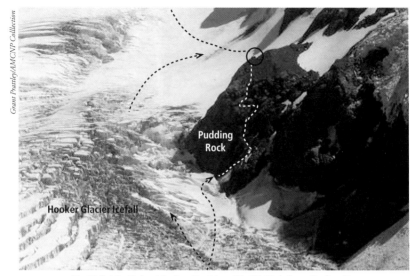

Fig. 10 Pudding Rock and Gardiner Hut (also see Fig. 11). Circle denotes Gardiner Hut.

this provides a good path across. The presence of a deep melt hole near the base of the waterfall indicates that access on to Pudding Rock will need to be gained to the left via seracs and ice boulders. Thirty metres of easy rock (possibly snow covered) needs to be negotiated before the obvious rock ledges and then slabs can be gained. Fixed cables, in three sections (installed in 2001), are attached to the rock via steel rods and bolts, and start from the base of the slabs. This Kiwi-style 'via ferrata' continues up through gullies and ledges. Use the wires for safety and assistance. At the top of the wires move up ~25m and traverse ~80m up-valley to the hut. When descending (abseil using the anchors) follow the wires to an abseil station positioned on the edge. The abseil to the glacier usually requires 2 x 50m ropes.

ii) If access from the ice onto Pudding Rock is too tricky then it is also possible to climb the rock right of the waterfall (difficult, and threatened).

iii) In winter or spring the wires on pudding rock may be covered by ice/ snow (some snow on the slabs is okay) and the climb will be very difficult or impassable. An alternative is to climb the waterfall gully if it is banked up with snow (beware of a schrund at the top of the snow cone).

Beatrice Peak 2528m

2.16   Grade 2-

The easiest route is via Baker Saddle (see the Strauchon Glacier Area section) and south along the Main Divide Ridge. The peak can also be climbed from the south via the Main Divide, via the ridge from the Hooker Valley onto Raureka (Route 2.15) or easily from Dilemma.

Peter Graham, Hugh Chambers, Dorothy Holdsworth, Jan 1914.

Fig. 11 Mt La Perouse, showing the South and East Faces.

Mt La Perouse 3078m

2.17   South Ridge   Grade 4+

From Gardiner Hut via Baker Saddle follow the snow arête until it runs out below icecliffs (beware of ice avalanches). Climb the rock buttresses to the left of the cliffs on sound rock or early in the summer follow an ice gully. Then following the winding arête to the summit. A dangerous route if the icecliffs are active.

Mike Gill, B Barrack, Jan 1960.

Phil Penney, Nick Cradock, Whitney Thurlow, Aug 1990.

East Face

2.18   Grade 4

The most elegant route is up a rounded rib that drops from the summit to the Hooker. From Gardiner Hut climb snow fields and rock ribs keeping an eye out for ice avalanches from cliffs to the right and left. Beware of soft snow slides later in the day in summer.

Hans Leitner, Eberhard von Terzi, Jan 1962.

Rob Hall, Steve & Michelle Lassche, Jun 1984.

A 'Baker Saddle East Face' variant. Adam Darragh, Parish Robbins, summer 1997.

2.19   Grade 4-

A route begins up under Mt Jellicoe and traverses up under Mt Low to the right of the summit of Mt La Perouse. There are a number of other variant routes on this face.

Gordon Hasell, A R Page, I R Seddon, Richard Tornquist, Jan 1958.

A variant using a rib on the East Face: Noel Sissons, J Keys, Dec 1971.

2.20   Divide Route   Grade 3

This route begins by climbing Mt Jellicoe either via the slopes under Mt Sturdee and up a Y-shaped couloir, via the rotten Divide ridge, via slopes on the west or via a prominent snow arête from the upper Hooker (A D Jackson, V I E Whitehead, 1941). Beyond Jellicoe either traverse Mt Low and the ridge to La Perouse or skirt below the ridge on the western slopes and up to the summit. This is a long climb but still the most common descent route.

Hugh Chambers, Peter Graham, Mar 1921 (La Perouse).

Bill McLeod, winter 1985.

Low 2932m

2.21   Grade 3

See Routes 2.19ii and 2.20

Hugh Chambers, Conrad Kain, Hugh Wright, Feb 1915.

(Possibly) Bill McLeod, 1985.

Jellicoe 2827m

2.22   Grade 3

See Routes 2.19ii and 2.20

Hugh Chambers, Conrad Kain, Hugh Wright, Feb 1915.

(Possibly) Bill McLeod, winter 1985.

Sturdee 2708m

2.23

The first ascent is unknown

2.24   West Rib

Three pitches of very good rock.

Bill McLeod, Mark Taylor, Sep 1989.

Harper Saddle 2585m

2.25

Ascend from the upper Hooker via a steep 150m snowface direct to the Saddle. If this route is cut off, then ways can be found to the right or left of Sturdee. A bolt abseil anchor can be found on the rock outcrop below and slightly right of Harper Saddle, on the Hooker Side.

2.26i   To reach the La Perouse Valley

Descend the icefalls below the saddle, probably on the true left - a very broken route, which may not be possible later in the summer (also see ii.)

2.26ii   To reach the La Perouse Glacier, Névé and the North Face of Hicks

Descend 200m from the saddle, keeping right, then ascend 150m snow or loose rock to the horizontal section of the ridge running down from Mt Hicks, reaching a small névé. At this point, to reach the La Perouse Glacier between the upper and lower icefalls, follow down snow slopes to the right of the diagonal ridge. Otherwise to reach the upper La Perouse Névé, cross a small névé towards the North Rib of Hicks, descend a short distance beneath a rock buttress and cross to a flat ridge. Using the left of two obvious notches descend 150m down a steep rotten rock gully (which usually requires an abseil) and snowslope to reach the main glacier below the North Face of Hicks. Time from Empress to the La Perouse Névé 2-4 hours.   Grade 3-

Mt Hicks 3198m

First ascended by Alex Graham, Henry Newton, R S Low, 1906. Their route via the west ridge has largely fallen away.

2.27   Curtain Route (Standard Route)   Grade 3

From Harper Saddle ascend the snowslope diagonally to the gap in the west ridge (beware rockfall from the Curtain). Continue up the ridge for 150m before crossing left to a major couloir. Ascend the couloir which comes out about 100m down the ridge from the final 40m rock wall below the summit.

George Lowe, Geof Milne, Jan 1949.

Bill Denz, A Jones, Jun 1972.

Descending. All the old fixed gear (pegs, chocks etc) in the Curtain/open book corner have fallen out or been removed. Bolt anchors can now be found in the standard descent couloir. Five abseils from the top of the couloir followed by an easy traverse across a rock ridge onto the slopes below the Curtain allows easy access to Harper Saddle. Do not rappel down the Curtain.

2.28   Divide Route   Grade 3+

From Harper Saddle head up on snow to the left of the Divide for a short distance before crossing onto the edge of the South Face. Follow up ledges and bluffs overlooking the South Face until the Divide flattens out, then follow the ridge up the final 40m wall to the summit.

Harry Ayres, Oscar Coberger, Feb 1951.

Chris Curry/Hedgehog House

Fig. 12 South Face of Mt Hicks, showing the routes on the left side (also see Fig. 13).

South Face

For the south face routes, where an almost 'ice crag' environment exists, some climbers have graded ice routes with waterfall ice (WI) or Scottish technical grades. These systems provide a more precise and comparable measure. Mt Cook grades, as used throughout the rest of this guide, have also been assigned.

From left to right:

★2.29   Dingle-Button   Grade 4-

Start at the second obvious gully right from Harper Saddle, 300m of moderately steep ice climbing leads to Route 2.28.

Ray Button, Graeme Dingle, Jun 1979.

A number of variations have been added left of the Dingle-Button (D-B) route, all appear to be about grade 3+.

2.30   Tales of Choss   Grade 4+

Start at the bottom of the D-B couloir and climb the rib on the right of the gully (crux 13). Join the Divide Route after six rope lengths.

Roger Parkyn, Andy MacFarlane, Feb 1984.

2.31   Deardissima   Grade 4

Gully immediately right of D-B. Rejoins D-B higher up.

Pat Deavol, Marty Beare, Jun 1999.

2.32   **King Hit**   Grade 5+

Follows a line of weakness through the steep area about 200m right of D-B but left of Heaven's Door. Can descend by traversing off via the snowslopes to the D-B route. Five or six pitches.

Dave Vass, Hugh Barnard, Jun 1995.

2.33   **Highway to Hell**   Grade 6

Start just left of HD in a right trending gully on 65-85 degree ice (probably thin) then traverse right across a snowslope and step into a narrow gully. Follow the obvious gully and short steep walls. After the first shelf continue up a narrow gully to the second shelf and easy ground. Move left across the shelf then up right through the rock band to gain the summit icefield. Thirteen pitches.

Hugh Grierson, Jade Pope, Dec 1996.

★ **2.34**   **Heaven's Door**   Grade 6

Start up steep loose ground 50m left of the Curver Route. Five pitches of hard climbing lead to some big ledges. Move right up mixed ground onto a second series of ledges and then up six pitches to reach the summit icefields.

Russell Braddock, Kim Logan, Jan 1983.

Nick Cradock, Paul Aubrey, Jul, 1987

A steep three pitch variation start to the right of *Heaven's Door* was put up by Craig Nottle and Roddy Mackenzie in January 1984.

★ **2.35**   **The Curver**   Grade 6-

Ascend two pitches of 70-80 degree ice to where the gully lies back a little, then follow the gully up a series of short ice walls as it tends left, then up to the summit icefield.

Nick Cradock, Tobin Sorenson, Aug 1979.

A four pitch variation start to the *Curver* was established by Lionel Clay and Richard Kirk in August 1986, Simon Middlemass with Marty Hunter did similar later.

★ **2.36**   **Original Gunbarrels**   Grade 6

Up two difficult pitches, into the bottom of the Curver Gully, then up three pitches until a diagonal gully cuts back right to the foot of the prominent double ice couloirs (the Gunbarrels). The first two or so original pitches fell off in 1999.

Jono Clarke, Mike Brown, Matt Quirke, Kester Brown, Nov 1999, WI 5- New Gunbarrels (First 2.5 pitches).

Bill Denz, Phil Herron, Murray Judge, Jun 1975.

★ **2.37**   **Yankee-Kiwi Couloir**   Grade 6+

Ascends Route 2.38, then up a steep ice couloir to the left of the Left Buttress to the base of the Gunbarrels, then as for Route 2.36.

Nick Cradock, Tobin Sorenson, Aug 1979.

Fig. 13 South Face of Mt Hicks.

2.45
2.44
2.43
2.42
2.41
2.39
2.38 & 2.37
2.36
2.35
2.34
2.33

Left Buttress

2.38 Direct Start   Grade 6

Head up a sustained wall with a small corner and cracks (about three pitches). Continue up prominent wide cracks in the bottom cliffs below the crest of the buttress (crux 18). Continue up Route 2.39.

Nick Cradock, Nic Kagan, Feb 1978.

★ 2.39 Original Route   Grade 5+

Ascend two pitches on the bottom wall nearer the Central Gullies, then traverse left directly below the main buttress to reach an ice ramp left of the buttress. Then either ascend directly up the buttress crest (crux 14/15), or up the ramp for a short distance before regaining the buttress, or up a short buttress left of the ramp before cutting back right again. Follow the buttress up progressively easier rock until the icefields. Then, depending on the state of the icecliffs, traverse left and up, or else through the cliffs. Superb.

Graeme Dingle, Murray Jones, Dec 1970.
Bill McLeod, Jun 1992.

2.40 Desolation Row   Grade 6

Start up Route 2.39, then traverse slightly right for 50m and up diagonally left for another 100m before ascending directly to emerge near the top of the Left Buttress.

Bill Denz, Nigel Perry, Jan 1981.

2.41 Central Gullies   Grade 6-

There are a number of variation starts and finishes. Choose a start and head up ice, sustained climbing through ice couloirs and icefields until easier 45° slopes lead to the icecliffs. Depending on the state of the cliffs, find a route through them to the summit.

Bill Denz, Peter Gough, Etienne Kummer, Nov 1972.

★ 2.42 Logan's Run (also known as Logan's Retreat)   Grade 6+

From the edge of the Central Gullies climb the major vertical couloir which runs up the left side of the Right Buttress. Very steep and sustained climbing. If sections are devoid of ice, then dry-tool (possibly on the 5th pitch). Near the top of the couloir it is possible to traverse onto the crest of the buttress. Finish up the Right Buttress route, or rappel off – there is some fixed gear. Nick Cradock and Kevin Boekholt later completed the top of the route, eliminating the aid used in the first ascent.

Kim Logan, Pete Sinclair, Dec 1983.
Bill McLeod, Steve Elder, Jul 1987.

2.43 Tingler   Grade 6+

Ascend the gully between Routes 2.42 and 2.44 for five and a half rope lengths of very steep, mixed ice and rock onto the Right Buttress.

Dave Fearnley, John McCallum, Oct 1987.

2.44 Right Buttress   Grade 5
Avoid the first 60m by using the icefield on the right. Traverse onto the crest of the buttress then directly up on or right of the crest (crux 14). Then head up the icefields and through the icecliffs.

Graeme Dingle, Noel Sissons, Dec 1972.

2.45 Right Icefields   Grade 5
Climb through the bottom cliffs which usually have two pitches of hard climbing, then up a sustained shield of ice. There are a number of variations.

Mick Browne, Keith Woodford, Nov 1972.

A route further right was soloed by Bernard Wietlisbach in Feb 1978.

Mt Dampier/Rakiroa 3440m

2.46   Grade 4-
Traverse from Hicks via the ridge avoiding two prominent towers on whichever side is best in prevailing conditions. Then go up the ridge to a schrund. From here continue up steep snow, through rocks, to the summit. It is also possible to cross the North Face to the North Ridge and then up to the summit.

Syd Brookes, Jack Cox, Marjorie Edgar-Jones, Jan 1938.

Bill Denz, Jun 1972.

★ 2.47 Hicks/Dampier Couloir   Grade 4-
From the Sheila Glacier ascend the right diagonal couloir onto the upper Hicks/Dampier ridge. About 2/3rds up the couloir it is possible to break left and follow an ice slope to the ridge line that leads to Hicks.

D Waugh, S Sweeney, Jan 1972.

2.48 Fantini/Dignan   Grade 5
Follow ice gullies left of the Maori Route which ultimately arrive on the Hicks/Dampier Ridge. This route is mostly out of the icecliff fall-line.

John Fantini, Tony Dignan, Jan 1987.

2.49 Maori Route   Grade 5
Ascend the gully in the centre of the face and connect with a snow ramp leading left. Then climb steep ice on the left edge of the icecliff. The route is threatened by falling ice.

Nic Kagan, Mark Whetu, Feb 1983.

2.50i Green Saddle Route   Grade 3+
From the upper Sheila Glacier head up the rib to the left of Fyfe's Gut - the narrow couloir directly below the saddle. It is possible to climb Fyfe's Gut but watch for stonefall. The route comes out above Green Saddle. Ascend rubbishy rock to the summit. A variant near the top involves moving left into a narrow ice couloir which leads to the summit ridge (grade 4).

Jack Clarke, Tom Fyfe, George Graham (when they climbed Aoraki/Mt Cook).

Bill McLeod, Jul 1984.

An alternative route crosses above the icecliffs to the Hicks/Dampier.
H P Barcham, J B Waterhouse, Jan 1955.

Aoraki/Mount Cook: High Peak 3754m

★ **2.51** **North Ridge** Grade 4
As for Green Saddle, then up three prominent steps on the ridge, the last
and more difficult ('Beare Step') being turned via a couloir on the Sheila
Face. A classic route used for the first ascent of Aoraki/Mt Cook. It was
descended by at least four parties on early ascents but this is not
recommended.
Jack Clarke, Tom Fyfe, George Graham, 25 Dec 1894.
Murray Judge, Dick Price, Aug 1978.
Beare Step: Marty Beare, Nick Cradock, Neal Whiston, crux 18/19, 4+, protection awk-
ward, Mar 1982.

Fig. 14 Sheila Face of Aoraki/Mt Cook.

Sheila Face

2.52 **Left Buttress** Grade 5
From the foot of Fyfe's Gut ascend the rib to the left of a wide gully via a
corner (crux 14). Ascend towards Fyfe's Gut and then follow the west of the
buttress until reaching a leftward traverse across a steep wall. Then follow
red slabs and possible ice leads to the North Ridge 150m from the summit.
Bill Denz, Peter Gough, Aug 1973.

2.53 Central Buttress — Grade 5-

The standard route begins close to the base of Fyfe's Gut. Two grade 12 pitches take you onto the buttress which is followed on relatively easy, occasionally loose rock. The rib is wide and there are a number of alternatives. 200m below the summit, the rib meets a 50m flat ridge. Above here follow either the buttress of good rock, or if iced, move left into a couloir to reach the summit.

Austin Brookes, Ron Dickie, Ralph Miller, Jan 1967.

Variations exist at the base of the Central Buttress, starting further right from the standard route and joining it 300m higher. Some grade 14 and harder rock pitches have been reported. Tobin Sorenson and John Allen climbed a variation to the right of the Central Buttress in August 1979.

Athol Whimp, Matt Evrard, Jul 1989.

2.54 Right Buttress — Grade 5

Follow the left crest of the buttress with a final pitch of grade 16, before joining Earle's Route. The first ascent tended out on the face on the right, with easier climbing.

Hugh Logan, David Pluth, Jan 1974.

Bill Atkinson, Pascal Sprungli, Jan 1980 (via the crest).

Bill McLeod, Simon Middlemass, winter 1989.

2.54i — Grade 5

The major gully between the Central Buttress and Right Buttress/Earles Route. Is usually well iced in winter.

Adrian (Ardi) Riechlin, Jun 1994 (killed after falling from the summit ridge).

2.55 Earle's Route — Grade 4-

Gain the ridge via the icefall on the left side of the Upper Empress Shelf. An alternative route is through a gap at the head of the Sheila Glacier but it involves a pitch of steep climbing. Follow the ill-defined ridge on poor rock. At about 3200m the ridge flattens out before meeting the final headwall. Depending on how iced the rocks are, either climb up steep ice gullies directly above or traverse left and use the Sheila Face exits, or even further left to the top of the North Ridge. The route faces north-west and hence can often be iced, making it a more serious undertaking than if the rock is clean.

Jack Clarke, Alex Graham, Peter Graham, Laurence Earle, Mar 1909.

Bill McLeod, 1985.

Hooker Face

A series of routes commencing from the Upper Empress Shelf.

2.56

To get onto the Upper Empress Shelf climb the glacier/icefall at the northern end where it descends to the Lower Empress Shelf, adjacent to Earle's Ridge. This route usually becomes impassable from January onward. As an alternative, use "Earle's Gap". This is the low point on the lower Earle's Ridge. From the upper Sheila Glacier climb a snow tongue (and possibly a pitch of rock) onto Earle's Ridge – above the gap. Once on the ridge it is usually necessary to climb along the ridge for a pitch or more to avoid the large glacial holes on the southern side.

2.57   Grade 4+

Ascend the couloir to the right of Earle's Route and through gullies on rock to the left of the main face to reach the summit ridge near the High Peak. Beware of rockfall in the gully.

2.57i

Two buttresses to the right of the gully were ascended by R Coombs and K Henshall, and B Dawkins and S Thompson in Dec 1969, but the first ascent of Route 2.57, which has been climbed a number of times, is unrecorded.

2.58   Grade 4+

Up a short steep gully onto a sustained iceshield, often of hard ice, which leads to the summit ridge. First ascent party unknown.

2.59   Grade 4

Via a short couloir and then either up good rock on the ribs to left or right (the standard Hooker Face route) or up the broad gully between the ribs.
H P Barcham, D Herron, Graham McCallum, Richard Tornquist, Dec 1956.

2.60   Grade 4+

Ascend a rock rib directly below the Middle Peak which leads to steep snowfields between the prominent icecliff under Porter Col and the icecliff on the Hooker Face.
Kevin Conaglen, Andy Harris, Feb 1983.

Empress Shelf

2.61   **Don't Call Me Dude**   Grade 4

Crest of the buttress between the upper and lower Empress Shelves. Excellent rock with no objective danger. 350m, crux 17. Descend via Earle's Gap (see Route 2.56) or glacier.
Peter Dickson, Feb 1992.

★ **2.62**   **Aoraki/Mount Cook Grand Traverse**   Grade 4-

A 'GT' involves traversing Low, Middle and High Peaks (or vice versa) of Aoraki/Mt Cook. The section from Low Peak to Porter Col involves some rock, whereas the rest of the traverse is ice (and this can be hard, especially in winter). The ridge line from Low to High Peak is New Zealand's highest and most exposed mile providing the most spectacular and famous traverse in the Southern Alps. In its day it was regarded as one of the most impressive achievements in world mountaineering.
Freda Du Faur, Peter Graham, Darby Thomson, Jan 1913.

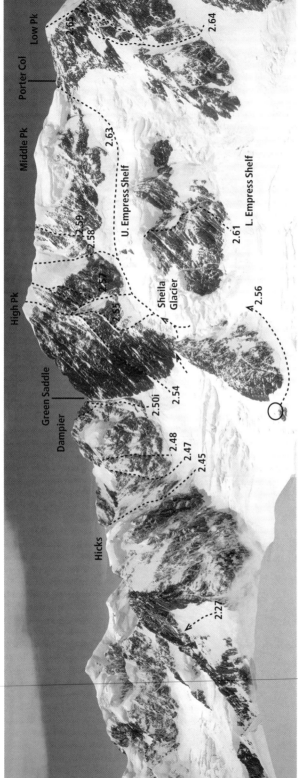

Fig. 15 The western side (Hooker Valley) of Aoraki/Mt Cook and Mts Hicks and Dampier. Circle denotes Empress Hut.

Aoraki/Mount Cook Middle Peak 3717m

★ **2.63 Porter Col Route** Grade 3

From the Upper Empress Shelf, ascend snowslopes and gain a short steep gully to the right of a large icecliff which leads to the col between the Middle and Low Peaks. This is a regular descent route (but often requires abseils on the first steep section). There is usually a schrund just above the col beneath the Middle Peak which is suitable for bivouacs ('Middle Peak Hotel', was the scene of Mark Inglis and Phil Doole's epic fortnight survival in 1982).

Tom Fyfe, George Graham, Dec 1894.

R Krauer, Kobi Bosshard, Aug 1963 (via Upper Empress shelf on skis).

Aoraki/Mount Cook Low Peak 3593m

2.64 North West Couloir Grade 3

This is a general term for a number of routes leading from the Lower Empress Shelf onto the West Ridge. The most regular routes are up either the narrow or the broad couloir in the NW Buttress, and then up a broad gully or the rocks further left to gain the West Ridge at about 3200m where it flattens out. A commonly used descent route – *but beware of rockfall in the lower part of the couloir – scene of a number of fatalities.*

Peter Graham, Freda Du Faur, Darby Thomson, Jan 1913, (as part of the first Grand Traverse).

Murray Cullen, John Entwisle, Aug 1977 (NW Couloir/West Ridge).

★ **2.65 West Ridge** Grade 3+

Commencing either at the foot of main West Ridge above Gardiner Hut, or gaining the ridge at certain points on the northern side, follow up on good rock. From Gardiner Hut the ridge is a long climb. The strata lead onto the South Face, so tend left until the ridge flattens at 3200m.

Peter Graham, Henrik Sillem, Mar 1906, (first ascent of the Low Peak).

Keith Thompson, Bob Cunninghame, Jun 1972.

South Face

2.66 The Creamer Grade 4+

200m left of Sweet Dreams.

Jo Kippax, John Smith, Jan 1990.

2.67 Sweet Dreams Grade 5

Ascend two rope lengths up Wet Dreams and then head left up an ice smear to broken ground onto the West Ridge.

Andy Harris, Mike Roberts, Pete Sinclair, Dec 1983.

2.68 Wet Dream Grade 5-

Start up a prominent gully 100m left of White Dream. The route follows a narrow gully which angles back to connect up with White Dream. In places it narrows to one metre in width. Mostly 50° angle but a few sections are

Colin Monteath/Hedgehog House

Fig. 16 *South Face of Aoraki/Mt Cook.*

steeper. The next section on rock and water ice can be hard to follow. The final third of the route follows a prominent gully that joins White Dream near to where the NW Couloir joins.

Kim Logan, Feb 1983.

★ **2.69** **White Dream** Grade 5

Commencing from the shelf above the Noeline Glacier, the route takes the easiest line up the mixed ground on the left of the face, linking two ice pitches passing just left of the left-most icecliff (crux). Continue up the icefield above to where the rock of the West Ridge meets the ice of the same ridge. Variation start: begin left of the route, following moderate ice gullies for three pitches, Marty Beare, Steve Erickson, 1983.

Colin Brodie, Nigel Perry, Dec 1980.

Pete Cammell, Charles Hornsby, Aug 1989.

2.70 **Slovenian Route** Grade 5-

From the shelf, head directly up the slopes beneath the two major icecliffs on the left of the face, up through a short rock band and between the cliffs. Then move back left and directly up above the left icecliff either to the top of the West Ridge or tending right again to Low Peak.

Vanya Furlen, Jan 1994.

2.71 **Original Route** Grade 4

From the prominent shelf gained from Gardiner Hut, climb up to the right across the face and then up beside the main rock rib on the right. Then gain the rib and ascend to the South Ridge below the final rock step.

Pete Strang, J R McKinnon, J Milne, R J Stewart, Nov 1962.

2.72 **Direct Route** Grade 5-

From the Noeline Glacier, ascend a 70° ice gully on the right of the main icecliffs, then directly up, turning the first prominent icecliffs on the left, and the next cliff on the right. A dangerous climb.

Bill Denz, Nov 1972.

2.73 **The Gates of Steel** Grade 5

Ascend the buttress right of the centre of the face, weave through icecliffs and then up the face to the South Ridge. The buttress is reportedly fairly safe but the rock is of mixed quality.

Bill Denz, Nigel Perry, Jan 1981.

Alex Palman, David Baguley, winter 1994 (buttress only).

★ **2.74** **David and Goliath** Grade 5

The prominent ice gully right of Route 2.73. 600 metres of good ice. Finishes at the top of the rock buttress of Gates of Steel, left of the big icecliff.

Paul Aubrey, Pete Axford, Nov 1987.

2.75   Nerve Runner   Grade 5+
Starting on the buttress immediately right of David and Goliath. Fifteen pitches straight up mixed ground with steep ice runnels. Good rock pro. Exit 200 metres left of Romeo and Juliet through icecliffs. Aptly named.
Nick Cradock, Bryan Dyson, Dec 1987.

2.76   Romeo and Juliet   Grade 5
Ascend the ice gully on the right side of the face, just right of the prominent icecliff and exit onto the South Ridge.
Lionel Clay, Anne Palmer, Dec 1987.

2.77   Sodom and Gomorrah   Grade 5+
Start up Romeo and Juliet, then continue up a ramp 100 metres towards the South Ridge, then straight up for five rope lengths to small snowfield to exit below the third step on the South Ridge.
Brian Alder, Dave Vass, Nov 1988.

2.78   South Ridge   Grade 4-
From the Noeline Glacier ascend to Endeavour Col (beware of rockfall – an alternative approach lies over Nazomi). Then ascend both the first and second steps on the east side. The third, crux step can be climbed direct. The rock is generally very loose. Then follow a classic arête to the summit.
Harry Ayres, Ruth Adams, Ed Hillary, Mick Sullivan, Jan 1948.
Graeme Dingle, Noel Sissons, Jul 1972.

Nazomi 2925m

Gledhill Buttress

★ 2.79   Terminator   Grade 5
Start climbing up the prow of the buttress, then continue up the slabby buttress above keeping well right of the corner. Twelve pitches of excellent sustained rockclimbing (crux 18/19, also pitches of 16). Phil Castle and Carol McDermott climbed this route in January 1985. The first two pitches climbed were in the corner just left of the buttress, they then moved right onto slabs between the corner and the buttress.
Hamish Dunn, Rob Staszewski, Feb 1985.

2.80   Xmas Sausage: Terminator Variant   Grade 4
Head up the Terminator and then straight up the slabby buttress above (crux 18).
Jeremy Strang, Dave Vass, Dec 1988.

2.81   Gledhill Route   Grade 4
Start right of the prow of the prominent buttress. Easy angled climbing leads up right into a corner and deep ugly gully. A crux near the top of the gully (two possible options, both grade 17) is followed by 200m of scrambling to the summit.
Alan & Geoff Gledhill, Feb 1973.
Direct variation start: Zane Williams, Bryan McArthur, Jan 1980.

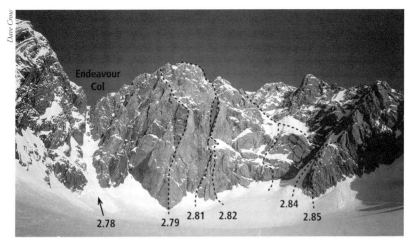

Dave Crow

Endeavour
Col

2.78

2.79   2.81   2.82

2.84

2.85

Fig. 17 Gledhill Buttress, Nazomi.

2.82   Tom and Bill   Grade 3+
On the buttress rib right of the *Gledhill* and *Terminator,* (crux 14, but might
be harder), limited protection.
Adrian Daly, Brendan Wilson, Jan 1988.

2.83   Variant   Grade 3+
Starts 70m right of the *Gledhill* line near a waterfall. Climb face to overhang,
then up groove and steep gully, and follow a rib to the top. Excellent rock,
crux 14 (possibly involves Route 2.82).
Matt Perchad, Garry Phillips, Feb 1996.

2.84   Noeline Couloir   Grade 2
Ascend the couloir and rock steps between the two summits. This is a standard
ascent and descent route. There are a considerable number of variations,
especially to the left of the couloir.
Freda Du Faur, Alex Graham, Peter Graham, Mar 1912.
Bill McLeod, Mark Taylor, Aug 1992.

2.85   Du Faur Ridge
The southern wall of the Noeline Glacier can be gained at various points
and although the upper portion has been climbed often, the ridge does not
appear to have been climbed in its entirety. Excellent rock buttresses are
found on the lower ridge.

Colin Monteath/Hedgehog House

The Gnome

2.94

2.93
2.92

2.91

2.89   2.90

Mona Glacier

Fig. 18 South Face of Nazomi.

2.86   Tim Jefferson Memorial Route   Grade 3
The obvious buttress clearly visible from Gardiner Hut on the western end
of the West Ridge of Nazomi. Climb the north side of the buttress using the
obvious left facing corner for three pitches, turning two large roofs on the
left. Move onto broken slabs of the west face through an overhanging 'V'
slot on the NW ridge (crux 16). Easy scrambling along the ridge then leads
to a point above a large snow slope leading down the north side to the
Noeline Glacier descent route.
Steve Upton, Mike Morrissey, Jan 1983.

★ **2.87   White-Vervoorn Buttress**   Grade 4
Gain the buttress from the Hooker Glacier below the Hooker Icefall 300m
of hard climbing on excellent rock (crux 15), which is reportedly far better
than Route 2.88, leads to lesser angled rock which a confident party can
climb unroped. To descend, walk off the top of the second buttress down
the Noeline Glacier.
Aat Vervoorn, David White, Nov 1972.
Bill Denz, Jun 1973.

2.88   MacInnes Ridge   Grade 4
Starting from the lower Hooker Glacier beside the stream from the Mona
Glacier, climb the first buttress, then onto the second buttress of good rock
(with a 50m cheval) and up to the "Gnome", from where a short descent
leads onto a small glacier below the final wall. An escape route exists to the
left round to Gardiner Hut. Otherwise straight up variable rock to the summit
ridge. This section can often be iced up.
Hamish MacInnes, Peter Robinson, Feb 1955.

South Face

2.89   Runts in Paradise   Grade 5-
Gullies left of Route 2.90, with a snow slope to start. This route climbs ice
to the left of the left rib and takes a left-hand variant gully at half height.
Graham Sanders, Rik Thwaites, Jan 1988.

2.90   Faintly French   Grade 3+
Climb the left rib, rock scrambling changing to steep climbing on an arête
(crux 15) followed by easier broken rock 200m below the summit.
Stu Skeen, Richard Howes, Feb 1984.

★ **2.91   Major Runt Route**   Grade 5
The obvious central couloir between the two major buttresses.
Russell Braddock, Nick Parks, Dec 1984.

2.92   Cormack-Wilson Rib   Grade 3+
Up the middle rib which steepens in the middle before reaching a shelf
below the final 150m of poor rock.
H W Cormack, L W Wilson, Dec 1936.

2.93   Slightly Scottish   Grade 5-
An ice climb up the couloir to right of Cormack-Wilson Rib. Where the
couloir cuts right to the South Ridge move left and up (crux) to reach the
shelf, then out onto the upper South Ridge.
Murray Ball, Bryan McArthur, Zane Williams, Jan 1980.
Andy MacFarlane, Jul 1993.

2.94   The Turkey Strikes Back (Right Rib)   Grade 3+
Third buttress right of the MacInness R. A rotten rock start leads to climbing
on sound compact rock with sustained difficulties (crux 13).
Roddy McKenzie, Craig Nottle, Graeme Saunders, Jan 1982.

2.95   South Ridge   Grade 3

The start from the head of the Mona Glacier névé is steep and has been avoided by using couloirs on the west to emerge where the ridge flattens. A prominent tower 200m below the summit is turned on the east. The rock is variable.

C J Burrows, W A Croll, Dec 1955.

Mt Pibrac 2514m

2.96   Grade 3-

From Hooker Glacier ascend via the Mona Glacier onto either the West Ridge, North Face, or North Ridge (Divide). The rock on Pibrac is good at the bottom but deteriorates markedly towards the top.

West Ridge: Freda Du Faur, Peter Graham, Dec 1912.

2.97

North from Ball Pass over Turner Peak.

Turner Peak 2338m

2.98i

Straightforward from most directions.

Darby Thomson, Samuel Turner, Feb 1913.

2.98ii   Grade 2

West Ridge: G Carr, K E Johnson, Jan 1965.

Ball Pass 2121m

★ 2.99   Grade 1+

From the East Hooker track. Follow the Hooker Valley track to the second swingbridge, don't cross it – instead continue up the eastern side of the Hooker valley, following a vague track marked occasionally with cairns. This track follows vegetated moraine terraces to a large shingle fan opposite Hooker Hut. To the north-east of this fan there is an obvious gully, ascend this to a relatively flat area under Mt Mabel known as the 'playing fields'. Continue up scree slopes to the east. These slopes snake upward between bluffs. Once above these slopes follow a ledge northward to the north-west ridge of Mt Mabel. This is the best route through the bluffs. Traversing northward again, cross rock slabs and descend around the ridge, west of Mt Rosa. Beyond Mt Rosa continue in a north-easterly direction across scree slopes to Ball Pass.

Ball Pass to Caroline Hut. Below the pass, descend the Ball Glacier a short distance before gaining the Ball Ridge to the south. Continue down this to Caroline Hut (~1790m, privately owned and locked, although an emergency shelter with a radio exists). To get to Ball Shelter, follow the Ball Ridge below the hut. Difficult sections can be avoided on the eastern side. Follow cairns until the track turns to the east, where the route descends boulder scree and alpine scrub to the shelf that Ball Shelter (~1020m) resides on. See Fig. 19.

Time: Village to Ball Shelter 8-10hrs, usually completed as a full day trip.

George Mannering, Arthur Harper, Jan 1890.

All the following peaks can be climbed with relative ease from the east side of the Hooker Valley.

Mt Rosa 2161m

R Moorhouse, E Studholme 1895.

Mt Mabel 2091m

James Annan, Malcolm Ross, Apr 1890.

Mt Kinsey 2083m

Peter Graham, Henrik Sillem, Feb 1906.

Mt Wakefield 2058m

Thomas Brodrick, Louis Sladden, 1889.

★ Guides Route

At least two of the ribs leading onto Wakefield from just above the second swingbridge were used as training climbs for guides in the 1930s. From the second swingbridge climb a very enjoyable ridge to the summit. The rock is good and the panoramic views including Sefton, the Main Divide and Aoraki are superb.

First ascent unknown.

There are also some good winter gully climbs on Mt Wakefield, starting from near the second swingbridge.

Strauchon Glacier Area

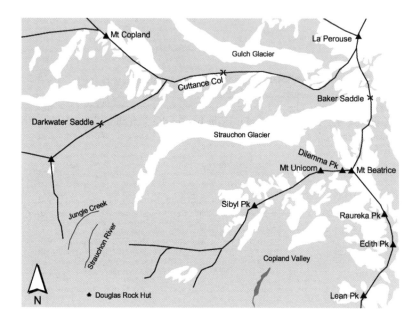

Strauchon Glacier Area

This small valley is renowned for outstanding rock climbing on the Dilemma-Unicorn massif. In addition, the lower valley is one of the most beautiful spots in the Mt Cook district. The tussock-covered old moraines and flats are framed by spectacular views of Mt La Perouse, Mt Cook, and the Dilemma group. The crossing of Baker Saddle provides a difficult but satisfying alpine trip.

Access

The quickest route is over Baker Saddle from the Hooker Glacier. There is a short steep snow climb on the east, and easy slopes on the west. Beware of ice avalanches on the west side of the saddle and also wet snow avalanches in the afternoon. The trip over Baker Saddle from Gardiner Hut to the base of the Strauchon Face takes two to four hours. From Douglas Rock Hut, in the Copland Valley, it takes between three and five hours.

From the Copland River below Douglas Rock Hut the lower Strauchon Valley can be reached by crossing the Copland River. Although the crossing is aided by a large vegetated rock island there is a cable across the Copland River, just above the junction with the Strauchon. Alternatively you can do a hideous bush-bash up the true right of the Copland River, from Welcome Flats Hut. Access up the lower Strauchon River however, is too difficult to be worthwhile and the best route is via Jungle Creek (one kilometre downstream from the Strauchon River). Jungle Creek leads onto terraces overlooking the glacier moraines.

Shelter

There are no huts but there may be bivouac rocks on the terraces.

Baker Saddle 2192m

3.0   Grade 2

From the Hooker Glacier as described above. Keep an eye on the icecliffs on La Perouse.

Henry Newton, Ebenezer Teichelmann, William Batson, Jack Clarke, Feb 1902.

Mt Dilemma 2602m

3.1   Grade 2+

Via Baker Saddle and Mt Beatrice, climb l00m of steep rotten rock to the East Summit. The ridge to the West Peak involves exposed scrambling on better rock.

East Peak (2594m): Hugh Chambers, Peter Graham, Dorothy Holdsworth, Jan 1914.
West Peak: Tom Fyfe, Conrad Kain, Mar 1914.

Fig. 19 Strauchon Glacier and Face. Aoraki/Mt Cook and Range behind.

Lloyd Homer/IGNS

Strauchon Face

3.2 Direttissima   Grade 5

Start at the top of the left hand snow cone, near the cascade draining from the hanging glacier. From the first bolts climb up the corner of a left-leading slab (14) for 2 pitches then up broken ground, next to the cascade, to a steep wall. Traverse right on a big ledge and up another slab to the rib below the hanging glacier. This is a good bivvy spot (5 pitches up). From the hanging glacier, start climbing up obvious large crack systems (not the Carter-Gough route) for a couple of pitches. Then head straight up though an obvious roof (3-4 pitches above the hanging glacier). Continue to sloping ledges. The Direct Route should be visible on the right: a left-facing corner that runs all the way up, just left of an overhang at the top. The bolt line climbs a jagged corner 30m left of this. Avoid a roof on the left (15 pitches above the ice) but climb through the next overhang (bolt runners, crux ~15/16). Continue up good slabs to flakey rock moving slightly to the right to reach the summit, 15m left of the Direct Route. Bolt belays (can be difficult to find). 40 pitches. There is a bivvy ledge 50m below the summit – *Hotel Hilti*.

Peter Dickson, Mar 1991.

★ **3.3 Direct**   Grade 5

From the lower Strauchon Glacier gain the hanging glacier on the face via a narrow gully to the right of the glacier to reach a shingle rib, or use the Direttissima start up the buttress. Cross to the glacier and start 50m to the left of the Dilemma-Unicorn corner. Climb easily up to a huge arch and tend left into a left-facing corner. The corner runs all the way up the face, passing beside an overhang near the top, to finish on the ridge right of the summit. A sustained ~30 pitch climb with crux pitches of 15. Anchors are sometimes hard to find.

Fred From, Murray Judge, Nic Kagan, Nov 1978.

★ **3.4 Carter-Gough**   Grade 5

Gain the hanging glacier but start 100m left of the Direct. Sustained slab climbing up irregular crack systems leads eventually to a prominent point four pitches left and below the summit. A fine climb with crux pitches of grade 15.

Brian Carter, Peter Gough, Jan 1973.

Direct to the summit: Marty Beare, Craig Hamilton, ~1981.

3.5 Misty Mountain Hop   Grade 5

Commencing on the left side of the hanging glacier ascend directly up the slabs left of the Carter-Gough route to reach the ridge running north-west from the summit. Once on the ridge, climb seven pitches to the summit.

John Goulstone, Mike Rockell, Feb 1983.

Mt Unicorn 2557m

Strauchon Face

The routes on Unicorn are harder and more exposed than those on Dilemma.

★ 3.6   Dilemma Traverse   Grade 3

From Dilemma climb down slabs on the Strauchon Face and then regain the ridge to ascend blocks onto Unicorn. An exposed climb, but still the easiest route off the peak. Highly recommended.

Frank Milne, Harold Porter, Jan 1924.

3.7   Classical Gas   Grade 6-

Ascend the left face of Unicorn following a distinct diagonal crack system which passes just left of the arching overhang. Start in the middle of the face, left of corners, up face to snow ledge. From ledge begin left of main crack, move up and gain crack as soon as practical. Follow line to summit ridge, traversing to the right at the top of face to the summit. Very sustained rock climbing (crux 16).

Bill McLeod, Peter Dickson, Dec 1992.

3.8   Original Route   Grade 5

As for Route 3.3 until the shingle rib is gained. From here move right into the major couloir and up for roughly 200m (beware of rockfall), then head left up the rock, towards an enormous corner where the left (main) face begins. Climb the left hand edge of the face immediately right of the corner to gain a large flattish snowfield, 300m below the top. There are good bivvy sites here. Climb the face above via crack systems that tend left to reach the ridge 60m below the summit (crux 16). Other variations are possible at the top.

Alan & Geoff Gledhill, Jan 1973.

3.9   Grade 5+

From the major couloir beneath the face climb up to the snowfield at the base of the great corner. Climb a hand crack 10-15 metres left of the big corner. After sustained climbing (crux 15) the crack runs out. Traverse right through the big corner at an obvious weakness to gain the flattish snowfield, and then to the top of the face via the Gledhill route.

Peter Dickson, Mar 1990.

3.10   West Ridge

Similar to the top of the Strauchon Face.

Descended by Alan & Geoff Gledhill, Jan 1973.

Getting off Dilemma:

The easiest way off Dilemma avoids the East Peak and rotten rock. From the West Peak scramble down the eastern edge of the Strauchon Face for 150m, then drop down a diagonal ledge system to snow 100 metres below. If the ledges are snowed up, abseil from the first notch between West and East Peaks, anchors in-situ (grade 2). Traverse across and up to a rock gendarme on the Main Divide, 100m north of Beatrice. Follow a snow ridge on the western side, passing under rock on the divide. At a rock rib that cuts westward, climb back to the divide, crossing it, and descend on the Hooker Valley side, traversing below the divide. This cross-over point is crucial. Continue along the crest over broken rock to Baker Saddle. It is also theoretically possible to rappel Route 3.2. This is not recommended as it would take all day and the bolts could be difficult to find, especially at night.

Other options: If descending from Beatrice, drop onto eastern snow slopes (go south first if necessary) and continue along snow to Baker Saddle.

Mt La Perouse 3078m

South Face

3.11   Bill and Ted's Excellent Adventure   Grade 6+...

Ascend the obvious main ice line that drips down the face. The upper section of the face is visible from Gardiner Hut. Near the top, gain the ramp of the slab route below the dormant(?) serac. Access to the base of the route may be threatened. Fourteen pitches. Two bivvies required. Probably the hardest route in the book.

Bill McLeod, Brian Alder, Aug 1993.

3.12   Slab Route   Grade 5-

Climb the diagonal slab that runs up the entire face (crux 14). The upper portion of the slab is usually snow covered and there may be a small icecliff to negotiate.

Peter Dickson, Bryan Moore, Jan 1988.

3.13   South West Ridge   Grade 4-

From the Strauchon Glacier ascend the Low Glacier onto the Navigator Range. Ascend on the Gulch Glacier side of the ridge. When the obvious rock step in the ridge is reached cut onto the Gulch Face and ascend directly on snow to where the South Ridge meets the South West Ridge. Also see the La Perouse Glacier section.

H T Barcham, Ash Cunningham, A Witten-Hannah, Jan 1953.

La Perouse Glacier Area

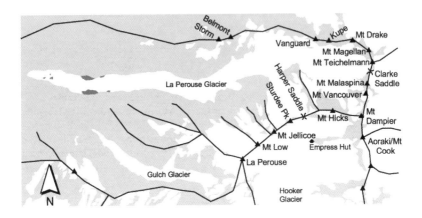

La Perouse Glacier Area

An inaccessible area reached either by intricate and involved climbing from the east or by a long two or three day struggle through thick forest up the Cook River. Once into this area, however, there is some superb climbing and a sense of remoteness.

Access

From the West Coast a hard two or three day bush tramp up the southern bank along a route marked by coloured blazes (but don't expect a track) leads onto the lower La Perouse Glacier.

From the Hooker Valley and Empress Hut cross Harper Saddle (refer to Routes 2.25, 2.26i & ii). From the Tasman Valley and the Grand Plateau, cross either Mt Malaspina or Clarke Saddle (6.19 & 6.20). The La Perouse side of the saddle is fairly easy, but the Plateau slopes are steep and crevassed. Another route from the Plateau lies up the spur of Mt Malaspina and then down the ridge to Clarke Saddle (which may involve an abseil) or down a steep couloir off the ridge.

The La Perouse Glacier itself is complicated by a lower and upper icefall which are both often heavily crevassed. The lower icefall can usually be avoided on its northern side, but the upper icefall can present difficulties, especially later in the summer.

Shelter

A number of bivouac rocks exist in the lower valley, (particularly on the walk in up the Cook River) and on the way to the West Ridge of La Perouse, but these can sometimes be hard to find. Many parties have snowcaved on the upper névé of the glacier.

Times

Up the Cook River to the La Perouse Névé 2-3 days.
Empress Hut to the La Perouse Névé via Harper Saddle 3-5 hours.
Plateau Hut to the La Perouse Névé via Clarke Saddle 5-6 hours.

Mt La Perouse 3078m

4.0 **West Ridge**   Grade 3
From the Gulch-La Perouse Glaciers junction ascend to a basin at 1550m where there are a number of natural rock shelters. From here ascend the ridge traversing several rotten rock steps. Then ascend a steep snowface onto the upper arête and follow this up onto the spacious summit area. A descent route has been made down the snow slopes to the north of the lower ridge.
Alex Graham, R S Low, Henry Newton, Ebenezer Teichelmann, Feb 1906.

4.1 **South West Ridge**   Grade 3
From the head of the narrow Gulch Glacier (beware of avalanches off the West Ridge) follow snow leads tending left to gain the ridge above the obvious rock step.
Dave Bamford, John Nankervis, Jan 1979

Fig. 20. North Face of Mt Hicks, Harper Saddle (obscured), Sturdee Peak and Mt La Perouse.

Jane Wright

Mt Hicks 3198m

4.2   **Red Wall**   Grade 4

An eight pitch route up red rock to the left of couloir on the Curtain Route (Route 2.27).

Mark Inglis, Richard Pears, Dec 1980.

4.3   **North Rib (also know as the Biscuit Tin route)**   Grade 4-

From the access route over Harper Saddle to the upper La Perouse Névé (Route 2.25) ascend good rock on the face to the right of the rib. The rib steepens towards the top, (crux 14/15). Then follow a flattening ridge for 250m to join the top of the couloir on the Curtain Route.

Peter Gough, P Barry, D Drake, Aat Vervoorn, Nov 1969.

Murray Ball, Paul Aubrey, Jul 1980.

North Face

4.4   **Book of Days**   Grade 5+

Next rock rib right of Right Buttress. Access is via snow slopes and a gully, which ends in a cul-de-sac, beside the Right Buttress (face between these routes was climbed by Marty Beare and Lindsay Main). Climb ramp right of corner to gain crest of rib. Follow crest to a striking red tower. Continue on crest to summit. The first pitch (crux 17) is followed by sustained climbing on solid red rock, which rarely relents. Thirteen pitches.

Bill McLeod, Mark Taylor, Jul 1992

4.5   **Right Buttress**   Grade 6+

Start up steep dark-coloured chimneys to the right of the prominent gully keeping left of the bottom. The first six pitches are sustained (crux 17), on excellent rock. The next eight pitches are easier and on good rock. Above the climbing becomes more broken.

Merv English, John Fantini, Noel Sissons, Jan 1975.

Bill McLeod, Mark Taylor, Aug 1989.

★ **4.6**   **Central Buttress**   Grade 6

Start up a crack on a small block below the main buttress, then right and into the obvious groove that takes you right up the climb. Hardest at the bottom (crux grade 15) except for a slight sting at the top. Good rock and classic climbing.

Bill Denz, Phil Herron, Murray Judge, Jun 1974.

4.7   **Variants on the Central Buttress**

i) Follow an obvious system of cracks parallel to and left of the main route. Sustained climbing with two harder pitches of grade 18-20. Good rock although shattered in places.

Monks & Sunderland, Feb 1996.

ii) Follow Route 4.6 for 3-4 pitches, then move right just before a widening chimney with an overhanging start. Continue 15m along ledge to steep crack system (~18). The route runs along the nose of buttress parallel to and right of Route 4.6, rejoining it after 8 pitches.

Andrew McAuley, Vera Wong, 1996.

4.8   **Weeping Gash**   Grade 6+

The gully between the Left and Central Buttresses. A startlingly steep couloir with frequent crux walls. Climbed in winter when the ice is solid. Required two bivvies.

Nick Cradock, Guy Cotter, Jul 1986.

4.9   **Left Buttress**   Grade 5+

Head up the obvious large five pitch corner on the right side of buttress, avoiding the roof by taking the right variant corner. 200m of easy climbing leads to a steep wall (crux 15) followed by easier climbing as the buttress lies back.

David Elphick, Barry Smith, Feb 1957 (avoided first five pitches).

Lindsay Main, Tim Wethey, Jan 1978 (entire buttress).

Bill McLeod, Mark Taylor, Aug 1989.

Mt Dampier/Rakiroa 3440m

4.10   **North West Flank**   Grade 3+

Start up an avalanche chute to the north of a large diamond buttress of rock below the summit. Move right to gain the edge of the buttress and then up a snow rib above. Traverse across a large snowfield and up to the major schrund below the final wall of Dampier. Move either left or right (the easiest way) to reach the Divide and then via the ridge to the summit. The normal descent route from Dampier lies down into the Grand Plateau, via the south ridge (Route 6.14).

Gordon Hasell, E R B Graham, T A Nuttall, Jan 1957.

Mt Vancouver 3309m

4.11   **West Buttress**   Grade 4-

Begin up slabs to the left of the buttress crest. Follow on up the edge of the buttress. The climbing becomes harder towards the top (crux 12). Then follow a snow arête to the summit.

John Fantini, Lindsay Main, Dec 1974.

4.12   Grade 3

Ascend from the La Perouse Glacier névé up into the cirque separating Malaspina and Vancouver. From here follow a gully onto Vancouver.

Bill King, Ian McAlpine, Steve Rawnsley, Feb 1985.

4.13   **Main Divide**

The ridge from Dampier is relatively straightforward (refer to Route 6.16) whereas from Malaspina requires traversing rock towers (Route 6.18).

Mt Malaspina 3042m

4.14   West Ridge   Grade 3+

Ascend a rock ridge onto a major bump in the ridge. Then across a sweeping snow saddle to a final buttress of four rope lengths which lead to the summit.

David Elphick, M White, Feb 1957 (Lower section).

Penny & Charles Webster, Feb 1984 (Upper section).

4.15

A prominent gully north of Mt Malaspina may provide a quick alternative to the route to the Grand Plateau over Clarke Saddle. See Routes 6.20 and 6.21

Teichelmann/Rakirua 3144m

4.16   South West Face   Grade 5+

Start up steep gullies at the bottom centre of the face. Two pitches of steep ice in these gullies are the crux. They can be avoided by traversing in from the right. Several pitches up steep icefields lead to steep gullies that run up to the South Ridge (13 pitches in total).

James Jenkins, Lindsay Main, Dec 1975.

Clarke Saddle and Ridge

Described under Route 6.20 and 6.21.

Magellan 3049m

4.17   Via Teichelmann   Grade 3

Traverse a sharp arête out to a prominent rock tower (not the summit), then down and along another sharp arête. A longer climb than it looks.

Harry Ayres, Bruce Gillies, D G Herron, Ed Hillary, Feb 1955.

4.18   South Face   Grade 4

Ascend a prominent rib that starts from the névé below the summit and leads out to the right of the summit. A short wall in the middle of the rib can be turned on the left. First climbed when well covered in snow.

Gordon Hasell, E R B Graham, T A Nuttall, Jan 1957.

Mt Drake 2960m

4.19   East Ridge   Grade 3+

The ridge from Mt Magellan is steep firm rock near Magellan but deteriorates as the col is approached. The section up to Drake is steep and loose.

Paul Aubrey, Richard Pears, Jan 1981.

South Face

4.20   Grade 3

Ascend the snowface to the left of the summit.

Gordon Hasell, E R B Graham, T A Nuttall, Jan 1957.

4.21   Grade 3
Start up the short rock face to the left of the snowface, then up the rock
ridge and snow arête to the summit. A good descent route.
David Elphick, Barry Smith, M R White, Jim Wilson, Feb 1957.

4.22   **West Ridge**   Grade 4
Descended as far as the final rise up to Mt Vanguard. After 500m a steep
knife-edge cheval presents difficult climbing.
Anton & Paul Wopereis, Jan 1980.

Kupe 2510m *Vanguard* 2331m
See Routes 15.41 - 15.45.

Lower Tasman Valley

The Tasman Glacier is the largest in New Zealand, and the Tasman Valley probably provides the greatest scope for general mountaineering in the country. The valley has been divided into four sections: the Lower Tasman, the Grand Plateau, the Upper Tasman, and a section called the Eastern Tasman describes the routes on Nun's Veil and neighbouring peaks.

The Lower Tasman

Encompassing the Mount Cook Range, this area contains generally easy climbing from the old Ball Hut road. The Ball Pass area is an excellent beginners' playground. Towards Mt Cook, however, the climbs are on a different scale.

Access

The Tasman Valley road that turns off Highway 80 is also known as the old Ball Road and allows vehicle access to Celmisia Flat, or to Husky Flat (if you have a 4WD). A transport service from the Tasman Valley Road to the Blue Lakes normally operates from either the Guide Shop or Hermitage during the summer. It is about two hours or so from Celmisia flat to **Ball Shelter** on foot. The track that follows along the moraine wall is made up of remnant sections of the old Ball Hut road, constructed during the depression years of the 1920s and 1930s and was used as a road up until the late 1970s. Above the Shelter, the climber has the alternative of descending a gully ('Garbage Gully') in the moraine wall onto the Tasman and hence to the Grand Plateau or Upper Tasman, or else ascending Ball Ridge to Ball Pass. The Ball Pass route is described in the Hooker Valley section.

The Tasman Glacier: access & travel

From Ball Shelter follow the track to the very end of the tussock terraces to the rocky slopes. Continue along these for about 60m to a marker post, this is the top of so-called 'Garbage Gully'. From this point both the Ball and Tasman glaciers should be visible. Descend the gully (despite its name the gully is quite straightforward) to the bottom where it meets the Tasman Glacier. The conditions at the margins of the glacier vary almost daily, but the best route on to the Tasman Glacier is generally directly below Garbage Gully. It involves heading toward the centre of the glacier for about 150-200m (effectively head east). Once clear of the holes, moulins and the difficult to pass ice/moraine slopes, turn up valley and begin the grind. From this point on the glacier, the options are as follows.

If you plan to use the Cinerama Col route to Plateau Hut you need to travel up the Tasman Glacier for only a short time (10-20 minutes) before veering left across to the scree slopes adjacent to the Ball/Tasman glacier junction (on the north side of the Ball Glacier). See Route 5.4 for the rest of the route to/from Plateau Hut.

For those heading to Haast Ridge, travel up the centre of the Tasman Glacier for about 20 minutes and then aim for the flat section of ice below the Hochstetter Icefall outflow. After this, continue up valley just past Haast Ridge until a suitable point to tackle the moraine wall becomes evident. See Grand Plateau section for details.

If your destination is the Beetham Valley, De La Beche Hut or Tasman Saddle head toward the east side of the glacier and travel up the white ice (you may see an occasional cairn, but don't count on it.)

Take some music.

Further descriptions can be found in the next section.

Shelter
Ball Shelter. A small comfortable shelter with a radio, water and two sleeping benches (with mattresses) for approximately eight people, but no kitchen equipment (~1020m, grid ref: 834-274).

Mt Wakefield 2058m

From the Tasman road bridge climb up the vegetated spur that eventually leads to the summit. This is an excellent day or overnight trip and could form the descent if the Guide Route (from the Hooker) is climbed. Panoramic views.

Mt Kinsey 2083m, *Mt Mabel* 2091m, *Mt Rosa* 2161m

The above peaks can all be climbed easily from the Tasman Valley. Mts Mabel and Rosa provide pleasant climbing up the valley above Husky Flat, but beware of avalanches in spring and early summer.

Ball Pass 2121m

The best route is via the ridge behind the Ball Hut over Furggens Knob and onto the Pass. The older route up the Ball Glacier (scene of New Zealand ski championships in the 1930s) has been affected by glacial recession. For descent to the Hooker Valley and other details see Route 2.99.

Mt Turner 2338m

Refer to Routes 2.98i and 2.98ii.

Mt Pibrac 2514m

The easiest routes are via Ball Pass either along the ridge or traversing around the Ball Glacier. This area was the scene of many ascents when guides were based at Ball Hut.

Nazomi 2925m

Via the South Ridge from Ball Pass: See Route 2.95.

5.0   East Face Routes   Grade 3
From the Ball Glacier gain the prominent shelf that runs below Nazomi and verges the Caroline Face by climbing 650m up a rib that starts from the Ball-Caroline glaciers junction. A number of routes exist from the shelf onto the crest of the Mt Aoraki/Cook Range:

i) to the base of the South Ridge of Nazomi.
Bruce Gillies, Roland Rodda, Dec 1942.

ii) A snow arête to the summit of Nazomi.
D C Ball, D G Herron, Phil Houghton, A R Page, Richard Tornquist, Jan 1959.

The shelf can also be used as an escape route from the Caroline Face of Mt Cook.

Aoraki/Mt Cook, Low Peak 3593m

South Ridge. Has been approached via Ball Pass, see Route 2.78.

Caroline Face

This 2000m climb, the biggest face in the region, requires good fitness. Significant avalanche danger exists in the lower sections – move quickly.

5.1   **The Denz Route**   Grade 5

Follow Route 5.2 to the shelf, then head across the shelf and ascend gullies and snowfields l000m to the Low Peak, meeting the South Ridge 40m below the summit.
Bill Denz, Nov 1972.
Glenn Pennycook, Jul 2001.
A Korean party may have climbed a route right (!) of Route 5.1 but details are lacking.

★**5.2**   **The Clit Route**   Grade 5

From the Caroline Glacier ascend an avalanche fan to gain the left side of three rock ribs that lead onto the large shelf. Above here follow the obvious arête up to the major icecliffs cutting across the face. Depending on their condition the cliffs can be the technical crux of the climb. Above here continue up a broad rib onto the summit icefields and head directly up the icefields to Porter Col if the icefields are in poor condition.
John Glasgow, Peter Gough, Nov 1970.
Rob Hall, Steve Lassche, Jun 1981.
The three initial rock faces have also been climbed.
Marty Beare, Lindsay Main, Colin Monteath, ~1985.

5.3   **Miroslav Route**   Grade 4+

Climb the snow rib right of the Clit Route (from the CR or from the Caroline Glacier directly). Continue through the icecliffs to join the East Ridge.
Adam Darragh, Rob Starmer, Jan 1988 (to the top of the rib and traversed onto the Clit Route).
Sveticic Slavko Miroslav, Mar 1990 (to the East Ridge).

Cinerama Col 2333m

5.4

This col is an access route to Plateau Hut, but it is more often used as a descent because of soft snow later in the day. *The following is a descent description.* From the Grand Plateau cross Cinerama Col and drop 150m down the Caroline Glacier, skirting left under the Anzac Peaks to the ridge line above the Boys Glacier (Boys Col). Descend the Boys (beware of wet snow avalanches here and on the traverse under the Anzacs), tending left to eventually meet low angle scree slopes. Follow the scree slopes down and traverse rightward along an obvious rocky shelf (a small waterfall is now on your right), marked with the odd cairn. A vague track leads to the large scree slopes below that drain almost all the way to the Ball/Tasman glacier junction. A large stream gut to the right provides access to the Tasman Glacier (beware of rockfall, especially during rain).

Anzac Peaks 2528m & 2513m

Grade 2-

These can be climbed from the Boys Glacier either via the ridge from Cinerama Col via a more demanding ridge from the Boys Col, or via the right side of the Boys Glacier.

Peter Graham, Hugh Chambers, Dorothy Theomin, Feb 1922 (via the latter route).

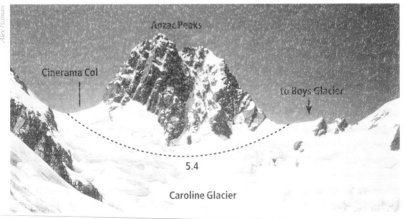

Fig. 21 Cinerama Col, Anzac Peaks and Boys Col.

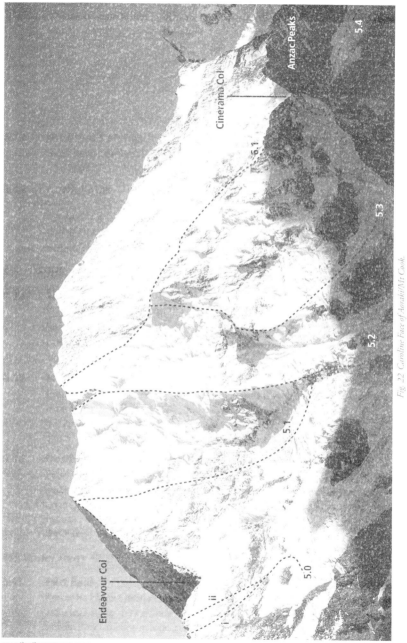

Anzac Peaks

5.4

Cinerama Col

6.1

5.3

5.2

5.1

Endeavour Col

5.0

i

ii

Fig. 22. Caroline Face of Aoraki/Mt Cook.

Grand Plateau

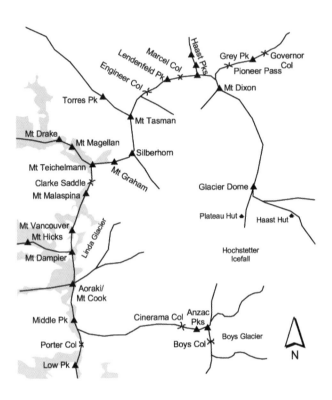

Grand Plateau

The Grand Plateau is notable for long demanding snow and ice climbs. The area provides the easiest access onto Aoraki/Mt Cook and as a result Plateau Hut is often full in the summer months. The climbs from this base require fitness and often involve a long day's climbing with a midnight/very early morning start.

Access

1. *Haast Ridge,* on the northern side of the Hochstetter Icefall. Gained from the Tasman Glacier. Despite being a regular access route the ridge is not easy and has seen at least three fatalities. Gain the ridge wherever a reasonable break exists in the moraine wall, usually further up the Tasman Glacier rather than at the toe of the ridge. Ascend the ridge, which narrows and steepens just before it reaches **Haast Hut**. Above the hut, use snowfields on the Hochstetter Icefall side to traverse up beneath the "Slipper" (a prominent rock gendarme ten minutes above the hut). Above a small col, near the Slipper, either head up on snow and traverse on the south side of Glacier Dome before descending to **Plateau Hut** or later in the season climb directly up from the col to the rocks of Glacier Dome, then drop down to Plateau Hut. Schrund conditions at the top of Haast Ridge can become troublesome late in the season.

2. *Via the Freshfield Glacier.* This is usually used as an alternative descent route below Glacier Dome, especially if Haast Ridge is snow covered. In the right conditions it is a quick descent route.

3. *Via Cinerama Col.* A scenic route and often used to descend from Plateau Hut. See Route 5.4.

4. *Anzac alternative.* A seldom used route exists round the eastern side of the Anzac Peaks and up the slopes next to the Hochstetter Icefall.

5. *Fly in.* It is possible to fly to the Grand Plateau by ski plane (or helicopter if planes are unable to fly/land). The landing strip for the planes is usually near to Mt Dixon, 10-20 minutes from Plateau Hut. For those arriving on the Plateau – rope-up for the walk to the hut.

Shelter

Haast Hut. A nine-bunk A-frame hut with a beautiful view, built on the site of the old Haast Hut (King Memorial) and near the historic Haast Ridge bivouac from which many of the early ascents of Aoraki/Mt Cook were made. Serviced with blankets, cooking utensils, and a radio (~1980m, grid ref: 836-323).

Plateau Hut. A three-room, 30 bunk hut with cooking utensils, a radio and solar lights. In summer check at the Visitor Centre to see how many are in the hut as it tends to become unpleasantly overcrowded. Some parties snowcave on the Plateau (~2210m, no cell coverage at the hut, but possible from Glacier Dome (025), grid ref: 826-322).

Times

From Ball Shelter to Plateau Hut via Cinerama Col 6-8 hours (depending on snow conditions). Descending is quicker but again is dependant on snow conditions – especially on the Plateau (hot tip: get away early).

From Ball Shelter to Haast Hut 7 hours (allow an extra 1-2 hours on to Plateau Hut).

Ski Touring Routes

• Freshfield Glacier. Access and descent route to/from Plateau. Very steep in places (C).

• Cinerama Col, Boys Glacier (C/D).

• Linda Glacier. Subject to crevasses and icefall (B/C).

Anzac Peaks 2528m & 2513m

6.0   Grade 1

Can be climbed with relative ease from the Plateau via a wide gully between the two peaks.

Samuel Turner, Feb 1917.

Aoraki/Mount Cook 3754m

★ **6.1**   **East Ridge**   Grade 4

A classic ice climb, perhaps the finest in New Zealand. The East Ridge joins Aoraki's summit ridge about 200m south of Middle Peak. The lower section of the ridge can be gained at a number of points. The conventional routes are:

i) From Cinerama Col, avoid the first 200m via the Plateau side, then head up slopes to gain the ridge. Follow the arête on up.

ii) Via the shelf below the East Face gain a snow ramp leading out left onto the ridge below a rock step before a prominent level section on the ridge (This section can be gained directly from the shelf). Beyond the level section, follow up the winding arête that merges into the upper Caroline Face and finishes near the Middle Peak. Ice on the upper section of the route is often hard.

Dan Bryant, Lud Mahan, Jan 1938.

Colin Monteath, Richard Schmidt, Steve Anderson, Greg Mortimer, Jul 1979.

East Face

Many variations exist on this 1600m high face. The routes are long sustained ice climbs and can involve high objective danger from rockfall. In 1991 a major rock avalanche swept down the face below High Peak, lowering its height by 10m. The debris jetted across the Plateau, spewed down the Hochstetter Icefall, across the Tasman Glacier and slightly up the moraine wall on the other side of the Tasman Valley. The most important routes are:

6.2 Great Gully
Grade 5

A prominent route parallel to the East Ridge.

Bill Atkinson, Rob Hall, Sep 1979.

A right side variant of the Atkinson/Hall line exists, finishing on Middle Peak.

Sveticic Slavko Miroslav, Mar 1990.

6.3 Rumblestiltzskin
Grade 6

Follows a prominent gully up through the rock buttress in a direct fall line from Middle Peak. Approach via the snow field under the Atkinson/Hall route, traversing right beneath the rock buttress. The gully involves steep climbing. Move right to a short snow slope, following its left edge to a final rock wall. Just right of the Middle Peak apex, ice formations lead through the rock - take the left branch to finish on Middle Peak.

Bill McLeod, Peter Dickson, Jul 1991.

6.4 Whiston Route
Grade 4+

Ascend mixed ground of icefields and rock ribs between the large gully on the left of the face and the Jones Route. A long climb subject to stonefall and rotten rock.

Murray Ball, Nick Cradock, Neal Whiston, Nov 1983.

6.5 Jones Route
Grade 4+

From the shelf head 900m up the left edge of the large snowface on the right of the face. Then out on a ramp leading left and up, joining the summit ridge just north of the Middle Peak. A variation heads straight up avoiding the ramp.

Murray Jones, Dec 1973.

High Peak Route

This route, and variations of it, were obliterated by the 1991 rock avalanche. (originally ascended by Don Cowie, Lyn Crawford, Pete Farrell, Vic Walsh, Nov 1961.

Bryan Pooley, Colin Dodge, Rob Rainsbury, John Visser, Jun 1973).

★ 6.6 Zurbriggen Ridge
Grade 3+

A classic Mt Cook climb. Ascend snow slopes on the edge of the East Face to gain the ridge 400m up, then up a rock step of poor rock (in certain conditions this can be sidled on the East Face). Above here follow snow slopes and the occasional rock pitch to gain the Summit Rocks where the standard Linda Glacier route is joined. Then ascend the north-east arête (commonly referred to as the 'ice cap') to the summit. The first three pitches of this route are the steepest, after which it relents a little.

Mattias Zurbriggen (with John Adamson to 3200m), Mar 1895.

Dave Vass, Dave Chowdhury, Alan Wood, Steve Hodgkinson, Jun 1983.

Fig. 23 East Face of Aoraki/Mt Cook.

6.7   **Bowie Couloir**   Grade 4-

Climb the prominent gully between the Bowie and Zurbriggen Ridges, following the right variation couloir at the top. Involves steep gully climbing and some rockfall danger.

J Barry, D Nicholls, Nov 1969.

Bowie Ridge

6.8   Grade 4-

The Lower Buttress can be climbed either from its toe in the Linda Glacier or just above Teichelmann's Corner (where the Linda turns towards Aoraki).

P Conaghan, R Cox, Feb 1962.

★**6.9**   Grade 4-

The Upper Buttress can be approached from either the upper Linda Glacier or from a subsidiary glacier between Zurbriggen and Bowie ridges and up a gully. The upper buttress has about nine pitches, consistently angled (crux 14), of good rock. Then traverse a ridge with gendarmes to join Zurbriggen Ridge.

Dick Irwin, Hamish MacInnes, Peter Robinson, Feb 1956.

Linking both buttresses - grade 4.

Bill McLeod, Peter Dickson, Jul 1991.

6.10   **Bowie Face**   Grade 5-

A route of 10 pitches ascends the left side of the top buttress of the Bowie Ridge. The route starts from the upper Linda Glacier and follows a narrow chimney (probably iced up)(crux 18). There are other routes further right. The rock is excellent.

Kevin Boekholt, Nick Cradock, Nov 1984.

★**6.11**   **Linda Glacier**   Grade 3

While this is the easiest and most climbed route on Aoraki/Mount Cook, it is also one of the most dangerous, being menaced by icecliffs. The lower glacier is often heavily crevassed and there is considerable danger from ice avalanches off the right (Divide) slopes. At the head of the glacier under the Gunbarrel (the prominent and active icecliffs of the Upper Linda), traverse left very quickly across the Linda Shelf to join Zurbriggen Ridge below the Summit Rocks (these provide access to the summit, which is over 400m above). A 150m gully that runs directly from the Linda Shelf to the start of the Summit Rocks is a popular alternative to traversing to the Zurbriggen junction. Climb the rocks - there is usually a series of ice gullies running up through the rocks which make for easier climbing. Late in the season parties may need to venture further toward the East Face. Once above the Summit Rocks follow the north-east ice cap to the summit. The easiest way to get onto the summit ridge is to traverse to the west, overlooking the North Ridge and Sheila Face, and climb a short step to follow a sustrugi filled ramp that leads to the top. Due to the 1991 avalanche the very top is probably not a smart place to stand and climbers are asked to respect the wishes of Ngai Tahu by not standing on the very top. The Linda Glacier is the most

Colin Monteath/Hedgehog House

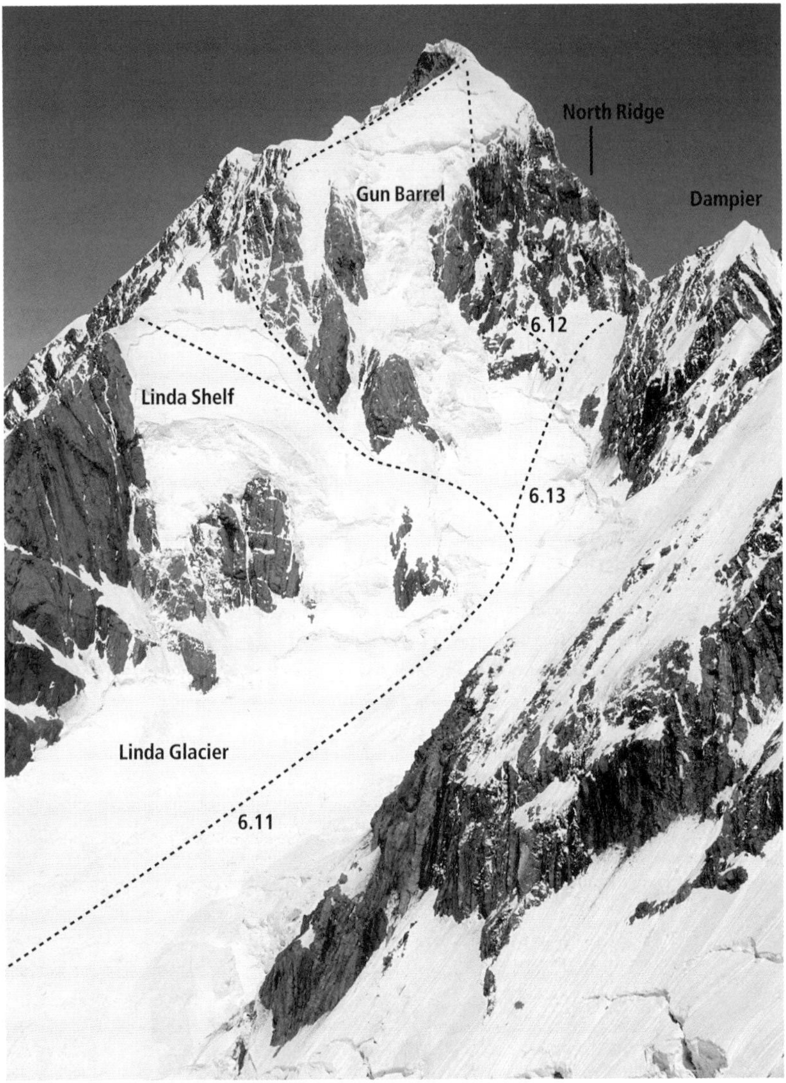

Fig. 24 Aoraki/Mt Cook from the north.

common descent route from Aoraki/Mount Cook. Most parties use two abseils (100m) when descending the Summit Rocks. As a result there can be a 'Christmas tree' of abandoned slings and other assorted anchors in the rock and ice. *Check these thoroughly before using them for abseiling.* There have been numerous falls on this part of the route. As a general rule, ascents of the 'Linda' take anywhere from 15-18hrs or more depending on conditions and the speed of the party. It's a big day out in any language. To make sure it's one to remember: get fit, plan, prepare and practice. If there are many parties intending to do the Linda (or Zurbriggen) - try to avoid a Summit Rocks bottleneck – and don't forget your camera.

A flat section on the Bowie Ridge above Teichelmann's Corner, accessible from the Linda Glacier, provides a relatively safe bivvy spot. There is also a schrund, uphill of the Linda Shelf, which has been used for shelter.

Hugh Chambers, Jack Clarke, Jim Murphy, Hugh Wright, Feb 1912.

Frank Milne, Norman Murrel, Rudolph Wigley, Aug 1923.

6.12	**Northern Icefields**	Grade 3

Rock buttresses and icefields right of the Gunbarrel.

John Fantini, Tony Dignan, Jan 1987.

★ 6.13	**North Ridge**	

Ascend to Green Saddle from the Linda Glacier (schrunds can be problem late in the season). Above here refer to Route 2.51.

First ascended from the Linda Glacier by Harry Ayres, Oscar Coberger, Dec 1951.

Beare Step: Bill McLeod, Peter Dickson, Jul 1991.

Mt Dampier/Rakiroa 3440m

6.14	**South Ridge**	Grade 3

Gained from the upper Linda Glacier either via the snowslope to Green Saddle or up a rib on the right. Thence up a steep rotten ridge. This route is possibly the best descent route off Dampier.

Freda Du Faur, Peter Graham, C Milne, Mar 1912.

6.15	**East Face**	Grade 3+

From the Linda Glacier it is possible to head up various routes on sound rock to arrive either on the south ridge or near the summit.

Syd Brookes, Jack Cox, Marjorie Edgar-Jones, Jan 1938.

There are also numerous interesting ice variants on the East Face.

6.16	**North Ridge, via Mt Vancouver**	Grade 3+

Follow the ridge to a prominent rock step, which can be climbed via a hidden gully on the eastern side. Climbers wishing to avoid this ridge can traverse across the North Face to the Hicks-Dampier Ridge. See Routes 4.12 and 6.17.

Bert Barley, J Forsyth, Mar 1950.

Mt Vancouver 3309m

6.17	**East Face**	Grade 3

From the Linda Glacier climb up diagonally to the right to gain a steep snow arête leading to the summit. Variations exist for this route on the snowslope to left. Nevertheless it is occasionally used as a descent route.

Bert Barley, J Forsyth, Mar 1950.

Fig. 25 Aoraki/Mt Cook, Mt Tasman and the Grand Plateau from the east. Circle denotes Plateau (L) abd Haast huts.

6.18 Main Divide Grade 3+

The ridge from Clarke Saddle over Mt Malaspina involves numerous rock towers and rock scrambling on unsound rock, which could prove time consuming for a slow party.

Mt Malaspina 3042m

6.19 East Spur Grade 2+

From the Linda Glacier opposite Teichelmann's Corner a broad snow shoulder leads up to just below the summit of Malaspina. This route provides a good access route to the La Perouse Glacier. From the summit follow the Main Divide to Clarke Saddle (an abseil may be necessary), but an alternative route to the La Perouse may lie down a dog-leg couloir closer to the summit of Malaspina

Neville Johnson, E Miller, A J Scott, Dec 1936.

Tony Teeling, Ken Joyce, Rob Young, Aug 1983.

Clarke Saddle 2978m

6.20 Grade 3-

The approach via the Linda Glacier is quite steep and often complicated with crevasses. The alternative approach over Malaspina may prove better in some conditions. The La Perouse side of the saddle is easier by comparison.

First reached by Dan Bryant and Lud Mahan in January 1933, from Teichelmann.

Mt Teichelmann/Rakirua 3144m

6.21 Grade 3-

Via Clarke Saddle, the route up the Main Divide to the peak is straightforward until the final summit cone where steep rock can be difficult and iced. If not covered by snow the rock is very loose.

Katie Gardiner, Harold Porter, Vic Williams, Feb 1929.

6.22 Grade 3-

From Mt Graham it is a simple climb until the exposed summit cone.

Dan Bryant, Lud Mahan, Jan 1933.

Erica Beuzenberg, Gottlieb Braun-Elwert, Jun 1989.

Mt Graham 3184m

6.23

A straightforward climb from either Mt Teichelmann or Silberhorn.

Dan Bryant, Lud Mahan, Jan 1933.

Ian Jowett, Noel Sissons, Aug 1971.

6.24 **Graham Spur** Grade 3+

From the Linda Glacier move leftwards (the route may change owing to glacier movements) onto the spur. Then head up the spur until 100m below the top where the route moves right up the final steep 50m of ice onto the ridge just north of the summit.

Paul Bieleski, A W Bowden, V R McGregor, Richard Tornquist, Dec 1962.

Silberhorn 3300m

★ 6.25 Grade 3

From the Grand Plateau head 200m up ice-avalanche-threatened slopes under Mt Tasman before turning left to gain the ridge, which is followed to the summit. The most popular approach route to Mt Tasman from the Grand Plateau.

Jack Clarke, Edward FitzGerald, Mattias Zurbriggen, Feb 1895.

Mt Tasman/Rarakiroa 3497m

★ 6.26 **Silberhorn Arête** Grade 3+

Climb to the Main Divide via Clarke Saddle, Graham Spur, or Silberhorn. Then ascend the final steep ice arête; a classically beautiful ice climb.

Jack Clarke, Edward FitzGerald, Mattias Zurbriggen, Feb 1895.

Harry Keys, Noel & Bryan Sissons, Ian Jowett, Keith McIvor, Keith Thompson, Aug 1971 (also Silberhorn).

East Face

Two recognised routes exist but the line of ascent may alter owing to changing ice conditions. Both routes are threatened by ice avalanches.

6.27 Grade 4-

Up directly to the col between Silberhorn and Mt Tasman.

Kobi Bosshard, Fritz Schaumburg, Jan 1962.

6.28 Grade 4

Up slopes under the summit of Mt Tasman parallel to Syme Ridge, finishing either directly to the summit or onto the North Shoulder.

Hans Leitner, Eberhard von Terzi, Jan 1960.

(John Pascoe, Duncan Hall and David Hall descended the majority of the face from under the summit in December 1938).

★ 6.29 **Syme Ridge** Grade 3+

Access onto the ridge is either up the slopes under the East Face (the 'Mad Mile'), up a broad gully on the toe of the ridge, or from the north-east side of the ridge (a rock section on the ridge has been crumbling away for some years but seems to be stable now). Then follow a narrow winding arête, which gradually broadens, to gain the North Shoulder of Mt Tasman. From here follow the Main Divide, which narrows before rising to the summit.

Dan Bryant, Rod Syme, 1930.

Bill McLeod, 1983.

Engineer Col 3093m

6.30

From the névé between Syme Ridge and Mt Dixon head straight up to the Col, icecliffs and crevasses permitting. From here it is possible to ascend the North Shoulder of Mt Tasman (see Routes 14.66 & 14.67), or Lendenfeld Peak.

Harold Porter, Marcel Kurz, Jan 1927 (Descended).

Lendenfeld Peak 3194m

6.31   From Engineer Col   Grade 2-

A straightforward climb.

6.32   From Marcel Col   Grade 2

An easy ascent. However, hard ice is common especially in winter. (See Routes 6.34 and 14.60)

6.33   East Face   Grade 3+

From the névé between Syme Ridge and Mt Dixon climb directly to the summit detouring where icecliffs dictate.

(Possibly) Rob Rainsbury, Dick Strong, Keith Thompson, John Visser, Dec 1970.

Don Bogie, Peter Sommerville, Aug 1977.

Marcel Col 2987m

6.34   Grade 3+

From the névé between Syme Ridge and Mt Dixon climb directly to the Col. The last 200m are steep. An easier route is via the East Face of Lendenfeld Peak. (Route 6.33).

Freda Du Faur, Peter Graham, C Milne, Apr 1912.

Mt Haast 3114m

6.35

From Marcel Col head up the Main Divide to a snow summit and then west along a rock ridge to the summit proper. See Routes 6.34 and 14.59.

_6.36_   South Face (Plateau Face)   Grade 4+

At least three variations exist, all commencing from the névé between Syme Ridge and Mt Dixon. Climb 400m of steepish ice and then, depending on conditions and inclination, either left through the ice bulge, directly up through the icecliff, or right via ice gullies through a rock band.

Mike Andrews, Colin Dodge, D Warren, Jan 1972.

6.37   Dixon-Haast Ridge   Grade 3

From the summit of Mt Dixon follow the rotten rock ridge over towers, usually turning difficulties on the east side.

Harry Ayres, Bruce Gillies, Feb 1953.

Fig. 26 West Face of Mt Dixon.

Mt Dixon 3004m

West Face

The névé between Syme Ridge and Mt Dixon provides access to the face. The prominent routes are described, and there are a number of other variations, especially in gullies further left towards Mt Haast.

6.38   Middle Class White Boys Get Away With Rape   Grade 4-
Ill-defined rock rib on left of face (crux 18).
Charlie Hobbs, Murray Ball, Dec 1986.

6.39   Left Buttress   Grade 4
Directly under the summit, ascend from a snow cone to gain a rock rib, which steepens in the middle before some interesting pitches on good rock below the summit.
Austin Brookes, Archie Simpson, Dec 1972.

★**6.40   Central Gully**   Grade 3+
Ascend a snow couloir and ice gully to the right of the buttress and finish up rock to emerge right of the summit.
Merv English, Peter Hillary, Nov 1976.

6.41   Right Buttress   Grade 3+
Ascend easy-angled, sound rock and finish near the top of the south ridge.
Jon Muir, Tom Scissons, Feb 1980.

6.42   White Spring   Grade 4+
South ridge/west face. 300m of mostly 60° ice with some steeper ground. A winter route.
John Fantini, Simon Parsons, Sep 1987.

6.43   No Way Out   Grade 4+
Start on the lower end of the south ridge, up a chimney (crux 18), head left onto the face, up an obvious rock gully, 15/16.
Cam Grierson, Guy White, Jan 1995.

★**6.44   South Ridge**   Grade 3-
Gain the ridge either via a steep 150m slope from the Grand Plateau or via the névé between Syme Ridge and Mt Dixon. Then head up a rock buttress and follow the winding arête to the summit.
F Gillett, T Newth, A Thompson, A P Thompson, M E Roberts, Dec 1936.

6.45   South East Face   Grade 3-
From the Grand Plateau turn the major icecliff on the left and head up. The route usually finishes high on the South Ridge. A somewhat dangerous climb.
B Biggs, L Duff, Dec 1973 (Possibly Jodine, Peter Holt, Jan 1973).
John Dale, Richard Pears, Jul 1976.

★ **6.46** **East Ridge** Grade 2+

Either follow the narrow broken ridge from Glacier Dome or climb up a narrow 80m gully from the Grand Plateau just beside the large icecliff. Then follow up easy slopes to the summit. The best descent route.

Dan Bryant, W A (Snow) Mace, Rod Syme, Jan 1931.

6.47 Grade 2+

From Pioneer Pass, climb up a snow gully onto the Haast-Dixon Ridge.

Graeme Dingle, Jill Tremain, Jan 1967.

Above Plateau Hut some short routes have been established on the rock outcrops on the ridge that continues to Dixon, particularly near Glacier Dome.

Fig. 27 Mt Dixon from Plateau Hut.

Pioneer Pass/Governor Col 2759m, 2834m

6.48 Grade 2

The crossing is accessible from either Haast Hut and the Freshfield Glacier, or Plateau Hut. From the Freshfield Glacier head diagonally up under the Dixon Ridge on the Haast Glacier. If the crevasses are open it is often necessary to climb a steep rock rib under the Dixon Ridge before traversing again over to beneath the Pioneer Pass. If a schrund cuts the pass off, head further right to Governor Col. From Plateau Hut follow the route onto the Dixon Ridge close to the South East Face and drop down onto the Upper Haast Glacier above the rock step. The Fox Glacier side is straightforward (but watch for cloud that can engulf the névé). Although technically a relatively easy crossing, this route is subject to windslab avalanches in winter, wet snow slides in summer, as well as serac collapse. There have been a number of fatalities from avalanches and failed abseil anchors on the rock rib.

Jack Clarke, Peter Graham, Ebenezer Teichelmann, Feb 1904.

Upper Tasman

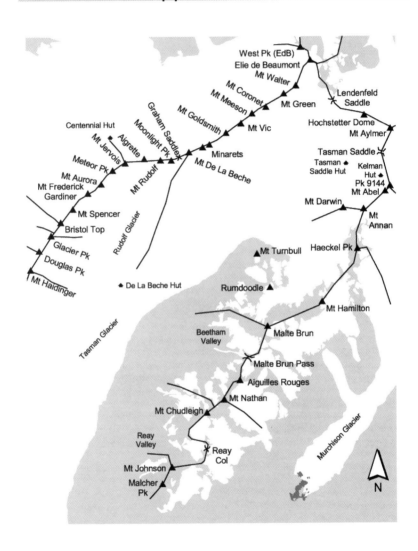

West Pk (EdB)
Elie de Beaumont
Mt Walter
Mt Coronet
Mt Meeson
Mt Green
Lendenfeld Saddle
Mt Goldsmith
Hochstetter Dome
Mt Aylmer
Centennial Hut
Graham Saddle
Moonlight Pk
Mt Jervois
Aigrette
Mt Vic
Minarets
Tasman Saddle
Meteor Pk
Mt Rudolf
Mt De La Beche
Tasman Saddle Hut
Kelman Hut
Mt Aurora
Pk 9144
Mt Frederick Gardiner
Mt Abel
Mt Darwin
Mt Spencer
Mt Annan
Bristol Top
Rudolf Glacier
Glacier Pk
Douglas Pk
Mt Turnbull
Haeckel Pk
Mt Haidinger
De La Beche Hut
Rumdoodle
Mt Hamilton
Tasman Glacier
Beetham Valley
Malte Brun
Malte Brun Pass
Aiguilles Rouges
Mt Nathan
Mt Chudleigh
Murchison Glacier
Reay Valley
Reay Col
Mt Johnson
Malcher Pk

N

Upper Tasman

Tremendous variety awaits the climber venturing up the well-trodden route from Ball Shelter. On the Main Divide there are long mixed and snow climbs of moderate difficulty, while on the Malte Brun Range there is a lot of good rock climbing away from the first onslaught of westerly weather. The Upper Tasman is a must for anyone who wants to savour the Aoraki/Mt Cook region. Whether it is alpine climbing or high level traverses over Graham Saddle, Tasman Saddle, or over the Malte Brun Range, the scope of options is almost limitless. The upper Tasman Glacier is also the main alpine skiing area of the Aoraki/Mt Cook district and is frequented by large parties of ski-plane-transported day skiers between July and October. The neighbouring Murchison Valley is also great ski country and can be gained easily via Tasman Saddle.

Access

On the east side of the Tasman Glacier the Reay Stream provides access to routes on Mts Johnson and Chudleigh. The best travel up the lower Reay is on the southern tussock slopes. Delightful campsites exist near the stream's junction with the Walpole tributary.

The next major stream up the Tasman on the east side is the Beetham. To reach the Beetham Valley traverse off the Tasman Glacier and onto easy rocky moraine slopes on the true left of the Beetham Stream. A few cairns and a vague track will become evident. Follow the track to a rock bluff where a three-wire bridge can be used to cross the Beetham Stream. In normal flow the stream may be crossable (400m upstream). However, there have been two fatalities here and so the bridge is strongly advised. If crossing the bridge in windy conditions use your harness and a sling for security. Beetham Hut was removed after it was damaged by an avalanche in 1995 and so tenting and hiding under rocks are the best options for accomodation. A cave in the scree slope across the river from the old hut site is reportedly worth a look (the old hut site is on a shelf above the basin containing excellent bouldering rocks).

To get to Malte Brun Pass, follow the south side of the Beetham Stream and then climb a long snowslope that lies under Aiguilles Rouges. To reach the western approaches to Malte Brun, head upstream from the old hut site for about 10-20mins before scrambling up scree slopes to a saddle on the lower West Ridge. On the northern side of the saddle descend to a rocky shelf and traverse to the Malte Brun Glacier.

Almost directly opposite the Beetham Stream at the junction of the Rudolf and Tasman Glaciers is **De la Beche Hut.** The hut cannot be seen from the Tasman; to reach it cut straight in from the Tasman white ice and ascend the easiest looking slope in the moraine wall. From the Beetham Valley or De la Beche Hut the upper Tasman Glacier provides good travelling to the Tasman Saddle. **Kelman Hut** is sited on the ridge between Mt Abel and Tasman Saddle. A bit over one kilometre west across the glacier is **Tasman Saddle Hut** situated spectacularly on a rock outcrop in the glacier. Final approaches to the hut should be made around under Mt Aylmer to the north or via the slopes from under Mt Green, Mt Walter, and Hochstetter Dome. There is a more direct route 400m west of the hut up a slope known as the Nose Dive, which runs through the icefalls. In winter beware of slab avalanche conditions on the Nose Dive and on the cornice slopes that run from below Tasman Saddle Hut towards Mt Aylmer. There are ski-plane landing strips opposite Climbers Col and at various points up the main glacier to the névé below Tasman Saddle.

Shelter
De la Beche Hut: An 8 bunk NZAC hut that has blankets, kitchen equipment, solar lights and a radio (~1420m, grid ref: 872-363).

Tasman Saddle Hut: A 14 bunk hut, owned and managed by AMCNP. Contents as above (~2300m, grid ref: 950-403).

Kelman Hut: A 30 bunk hut owned and managed by AMCNP. Contents as above (~2460m, cell coverage (025), grid ref: 966-398).

Times
From Ball Shelter to the Beetham Valley 5-7 hours.
From Ball Shelter to the De la Beche Hut ~6 hours.
From Ball Shelter to Tasman Saddle Hut or Kelman Hut ~10 hours.

Ski Touring Routes
- Minarets from De la Beche Hut, via Ranfurly Glacier. Very steep traverses on lee slopes. Upper section very crevassed (C).
- Mt Hamilton via Darwin Glacier. Steep skiing (C).
- Darwin and Bonney Glacier. Very scenic, great views of Main Divide peaks, away from the traffic. Subject to crevasses (B).
- Turnbull Glacier. Steep (C).
- Hochstetter Dome, via 'Aylmer Col' (A).
- Hochstetter Dome, via glacier and Lendenfeld Saddle (B).
- Elie de Beaumont. Subject to large crevasses on the Anna Glacier (B/C).
- Glacier, en route to Tasman Saddle Hut, under Green and Walter (A).
- Upper Névé, toward Kelman Hut (A).

Haidinger 3070m

South Ridge
See Route 14.39.

7.0 East Face Route   Grade 3
Climb the ridge immediately north of the Haast Glacier, overcoming a final large bump to reach the Upper Haast Glacier. From here the route heads up the snowface onto the South Ridge. Other more difficult routes may exist to the right on the upper face.
Dick Strong, Keith Thompson, Dec 1970.

7.1   East Spur   Grade 3+

This consists of a 400m buttress of relatively loose rock, dropping from the North Peak. The spur has been gained by two routes.

i) Via a rock and scree rib separating the two arms of the Kaufmann Glacier.

D C Ball, Bob Cunninghame, Jan 1960.

ii) Up scree and rock south of the Forrest-Ross Glacier to a small snow basin.

Tom Fyfe, Malcolm Ross, Feb 1897.

7.2   East Ridge/North East Face   Grade 3

These short 350m routes are gained by climbing scree slopes and a rotten ridge onto Emas Dome, then dropping to Forrest-Ross Glacier névé. Cross the névé to gain either the ridge or the face that meets the Main Divide, some distance north of the North Peak.

Jack Clarke, J R Simpson, Mar 1913.

Colin Monteath/Hedgehog House

Fig. 28 Mt Haidinger and Douglas Peak from the east.

Douglas Peak 3077m

7.3   Grade 3

This peak is usually climbed from the Tasman Glacier via Glacier Peak. Access from the Forrest-Ross Névé onto the south (Ayres) ridge is quite feasible. Another route exists from the névé, which ascends up under the summit before cutting right to the col with Glacier Peak.

L J Dumbleton, Neville Johnson, J D Willis, Dec 1935.

Glacier Peak 3002m

7.4   Grade 3

The usual route is over Emas Dome (see Route 7.2) and up the elegant East Ridge arête to the summit. It is also possible to climb the iceface north of the ridge from a small névé below and north of Emas Dome.

Bill Beaven, F Gibbs, Feb 1950 (via the East Ridge).

Harold Porter, Vic Williams, Dec 1930 (via the iceface).

7.5   South East Face   Grade 3

From Emas Dome descend to the Forrest-Ross Névé and then find a route through the schrunds. Ascend the face, gaining the East Ridge near the summit.

David Jewell, Jan 2001.

Bristol Top 2891m

7.6

The only existing routes follow the Main Divide. The Divide is relatively easy but on the Glacier Peak side there are towers (refer to Routes 14.19 & 14.20).

Conway Peak 2899m

7.7   Grade 3

Follow the Main Divide from either Bristol Top or Frenchay Col. Conway itself is just off the Divide to the west. See Routes 13.17 and 14.18.

Frank Milne, Harold Porter, Mar 1925.

Mt Spencer 2788m

7.8   Grade 3

A route lies up the icefalls well north of the Grant Duff Glacier and then up a rib of steep shattered rock and snow directly to the summit. The rock on the Main Divide is notoriously loose in this area. Also see the Franz Josef Glacier section.

Tim Barfoot, John Luxton, Richard Tornquist, Jan 1962.

Mt Frederick Gardiner 2680m

7.9   Rudolf Rib   Grade 3+

Climb a loose rock rib from the Rudolf Glacier (avoiding a small icecliff near the top) to reach a snow basin. Staying clear of an icecliff near the peak, head right up to the Main Divide between Mts Frederick Gardiner and Aurora. The final ridge to the summit is steep and loose.

Mike Andrews, Bill King, Jan 1981.

Mt Aurora 2663m

7.10   Grade 3+

As for the climb of Mt Frederick Gardiner via Route 7.9 but once on the Main Divide head north up Aurora instead. Also see the Franz Josef Glacier section.

Mike Andrews, Bill King, Jan 1981.

Mt Meteor 2624m, *Mt Jervois* 2630m, *Mt Aigrette* 2665m and *Mt Rudolf* 2743m

All appear to be unclimbed directly from the Tasman Glacier.

Moonlight Peak 2670m

An easy ascent from Graham Saddle.

Fig. 29 *Mt De la Beche and the Minarets. Circle denotes De la Beche Hut.*

Graham Saddle 2635m

7.11   Grade 1+

From De la Beche Hut descend the moraine wall and head up the Rudolf Glacier for three kilometres until a major icefall is reached. Climb the snowslope to the right of the icefall to gain a rock rib (beware rockfall). Climb easily up the rock rib heading out left before the top and traverse round snowslopes just above the icefall. Then head up a long easy-angled snowfield to the Saddle. An alternative but more difficult route lies up the De la Beche ridge behind the hut, avoiding the lower Rudolf Glacier and rock rib. On the West Coast side, head down the Franz Josef Névé and turn south-west under the North West Ridge of Mt Rudolf, to head for Centennial Hut, situated on a rock buttress below Mt Jervois. Alternatively, if Almer

Hut is the destination, continue down the Franz, passing the Mackay Rocks on the right. Later in the season crevasses may prove troublesome. Follow snowslopes to Almer Hut. Also see the Franz Josef Glacier section.

First gained by George Graham and Tom Fyfe in 1894 en route to De la Beche. A year later Mattias Zurbriggen, Arthur Harper and Edward FitzGerald crossed it in March. Named by Fyfe after Graham.

De la Beche Hut to Centennial Hut allow 8 hours
De la Beche Hut to Almer Hut 8-10 hours

Mt De la Beche 2950m

From the upper Rudolf Glacier and Graham Saddle, the West Ridge, West Rib (Route 7.12) and South Ridge (Route 7.13) of Mt De la Beche all provide short pleasant climbs. The West Rib contains some slightly more technical climbing than the other two routes.

7.14   De la Beche Ridge   Grade 2

From De la Beche Hut, head up the ridge for 400m and then traverse on the eastern snowslopes and basins up to the plateau between De la Beche and the Minarets. Then up either the South Ridge or North East Rib.

Tom Fyfe, George Graham, Feb 1894.

★ *The Minarets* 3031m (west), 3040m (east)   Grade 2

A very short climb from the plateau between Mt De la Beche and the Minarets. The plateau is reached by Routes: 7.11, 7.13 or 13.3.

Tom Fyfe, Malcolm Ross, Feb 1897.
R & N Rodda, Aug 1962.

7.15   The Ranfurly Glacier   Grade 2+

From the Tasman Glacier there are a number of variations ascending the glacier, the most usual being a prominent spur leading up under Mt De la Beche.

Freda Du Faur, Laurence Earle, Peter Graham, B Spencer, Jan 1910.

7.16   North Ridge   Grade 3+

Although not a difficult climb access is a problem as it is necessary to approach the ridge over Mts Coronet, Meeson, Vic and Goldsmith. The ridge crest can be followed except for one or two places where a traverse on the west is necessary.

Harry Ayres, Mick Bowie, F F Simmons, Jan 1938.

Mt Goldsmith 2909m

Unclimbed directly from the Tasman Glacier. The ridge connecting Mt Vic and the Minarets is not very difficult, and the western slopes usually provide alternatives to any problems encountered. See Route 12.18.

Mt Vic 2807m   Grade 3-

Unclimbed directly from the Tasman Glacier. Ascend via Route 7.17 and Mt Meeson.

Frank Alack, Katie Gardiner, Vic Williams, Feb 1934.

Fig. 30 Upper Tasman Glacier and Darwin Glacier.

Mt Meeson 2716m
Grade 2+

Using the access routes onto Mt Coronet, either cross the basin underneath Mt Coronet up onto the Main Divide or use the Main Divide from Mt Coronet itself and ascend to Mt Meeson.

Hugh Chambers, Conrad Kain, Prof. Robinson, J Robertson, Hugh Wright, Feb 1915.

Mt Coronet 2651m

7.17
Grade 4+

From the Tasman Glacier, ascend the East Ridge up a snow and rock ridge until a broad plateau. From here ascend either to the summit direct or gain the ridge south of the summit. This is a good descent route.

Peter Graham, Claude Macdonald, Jim Murphy, Feb 1909.

7.18
Grade 2+

Via the Divide Ridge from Climbers Col, ascend a mixed snow and ice ridge with rock of varying quality. Traverse any difficulties on the west.

Graham McCallum, H P Barcham, P C Gardiner, J B Waterhouse, Dec 1954.

Mt Green 2837m

7.19   South Ridge
Grade 3+

From Climbers Col (access may be cut off late in the season) climb the first rock step direct then along a horizontal arête and up the second step to where the ridge flattens. Then up a blocky ridge to summit.

D Dawe, Hamish MacInnes, Dick Irwin, Feb 1956.

7.20   South East Face
Grade 3+

Take the gully in the centre of the face, depending on the condition of the upper face, join either the South Ridge or South East Buttress.

Kevin Carroll, John Andrews, Jan 1971.

7.21   South East Buttress
Grade 3+

From the basin below Climbers Col head right and gain the prominent rib. Move up steep loose rock until some grey slabs (the Cod Piece) are met halfway up. Then continue up steep loose ground onto the upper part of the South Ridge.

Ian Cave, Mike Gill, John Nichols, Feb 1960.

East Face

A number of variations exist, including:

7.22   Left Hand Trinity
Grade 5-

Take the obvious deep cut couloir on the left hand side of the face. Seven pitches, with occasional 80° sections, top out on the south ridge 3-4 pitches from the summit.

Mike Smith, Tony Dignan, Oct 1986.

7.23   East Face NE Ridge (Main Divide)   Grade 2

Climb up the broad plateau between Mts Green and Walter via the prominent SE ridge. Alternative routes onto the plateau exist, but the ridge is the best. Then either head up snowslopes on the East Face or the mixed snow/rock of the North East Ridge.

Alex Graham, Peter Graham, Ebenezer Teichelmann, F W Vollmann, Feb 1909 (NE Ridge).

Divers Col 2681m

7.24   Grade 2

A good route to the upper Spencer Glacier, giving access to the climbs from that area. Use Route 7.23 to reach the Col, then descend to the Spencer Glacier.

Fig. 31 East Face of Mt Walter.

Mt Walter 2905m

7.25 South Ridge Grade 2-
From plateau between Mts Green and Walter, ascend the easy snow ridge.
Alex Graham, Peter Graham, Ebenezer Teichelmann, F W Vollmann, Feb 1909.

East Face

7.26 Geriatric Grade 5
A thirteen pitch route starting just right and below where the major icecliffs begin to develop. The route follows a right ascending traverse after four pitches and then heads straight up steep ice onto the ridge 200m from the summit of Mt Walter.
Russell Braddock, Paul Brailsford, Aug 1983.

★ 7.27 Ice Creme Grade 5
Ascend an obvious gully for eight pitches, which broadens out to join the snowfields left of the summit.
Paul Bayne, Shaun Norman, June 1983.

7.28 Curtains Grade 5
Climb a steep ice curtain, which leads into a broad gully. The gully leads left and finishes directly at the summit.
James Jenkins, S Parkes, Aug 1981.

7.29 Original Grade 5
Ascend a steep couloir on the right side of the face for three pitches. Then traverse left into the same gully ascended by Route 7.28.
Nick Cradock, Barry Jury, Nic Kagan, Jun 1977.

7.30 North East Ridge Grade 2
From the col between Mts Walter and Elie de Beaumont, head up over the rock step to the summit.
C J Read, G S J Read, K Suter, Feb 1934.

Mt Elie de Beaumont 3109m (East Peak), 3054m (West Peak)

★ 7.31 Anna Glacier Grade 2+
Head up the glacier (which later in the season can be cut off by crevasses) usually keeping close under Mt Walter. Then ascend slopes onto the col between Mts Walter and Elie de Beaumont. Follow an easy snow ridge up to the summit (but watch out for hard ice just above the col). This is the usual descent route. Routes can be pushed directly up the Anna Glacier to the summit in good snow conditions. If the Anna Glacier is badly crevassed and the col between Mts Walter and Elie de Beaumont is cut off, traverse from Divers Col over Mt Walter to Elie de Beaumont.
Peter Graham, Henrick Sillem, Feb 1906.

Alex Palman

Mt Sefton makes a stunning backdrop for bouldering as Nick Douglas discovers Sefton Bivvy Rock, Hooker Valley.

Hogbacks hover over Aoraki/Mount Cook village and Lake Pukaki, as seen from the summit of The Footstool.

Anjali Pande ploughs through November snow en route to the top of Aoraki/Mt Cook.
Photo taken on the ice cap above the summit rocks, Grand Plateau.

Warren Jacobs

The Hidden (L) and Balfour Faces of Mt Tasman.

Peter Dickson

Alex Palman leads up Mt Drake's West Wall, Balfour Glacier.

Alex Palman

The Godley Valley cloaked in winter snow.

Sam Bosshard

The late Andy MacFarlane enjoys the ice on the first ascent of the "Cave Route", Brunner Col, Mueller Glacier Area.

Brian Alder

Bill McLeod gets started on the first ascent of "Bill & Ted's Excellent Adventure",
South Face of La Perouse. Strauchon Glacier Area.

The top of the amazing Strauchon Face of Dilemma as seen from Unicorn. Strauchon Glacier Area.

Two climbers look for a way to the upper Empress Shelf, on Aoraki/Mt Cook. Mt Sefton in the distance. Hooker Valley.

Looking down the URGA Memorial Route from above the roof (crux). Mt Drake, Balfour Glacier.

Fig. 32 Mt Elie de Beaumont and the Anna Glacier.

7.32   **South East Ridge**   Grade 3-
From Lendenfeld Saddle climb the sharp and undulating ridge onto the
upper Anna Plateau (there may be an unpleasant icecliff here) and easily
onto the summit.
Mavis Davidson, Rod Hewitt, Priestly Thompson, Jan 1954.

7.33   **West Peak**   Grade 3+
A highly recommended and exhilarating addition to climbing the main
summit of Mt Elie de Beaumont. From the main summit, descend and
head west along a sharp, very exposed, undulating arête, traversing around a
number of gendarmes, usually on the south side, before reaching the West
Peak.
Mick Bowie, Colin Wyatt, Jul 1936.

145

Lendenfeld Saddle 2419m

7.34

The saddle was first reached by Dr von Lendenfeld's party in 1884 and first crossed by Tom Fyfe and Malcolm Ross in 1897.

Hochstetter Dome 2827m

7.35   Grade 1

The south-east and north-west ridges (Route 7.36) are easily climbed. The shoulder on the south-east ridge above Lendenfeld Saddle is a regular ski run.

Dr and Anna von Lendenfeld, H Dew, Mar 1884.

7.36   Grade 2

The small buttress on the south face of Hochstetter Dome visible from Tasman Saddle Hut has also been climbed.

First ascent party unknown

(The 1500m North Face (Whataroa) of Hochstetter Dome is one of New Zealand's largest unclimbed faces.)

Fig. 33 Whymper Spur (Route 12.0) and the Maximilian Ridge on Mt Elie de Beaumont.

Mt Aylmer 2699m

7.37   Grade 1

Easily climbed from either 'Aylmer Col' (between Aylmer and Hochstetter Dome) or Tasman Saddle. The short, steep south face has been skied.

Barbara, Jim & George Dennistoun, Ada Julius, Jack Clarke, Dec 1910.

Tasman Saddle 2435m

7.38   Grade 1+

A regular crossing route from the Tasman to the Murchison Valley. From the Tasman Valley, use the obvious saddle nearest Mt Aylmer and descend onto the Murchison Glacier down the "Murchison Headwall". Beware of avalanche danger here in winter.

Peter Graham, Jack Clarke, George Rose, Apr 1906.

Peak 9144 2669m

Being close to Kelman and Tasman Saddle huts, this peak has a number of short popular routes on it:

7.39   Grade 2-

From Tasman Saddle.

7.40   Grade 2-

Via the couloir on the West Face or the rock buttresses on either side.

Fig. 34 Mts Annan and Darwin from the Upper Tasman Glacier.

147

7.41   Grade 2

Up the southern ridge.

Jack Clarke, Laurence Earle, Jan 1910.

Mt Abel 2688m

An easy ascent from either the col next to Peak 9144 or the Mt Annan side.

Jack Clarke, Laurence Earle, Feb 1910.

Mt Annan 2934m

From the Tasman Glacier:

7.42   North East Ridge   Grade 2

Ascend easy rock. This is a good descent route.

Hugh Chambers, Jack Clarke, Feb 1912.

7.43   Couloir Route   Grade 2+

Ascend the gully beside the North East Ridge.

J B Waterhouse, Feb 1966.

Paul Caffyn, R & M Smith, Aug 1977.

7.44   Annan Buttress   Grade 3+

Ascend three prominent rocksteps on good rock, interspersed with short snow sections between the rock steps.

B Dawkins, Bob McKegg, B Poppelwell, W Stephenson, Dec 1968.

7.45   Annan-Darwin Traverse   Grade 3+

A long rock ridge involving five (but you might find more) major rock steps of dubious quality rock.

D Smyth, J B Waterhouse, Feb 1966.

From the Darwin Glacier

7.46   South East Ridge   Grade 2

This is reached from the glacier via the saddle at the head of the Darwin Glacier, or over Haeckel Peak, and provides little difficulty.

R M Crockett, W G McClymont, F F Simmons, Dec 1934 (via Haeckel Peak).

Mt Darwin 2952m

From the Tasman Glacier, Annan-Darwin Ridge (see Route 7.45).

Darwin Buttresses

7.47   Horn/McLean Rib   Grade 4

Ascend the prominent rib onto the Annan-Darwin Ridge. The lower half of the rib is good rock (crux 12), but the upper section contains some evil looking, loose black gullies.

R Horn, D McLean, Dec 1969.

7.48   **Couloir Route**   Grade 3+

Climb the obvious couloir between the Horn/McLean Rib and the Original route.

Andrew Lock, Luke Trehey, Nov 1990

7.49   **Original Route**   Grade 4-

Commence up firm rock from the right toe of the buttress and ascend to the first snowfield. Then traverse right and up to a second snowfield before taking the left of two prominent buttresses (crux 12). Above here the climbing becomes easy scrambling on broken rock.

Geoff Wayatt, A Cross, M Douglas, T Terry, R Smith, Jan 1967.

Etienne Kummer, Joos Flutsch, Bruno Sprecher, Aug 1974.

7.50   **Lost Bolt Buttress**   Grade 4

Ascend the original route but take the right of the two prominent buttresses. So named because somewhere here a Japanese party placed a bolt ladder that no one has found again (crux 14).

R Aitken, S Firth, Dec 1973.

7.51   **North West Arête**   Grade 2

Ascend the prominent rock spur leading up onto the West Ridge. Between here and the buttresses are a number of descent routes, but be careful as certain couloirs end in bluffs.

Sydney King, Darby Thomson, Feb 1914.

7.52   **West Ridge**   Grade 2

A long but easy climb gained from the névé feeding the Tasman Glacier above Darwin Corner.

Jack Clarke, Tom Fyfe, Franz Von Kronecker, Mar 1894.

7.53   **South Face**   Grade 3

Head up to the left of a small icefall on the left of the face, then wind through cliffs onto snowslopes on the far left of the face. Finish onto the West Ridge via a wide couloir.

R Arbon, J B Waterhouse, Jan 1979.

7.54   **Darwin Route**   Grade 2+

Ascend towards the saddle at the head of the Darwin Glacier and then cut off up snowslopes towards the summit.

B Carter, J Cruse, R H Peate, J M Rowe, Dec 1955.

Haeckel Peak 2965m

7.55   **North Ridge**   Grade 2

From the saddle at the head of the Darwin Glacier follow the rubbly but straightforward ridge.

R M. Crockett, W G McClymont, F F Simmons, Dec 1934 (Descended).

Lloyd Homer/IGNS

Fig. 35 Mt Annan – Malte Brun. Left circle denotes Tasman Saddle Hut.

7.56   **West Face**   Grade 2+
Ascend the rock spur separating a feeder glacier from the main Darwin
Glacier, cross the feeder where it flattens slightly, and ascend to a square
snow patch on the west face, then onto the top of the south-west ridge.
Otto Frind, Conrad Kain, Mar 1914 (Descended).
Mick Bowie, C Irving, Jan 1933.

7.57   **South West Ridge**   Grade 2
Reach the col between Hamilton and Haeckel, either from the Bonney
Glacier and across the North West Ridge of Hamilton, or else ascend the
lower North West Ridge; or ascend the feeder glacier of the Darwin Glacier.
The rock on the ridge is loose.
Jack Clarke, Bernard Head, Jim Murphy, Jan 1912.

Mt Hamilton 3025m

7.58   Grade 2
Ascend the Bonney Glacier and head up snowslopes to a prominent col on
the North West Ridge. Then either ascend the ridge, the snow gully on the
left, or else cross to the North Ridge, which is a narrow affair that gradually
broadens. These routes join the summit ridge 200m north of the summit.
Jack Clarke, Laurence Earle, Alex Graham, Dec 1909.
Gordon Hasell, Alan Brown, Roland & N Rodda, Aug 1961.

7.59   **West Gut**   Grade 3+
From above the first icefall in the Bonney Glacier ascend the obvious gut in
the west flank for 10 rope lengths coming out on a snow slope near the top
of the North West Ridge.
Kevin Boekholt, Chris Morris, Dec 1985.

7.60   **South Ridge**   Grade 3
Usually descended in conjunction with a climb of the North East Ridge of
Mt Malte Brun and hence is a long climb. The ridge is relatively easy but
becomes rotten near the Hamilton-Malte Brun col. A route onto the col
ascends a narrow couloir from the Bonney Glacier.
Harry Ayres, Bruce Gillies, Feb 1951 (Descended).
Alex Parton, Jim Tobin, Jan 1976.

Mt Turnbull 2265m

7.61
Easily climbed from beside the Turnbull Glacier. Many ascents have been
made from all directions.
(Possibly) Tom Fyfe, Mar 1894.
(or J W Brown, Malcolm Ross, Miss J E Turnbull, Feb 1910.)

Mt Rumdoodle 2706m

7.62   Grade 2

The easiest way to climb this peak is from the Bonney Glacier but ascents have been made from all directions.

7.63   Grade 3-

A rock route on the west face.
Stella Sweney, Stuart Eadie, Jan 1978.

An enjoyable ice gully route exists on the south-west aspect, gained from the top of the Malte Brun Glacier (grade 3).
First ascent unknown.

Mt Malte Brun 3199m

The routes on the western side of Mt Malte Brun provide good rock climbing and can be gained either via the Turnbull Glacier, which joins the upper Bonney Glacier, or up the Malte Brun Glacier.

7.64   North East Ridge   Grade 3+

Descend from Mt Hamilton to a narrow rubbly notch and climb up a steep slab for 150m, then on up the ridge, which rises in a series of short steps of good rock.
Harry Ayres, Bruce Gillies, Feb 1951.

7.65   North Face   Grade 3+

From the lower Bonney Glacier ascend the ribs and slabs of excellent rock between the North East and North Ridges. There is plenty of room for variations.
A C Rattray, J C Stamers-Smith, Dec 1958.

7.66   North Ridge   Grade 3

This route usually commences from the Bonney Glacier just above the small icefall but there is wide scope for variations especially from below the icefall. The rock on the ridge is good and the climbing pleasantly interesting but nowhere difficult. An enjoyable climb for a sunny day.
Peter Graham, Henrik Sillem, Mar 1906.

★ 7.67   North West Face   Grade 3+

Scene of Tom Fyfe's remarkable 1894 solo climb. Fyfe's route ascends to the left of a shallow couloir in the centre of the face. Other routes ascend to the right of the couloir while some variations keep closer to the North Ridge. Although the climbing is not very difficult, it is still quite sustained.
Tom Fyfe, Mar 1894.
Etienne Kummer, Bruno Sprecher, Joos Flutsch, Jul 1974.

7.68   Fyfe's Couloir   Grade 3

From the névé of the Bonney Glacier, ascend the snow and ice couloir to within l00m of the summit. This can make a quick descent route, but it is a natural funnel for rock fall and avalanches.
F McMahon, A Simpson, R Yates, Dec 1964.

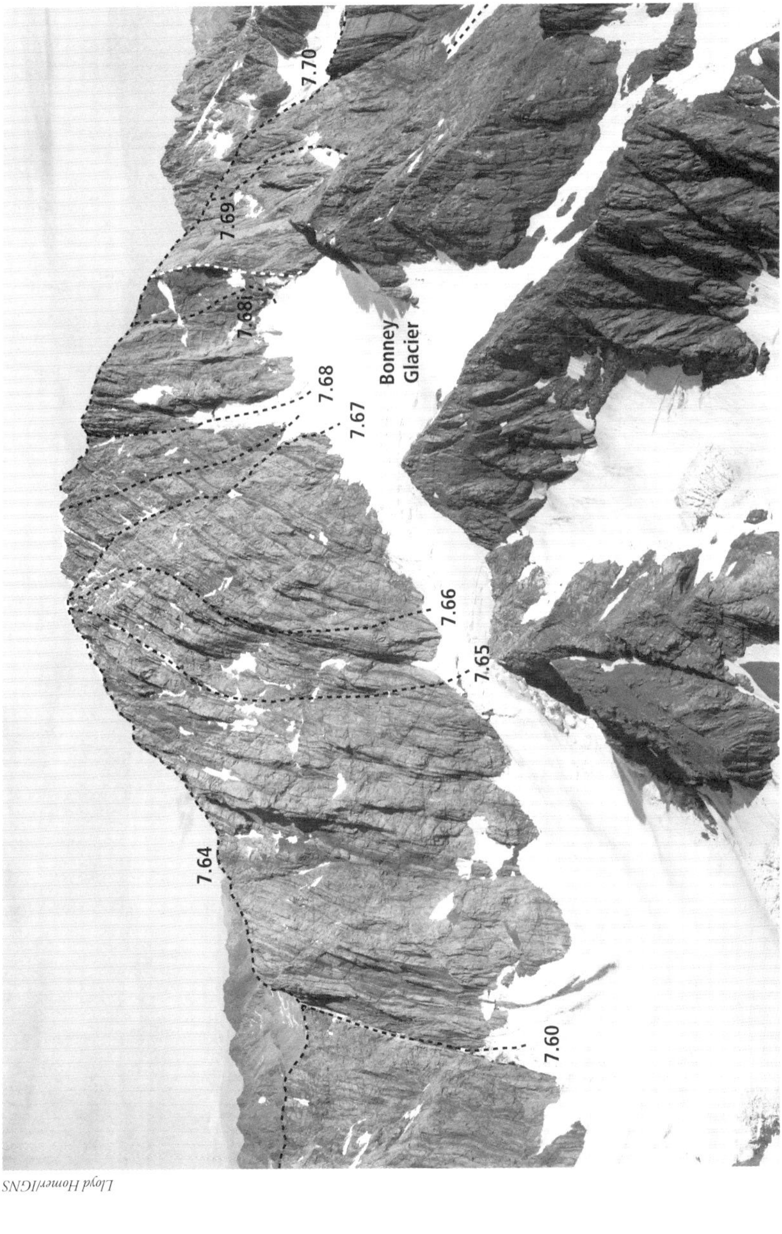

Fig. 36 North-western side of Malte Brun.

Lloyd Homer/IGNS

153

7.68i Bonney Headwall — Grade 4

From the Bonney Glacier climb compact rock that steepens progressively to a crux before a snowcovered ledge Access the ledge toward either the left or the right. Continue up rock directly to the Cheval or follow the ledge which ramps to the right, arriving on the West Ridge about 60m west of the Cheval. Not recommended as a descent.

Brendan Gaynor, Ewan Reid, John Zapp, John Menin, Dec 1971.

★ 7.69 West Ridge — Grade 3

This route, or rather series of routes, starts from the head of the Malte Brun Glacier and joins the West Ridge proper well before the "Cheval", a famous and spectacular narrow section of ridge. The easiest route begins by cutting left from the head of the Malte Brun Glacier up one of a series of couloirs onto a small snowfield and then up a short rock face onto the ridge. An enjoyable alternative, however, is to climb the beautiful rock rib from the col which separates the Malte Brun and Bonney Glaciers. The climbing on these routes is exposed, but not too difficult. On reaching the true West Ridge negotiate the Cheval and then up 200m to the summit. This route is used regularly for descents but be sure to remember where to turn off the West Ridge in order to reach the head of the Malte Brun Glacier.

Hugh Chambers, Jack Clarke, Feb 1912.

7.70 Full West Ridge — Grade 3+

From the Beetham Valley the best route is probably to cut across the toe of West Ridge and ascend above the old Malte Brun Hut site, regaining the ridge at a col at 2300m. Follow the ridge on generally good rock. The climb steepens and provides some difficulty before easing off where Route 7.69 is joined. Cross the Cheval and continue up 200m to the summit.

Laurence Earle, Freda Du Faur, Peter Graham, Jan 1910.

At least one of the pillars on the north side of the lower ridge has been climbed, and provides excellent climbing (crux 16).

Max Dorflinger, Otto Von Allmen, Dec 1972.

South Face

7.71 Moore Gully — Grade 4

Ascend the prominent gully on the left side of the face to reach the West Ridge below the Cheval.

Peter Moore, Dec 1973.

7.72 Central Rib — Grade 4

From halfway up the Beetham Glacier ascend broken spurs and ridges on the left side of the prominent central rib.

Ian Cave, Mike Gill, John Nichols, Feb 1960.

7.73 The Christmas Turkey — Grade 4

Start up a prominent couloir on the face 200m right of the original route and ascend until the couloir peters out. Traverse left around the buttress and ascend gullies to the West Ridge.

Roddie MacKenzie, Craig Nottle, Graham Sanders, Dec 1981.

7.74   Rock and Roll   Grade 4

Ascend the third prominent snow cone left of the South Ridge and on up mixed snow and rock, with two short steep steps. After 200m, easier ground leads up rightwards towards the summit. If clear of snow and ice, the rock is not very sound.

Dave Fearnley, Fiona MacKenzie, Craig Nottle, Dec 1983.

7.75   Rock n Roll Pt 2   Grade 4

Starts left of the direct route. When good ice covers the "forgettable rock" then this route could be worth a look, otherwise probably not.

Craig Nottle, Dave Fearnley, Fiona MacKenzie, Jan 1984.

(A route between 7.75 and 7.76 was soloed by Greg Aimer in late 1984, which may have involved 7.76)

★ 7.76   Rightside Direct   Grade 4+

Ascend the second prominent snow cone left of the South Ridge and, ignoring a ramp leading right to the Zig Zag route, ascend five steep ice pitches to reach easier-angled snow slopes leading to the summit.

Duncan Ritchie, Judith Terpestra, Jan 1983.

Hugh Logan, Lindsay Main, Jun 1983.

Fig. 37 South Face of Malte Brun.

★ 7.77   Zig Zag   Grade 4-
Ascend the second prominent snow cone from the South Ridge and follow
a ramp out right and into an amphitheatre. Move up left onto the crest of a
buttress and then follow snowfields to the summit.
Nigel Perry, Richard Mortenson, Jan 1981.
Dave Crow, Jun 1991.

7.78   South Ridge   Grade 3
From Malte Brun Pass head up the ridge, skirting the first few pinnacles on
the west side, and then up the crest of the ridge, which rises in two long
steps. The rock is highly variable and in parts the ridge is quite exposed.
Despite this most of the route is on snow and ice.
Peter Graham, Claude Macdonald, Jim Murphy, Feb 1909.
Hugh Logan, Lindsay Main, Jun 1983 (Descended).

Malte Brun Pass 2483m

7.79   Grade 2-
From the Beetham Valley follow the stream up past the tributary from the
main Beetham Glacier then turn up the next major gully descending from
the Pass on the south side of a small ridge sticking out from the pass.
Snowslopes or scree lead up under Aiguilles Rouges onto the extensive plateau
of the pass. The descent onto the Cascade Glacier is straightforward. To
reach the Murchison Glacier either ascend from the lower Cascade Glacier
up 250m of gullies onto the lower East Ridge of Aiguilles Rouges or else
sidle around down the side of the snout of the Cascade Glacier. (See also the
Murchison Glacier section).
Otto Frind, Conrad Kain, 1914.

Aiguilles Rouges 2950m

Most of the routes described can be reached via the Malte Brun Pass but
Routes 7.86 and 7.87 are approached from the upper Beetham Valley.

7.80   North East Ridge   Grade 2
Ascend from the pass onto this ridge climbing good rock over the East Peak
and on to the high peak. The ridge starts in the Cascade Glacier but is
gained at half height from Malte Brun Pass.
Laurence Earle, Peter Graham, Mar 1909 (Descended).

7.81   North East Flank   Grade 2
There are two narrowish couloirs, the left one leading up to near the East
Peak, and the right one providing access to broad snowslopes leading to the
main summit. A good descent route.
Freda Du Faur, Peter Graham, Mar 1913.

★ 7.82   North Ridge   Grade 2
From the Pass ascend the ridge to the right of Route 7.81. Excellent rock.
Farther right are steeper variations with good climbing.
Laurence Earle, Peter Graham, Mar 1909.
Duncan Ritchie, Adrian Daly, Jun 1977.

7.83 **North West Ridge** Grade 3+

It is possible to start from the upper Beetham Stream climbing the lower buttress (crux 16) up to shingle ledges, and then up the upper ridge, which has slightly easier climbing.

Greg Mortimer, S Parkes, Apr 1980.

7.83i Grade 3-

Starting right of Route 7.83, from the upper Beetham Stream, climb up a ridge crossing the occasional shingle covered ledge. Continue up the snow slope to link with the small ridge between Routes 7.83 and 7.85. Joins the North East Ridge below the summit.

(Possibly) Ross Cullen, Chris Knol, Jan 1982.

7.84 **Central Gully** Grade 3-

Climb the gully between the two rock buttresses on the west face. Left of 7.85. Climbed with snow/ice in the gully.

(Possibly) Ako Groot, Hawke Groot, Jan 1991.

7.85 **West Ridge** Grade 3+

From Malte Brun Pass traverse across scree ledges to gain the ridge at half height. Ascend good rock with some surprisingly difficult sections.

Ian Cave, Mike Gill, John Nichols, Feb 1960.

7.86 **Tiddley Pom** Grade 3-

Ascend the prominent couloir on the south-west face.

Jo Kippax, Sean Waters, Aug 1992.

7.87 **South Ridge** Grade 2+

Gained by a large winding couloir (prone to rockfall), which ends in a short rotten rock face. The ridge is rather rotten at first and then improves.

J Boyd, M McPhail, John Nankervis, Jan 1973.

Beetham Crag, the Lower Cliff and the Langdale Buttress

The *Beetham Crag* is about 200m above the Beetham Hut site and south a little, overlooking the Tasman Glacier. The crag was developed in the early eighties. Nick Banks established a few routes in the summer of 1983 and later that season participants on a guides course added more routes. Apparently there are about a dozen routes but records are sketchy, despite this the rock is superb and the setting is without compare. To get to the *Lower Cliff*, sidle around from the Beetham Crag, crossing the small stream above the gorge. Continue sidling around and down to the crag. There are also some excellent short-medium length rock routes on the *Langdale Buttress*, situated 2hrs from the Beetham Valley, at the foot of the Mt Chudleigh's North West Ridge (map 260-H36; grid ref: 898-329).

Beetham Crag

Celibate Slanter (21)

Up the crack to roof (hard move through roof). Follow the line up and right. John Entwisle.

7.90

7.91

7.89

7.87

7.86

7.82

7.81

James Wright

Beetham Valley

7.83i

7.83i

7.84

7.83i

7.85

7.83

To White-Brun Pass

7.80

7.82

Lloyd Homer/IGNS

Flower Presser (20)
The crack right of Celibate S'. John Entwisle.

Aoraki Without Oxygen (19)
The first crack to the right of an obvious large roof. Marty Beare.

Mechanical Seagull (19)
Up the right-leaning crack, move a little to the left and over the small overlap. Peter Taw.

Banksruptcy (18)
The obvious corner. Exit left via twin cracks to the arête. Nick Banks.

Banksquet (14)
Around from the previous climbs is this obvious corner. Nick Banks.

Screaming Feat (18)
Nick Banks and Geoff Ward.

Lower Cliff

Blanks (13)
A short crack. Nick Banks.

Wislestop (17)
A wall eliminate. No pro. John Entwisle.

Telebanks (15)
Nick Banks.

Ewbanks (14)
Nick Banks

Langdale Buttress
See Fig. 40 for route locations.

A Mark Time (16)
Mark Whetu

B Beggar For Punishment (16)
Dave Begg

C Red Right Hand
Kevin Boekholt, Marty Beare, 1983

D The Big Red Engine
Just to the right of the lowest part of the Langdale Buttress is an obvious arête (crux 17, 7 pitches). Marty Beare, Rob Collister, 1988.

Mt Nathan 2868m

7.88   North East Ridge   Grade 2+
Rather loose, exposed climbing.
Mike Andrews, Donald Cargo, Feb 1973 (Descended).

7.89   Beetham Buttress   Grade 3
Ascend the buttress right of the central gully on Barkley Face on mediocre quality rock.
Harry Clark, Craig Nottle, Dec 1982.

7.90 **South West Ridge** Grade 2+

Gained either by the Barkley Glacier and a couloir to the low point in the ridge between Mts Nathan and Chudleigh, or via the North West Ridge of Mt Chudleigh to the head of the Barkley Glacier, and then up the couloir. From here follow the ridge up loose rock to the summit. Probably the easiest descent route.

Samuel Turner, Feb 1918.

Mt Chudleigh 2966m

High Peak

7.91 **North East Ridge** Grade 2+

From the Barkley Glacier, ascend a couloir to the low point in the ridge and climb the ridge, which is at first pinnacled and then rises steadily. The rock is loose.

Mike Andrews, Donald Cargo, Feb 1973 (Descended).

7.92 **North Face** Grade 3

From the left side of the top of the Barkley Glacier head up a small ice ramp to the main North Face. Ascend this to join the top of the NW ridge.

S Hancock, T Murray, Jan 1988.

★ **7.93** **North West Ridge** Grade 2+

Reached from the Barkley, Langdale, or Walpole Glaciers, the ridge turns into a pleasant snow arête which leads high onto the mountain and is followed by a short stretch of rotten rock to the summit. A good descent route.

Hugh Chambers, Freda Du Faur, Jim Murphy, Jan 1911.

Middle Peak 2913m

The Middle Peak was first climbed by Alex Graham, Peter Graham, Ebenezer Teichelmann, Feb 1910 via Route 8.1.

7.94 Grade 3

Ascend poor rock on the left side of the buttress that leads up to the summit ridge just left of the Middle Peak.

Roger Foley, Simon Carr, Jan 1984.

South Peak 2617m

7.95 **West Face** Grade 3-

From the Walpole Glacier ascend the rock face to the summit.

I B Pledger, K Suter, P C Weenink, Dec 1934.

7.96 **West Ridge** Grade 3

If climbed from the corner of the Walpole Valley the ridge provides a varied fare of rock climbing over pinnacles, across chevals, and up short walls. The rock is variable and in places offers some difficult moves. The final rise to the South Peak is up short slabs interspersed with ledges. The climbing here is easier than lower on the ridge.

C Lake, R Thompson, Feb 1976.

Fig. 39 Mt Chudleigh from the west.

Fig. 40 Langdale Buttress.

Reay Face

The face consists of three buttresses - Left, Central, and Main.

7.97   Left Buttress   Grade 3

Right Pillar - enjoyable rockclimbing (crux 13) for ten pitches.

Dave Begg, Hugh Logan, E Neve, N Reeves, Nov 1977.

7.98   Central Buttress   Grade 3+

Climb the line of weakness up the obvious slabs on the right of the buttress. Five pitches of good rock of mostly grade 12 (cruxes: 14, 18, although avoidable) are followed by 12 pitches of very loose rock (crux 17). First ascensionists descended a gully between the Left and Central Buttresses.

Steve Elder, Steve Eiseman, Mar 1986.

Main Buttress

There are two routes:

7.99   Grade 3

The route meanders from the Central Buttress to the left side of the Main Buttress.

Mike Browne, Keith Woodford, Dec 1971.

8.0   Grade 3+

Up the centre of the buttress. The crux (13) of the route is up high.

Lindsay Main, Darby Thomson, Mar 1974.

8.1   Reay Glacier Route   Grade 2-

Ascend the Reay Glacier keeping on the right until overlooking the Murchison Valley and then up easy snowslopes to the South Peak. A quick and easy descent route.

Alex Graham, Peter Graham, Ebenezer Teichelmann, Feb 1910.

Reay Col 2455m

Reached from the Reay Valley by sidling on scree on the north side of the valley, climbing up to the Reay Glacier, and then through a rock notch in the ridge 200m south from where the glacier swings up Mt Chudleigh. See Route 9.5.

Mt Johnson 2692m

8.2   North West Ridge   Grade 2-

From the Reay Valley head up couloirs onto the upper North West Ridge then on to the summit.

First ascent party unknown.

The red rock pillars of the lower North West Ridge above the Reay Valley are believed to be unclimbed but show great promise as a rock-climbing area. The lower Reay Valley contains some small bivouac rocks and excellent camping amongst snowgrass.

8.3　　**Dorothy Glacier Route**　　　　　　　　　　Grade 2-

From the moraine hollow south of the Dorothy Stream, gain height, climbing past a waterfall, and traverse across onto the Dorothy Glacier. Ascend to col and up the North West Ridge.

First ascent unknown.

8.4　　**West Face**　　　　　　　　　　　　　　　Grade 2

As for Route 8.3 but before the Dorothy Glacier is reached head straight up good, fairly easy rock to the summit.

Samuel Turner, Darby Thomson, Feb 1913.

8.5　　**South West Ridge**　　　　　　　　　　　Grade 2-

Climb to summit between Mts Malcher and Johnson, then climb along the undulating ridge to summit.

First ascent party unknown.

Mt Malcher 2502m

8.6　　　　　　　　　　　　　　　　　　　　　Grade 2-

Easily climbed from the Tasman Glacier.

Franz & Julius Malcher, Feb 1914.

Novara Peak (The Twins) 2326m, 2298m

8.7　　　　　　　　　　　　　　　　　　　　　Grade 1+

Easily climbed from the moraine hollow beside the Tasman Glacier, or else from the junction of the Tasman and Murchison valleys.

Franz & Julius Malcher, Feb 1914.

Murchison Valley

Murchison Valley

The climbs of the eastern Malte Brun Range, at the head of the Murchison Glacier and those on the Liebig Range, north of Nun's Veil, are described here. The Murchison Valley, a strangely neglected area, provides good climbing. The peaks of the Liebig Range are generally easy, but Mts Ronald Adair and Conrad offer promising rock routes. On the Malte Brun Range the climbs are long, mixed snow and rock routes of excellent quality. Some winter ice lines have also been developed (Mt Chudleigh). The head of the valley is heavily glaciated and the routes are predominantly moderate snow climbs. It is a ski touring region *par excellence,* with the run down the Mannering Glacier, in particular, standing out. Expansive transalpine and ski touring trips are also possible, such as those taking in the Godley – Murchison – Tasman – Franz Josef (and Fox) glaciers.

An advantage of the Murchison Valley is that the weather can be quite good when poor elsewhere in the Aoraki/Mt Cook region.

Access

Glacier Explorers Ltd run guided boat excursions on the Tasman Lake and can provide transport to the Murchison side for climbers. At the time of printing an arm of the lake had extended toward the Murchison Valley and saves some walking. Boat rides are only possible when normal trips are running and these can be arranged at the Hermitage. Once on the other side, parties can cross the Murchison River if it is low. Alternatively, follow the river to the Murchison Valley and find crossings there. There is no longer a bridge across the Murchison River. Crossings are possible further up on the broader river flats. Beyond these, easy river beds lead up the south-east of the valley to **Liebig Hut.** Alternatively, the lower Murchison Valley can be reached from the Ball Hut road by crossing the Tasman Glacier from Celmisia Flat. It is possible to fly by helicopter to this hut. If the north-western side of the river is followed, travel is easy until just before **Onslow Hut.** At this point it may be possible to sneak around the water's edge. If not, use a high sidle around a steep gut, to avoid the river. The river itself is often hard to cross (but have a look just in case it is low), and the travel between Liebig and Onslow Huts may involve traversing round the head of the large glacial lake at the toe of the Murchison Glacier. Travel up the main glacier is desperately tedious. It is probably just as easy to reach the head of the glacier via the Tasman Glacier and Tasman Saddle, or even better, by ski-plane. **Murchison Hut** is located on the north-east side of Mt Cooper.

Shelter

Liebig Hut. Owned and operated by AMCNP. It has six bunks, blankets, a radio, and some kitchen equipment (~1000m, grid ref: 928-274).

Onslow Hut. A small 6 bunk hut owned by the NZ Deerstalkers Association. Few facilities and there is *no radio*. This hut is sometimes referred to as Steffan Memorial Hut (~1040m, grid ref: 926-296).

Murchison Hut. A 10 bunk hut owned by the NZAC, kitchen equipment, and a radio (~1900m, grid ref: 994-399).

Classen Saddle

Crossing Point

Sydney King

Phyllis

Acland

Richmond

Liebig Range

The Ant-hill

Armadillo Saddle

Conrad

Godley Pass

Ronald Adair

Coopers Mate

Murchison Glacier

Onslow Hut

Fig. 41 *Murchison Valley and Liebig Range.*

Times

From Celmisia Flat to the Liebig Hut 5-6 hours.
From Liebig Hut to Murchison Hut 6-8 hours.
From Tasman Saddle to Murchison Hut ~2 hours.

Ski Touring Routes

- Murchison Headwall (subject to slab avalanche danger) - Mannering Glacier (B/C).
- Mt Sydney King. Subject to crevasses on the Aida Glacier. (B)
- Mt Phyllis/Classen Saddle (B).
- The Ant-hill - Mt Richmond - Mt Acland -Aida Glacier round trip (B/C).
- Rutherford Stream - saddle west of The Ant-hill - Murchison Glacier. Ascent through the Rutherford is subject to avalanches after fresh snow (!!). Descent from saddle west of Ant-hill to the Murchison requires good route finding through the bluffs (C).

Malte Brun Range

Novara Peak

South Twin 2298m

9.0   East Ridge   Grade 1+

Starting from the Murchison Valley ascend an easy rib to reach the divide a little south of the peak.

J B Waterhouse, Dec 1985.

Colin Monteath, Nick Groves, Jun 1994.

North Twin 2326m

9.1   North East Ridge   Grade 1

From the Burnett Falls ascend the ridge heading directly to the summit.

J B Waterhouse, Dec 1985.

Mt Malcher 2502m

9.2   East Rib   Grade 2

From the Burnett Glacier ascend the rib that reaches the Divide just south of the summit.

J B Waterhouse, Dec 1985.

Access to the terraces beneath Novara Peak and Mt Johnson can be found up the slopes beside the Burnett Glacier. Between the Burnett and Lecky glaciers are a number of tussock basins with good campsites, but there are steep walls leading from the terraces down to the river.

Mt Johnson 2692m

South Face
9.3   Grade 4

Commencing from the Burnett Glacier, ascend the prominent rock rib leading to the summit.

Rob Blackburne, Mike Brosnahan, Ross Cullen, Nick Shearer, Mar 1983.

9.4   North East Ridge   Grade 3+

Ascend to the saddle between Mts Johnson and Chudleigh either via the Lecky Glacier or the ridge on the left. From the saddle traverse a 2km ridge of jumbled rock with steps becoming increasingly harder. From a sharp notch just north of the summit, ascend final face of three pitches (crux 13) to the summit.

R Arbon, Lindsay Main, J B Waterhouse, Dec 1978.

Reay Col 2455m
9.5   Grade 1+

Ascend just behind the Onslow Hut up snowgrass slopes and bluffs to the Lecky Glacier. An easy scenic crossing can be made from here through the rock notch of the Reay Col.

Arthur Harper, Percy Johnson, 1891.

Mt Chudleigh 2966m
9.6   Grade 2+

Ascend toward Reay Col but 200m below the Col head straight up steep snow, keeping left of some icecliffs to join up with the Reay Glacier route on Mt Chudleigh.

B Barton and others, Jan 1974.

East Face

9.7   Walking The Dog   Grade 4-

From the névé of the Lecky Glacier ascend mixed ground on the left of the face, and then ascend and traverse right to an arête, topped by an exit gully 100m north of the summit.

Rob Blackburne, Duncan Ritchie, Apr 1984.

9.8   Direct Route   Grade 5-

This line bisects Routes 9.7 and 9.9. Eleven pitches of snow and ice. The crux, about 80m in length, is steep mixed ground with limited protection. The route tops out slightly north, and 40m lower than the high peak.

Jono Clarke, Pete Barnes, Nov 1996.

9.9   Spaghetti Route   Grade 4

Ascend steep mixed ground directly under the summit to gain a snowfield. Traverse left and up to gain the prominent snow arête, and then finish up gullies to just north of the summit.

Ross Cullen, Dave Wills, Apr 1984.

Fig. 42 Eastern aspect of the Malte Brun Range including Mts Chudleigh - Hamilton.

Colin Monteath/Hedgehog House

9.10   East Ridge Variation   Grade 3

Climb onto the ridge where it begins the final sweep to the summit. Ascend for 300m and then traverse diagonally left for at least five rope lengths to finish up route 9.9.

Jim Jolly, John Nankervis, Jan 1984.

Mt Nathan 2868m

Believed to be unclimbed directly from the Murchison.

Aiguilles Rouges 2950m

9.11   South Face   Grade 3+

Traverse across the Onslow Glacier to gain the broad rib on the right side of the Face. Head up the rib, which eventually merges into the 45-50 degree slopes of the upper face, arriving on the summit ridge between the East and High Peaks.

Dave Bamford, John Nankervis, Jan 1980.

9.12   East Ridge   Grade 2+

An enjoyable climb with plenty of variety. Access from Onslow Hut is easy except for a short section of rotten rock. The lower flat sections of the ridge can be avoided by keeping to the Onslow Glacier, but two prominent rock steps have to be climbed where the ridge begins to steepen, and after another 200m a snow bulge is climbed. The route then gradually lies back up to the East Peak. It is roughly 25 minutes from here to the Main Peak.

M J P Glasgow, Harry Stevenson, Dec 1951.

Malte Brun Pass 2455m   Grade 2-

The pass can be reached either via the lower sections of the East Ridge of the Aiguilles Rouges by dropping down a steep gut onto the Cascade Glacier or by travelling up the Murchison Glacier and climbing up the Cascade Stream, gaining the south side of the glacier. Ascend the Cascade Glacier up easy slopes to the pass. After crossing the broad expanse of the pass, descend either snow or, in late summer, rock and scree to the Beetham Valley. Refer to Route 7.79.

Frind Peak 2448m

9.13   Grade 2-

Easily climbed from either the Cascade Glacier or by the ridge from the Murchison Glacier. The ridge from the Murchison Glacier has a small notch in it.

R M Crockett, W G McClymont, J H Rose, F F Simmons, Dec 1934.

9.14   North Face   Grade 2

From the Baker Glacier, direct to summit.

B Waterhouse, Dec 1986

Malte Brun 3199m

South Ridge, from Malte Brun Pass. See Route 7.78.

East Face

9.15   Grade 4

From the névé of the Baker Glacier head up steepish ice (up to 55 degrees) to the right of the prominent rock rib in the centre of the face, move rightwards and up, keeping an eye open for ice avalanches and rockfall. A route best done fairly quickly.

Richard Hancock, John Nankervis, Jan 1978.

9.16   Grade 3+

From the névé of the Baker Glacier ascend the snowslope to the left of the East Rib into an ice couloir that leads onto the upper East Rib. Beware of soft snow avalanches later in the day.

Bernie Gunn, Fred Hollows, Barrie Jackson, Gillian Soper, Dec 1952.

★ 9.17   **East Rib**   Grade 3+

From the névé of the Baker Glacier, gain the rib via snowslopes on the left and ascend the mixed snow and rock steps. The rib eases into a snow arête and joins the top of the North East Ridge. A classic route.

Bill Beaven, Ian Gibbs, Earle Riddiford, Hugh Tyndale-Biscoe, Jan 1953.

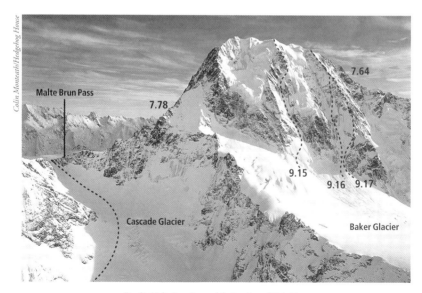

Fig. 43 Malte Brun Pass and the East Face of Malte Brun.

Mt Hamilton 3025m

9.18   South East Arête   Grade 3+
From the valley floor ascend the ridge out of the Baker Glacier onto a subsidiary peak. Then up the arête to an ice bulge. Ice changes may have made this part of the climb difficult. Continue up the face to the summit. A rarely climbed but beautiful line.
Bernie Gunn, Fred Hollows, Barrie Jackson, Gillian Soper, Dec 1952.

Rose Peak 2508m

9.19   Grade 2-
Climbed easily via the lower Dixon Glacier and a slope leading onto the South East Ridge. Gives access to Mt Haeckel.
R M Crockett, W G McClymont, F F Simmons, Dec 1934.

Mt Haeckel 2965m

9.20   East Ridge   Grade 3-
Gained either via the upper Mannering Icefall (on the rocks on the left if the icefall is broken), the Dixon Glacier, or over Rose Peak, then up easily angled snow, or rock, or both, to the summit.
R M Crockett, W G McClymont, F F Simmons, Dec 1934.

Mt Annan 2934m

9.21   East Rib   Grade 3
After negotiating the step between the two arms of the Mannering Glacier, move quickly onto the rib via slopes between Mt Annan and Peak 9144, to gain the crest of the rib. Head up wide snow slopes interspersed with rock bands to arrive within a few feet of the summit.
Bob Gunn, John Nankervis, John Wild, Dec 1968.

Mt Abel 2688m
Unclimbed directly from the Mannering.

Peak 9144 2669m

9.22   East Ridge   Grade 2+
From Starvation Saddle ascend 50m of loose rock to a broad snow ridge below the first buttress of 160m. Then follow another snow ridge to the final rock ridge leading up 250m to the summit. The rock is generally loose.
F J Austin, J B Butchers, J C Mathews, Dec 1957.

Mt Cooper 2362m

9.23 Grade 1

An easy climb from all directions: from Starvation Saddle, the Mannering Névé or via number of options from the slopes above Murchison Hut.

M Barford, J Moore, Dec 1943.

Starvation Saddle 2204m

Can be accessed from either the Mannering Névé or easily from the upper Murchison Glacier.

Tasman Saddle 2435m

9.24

From Murchison Hut descend to the glacier or traverse snow slopes and travel around northern edge of central icefall and up towards the saddle. The final 150m is relatively steep. If descending to the east note that the central icefall is not immediately evident from the Murchison Névé.

Mt Aylmer 2699m

9.25 North East Ridge

Gain the ridge from nearer to Graceful Peak. Very loose rock reported. (also see Route 7.37).

Keith McNaughton, John Gamlen, Dec 1966 (involving a traverse from Graceful Pk).

Graceful Peak 2457m

9.26 North East Ridge Grade 2+

From Whymper Saddle climb a steep snow slope west of the saddle to reach a rock ridge to the north-east. Follow this narrow and loose ridge to the summit.

N H Hamilton, M Hamilton, B W Patterson, Dec 1942.

9.27

From the Murchison Névé gain the col between Aylmer and Graceful, then follow the Main Divide (rock) to the summit.

Whymper Saddle 2223m

9.28

From the Murchison Névé, navigate the crevasses to the saddle.

Brodrick Peak 2669m

(also see Routes 11.6 - 11.9)

Annan

Abel

Elie de Beaumont

Whymper Saddle

Aylmer

Graceful

Brodrick

Whataroa
Saddle

Crossing
Point

CS

TS

SS

Cooper

Murchison
Glacier

Mannering
Glacier

Fig. 44 The head of the Murchison Glacier. Circle denotes Murchison Hut. TS, SS and CS denote Tasman, Starvation and Classen Saddles.

9.29

From Whymper Saddle follow the Main Divide firstly on snow then rock to the Low Peak.

D W Beatty, P A L Fraser, A W McNaught, J V McNulty, Jan 1955 (Low Pk).

9.30 South West Ridge

The vague feature on the left side of the peak seen from Murchison Hut.

John Gamlen, Keith McNaughton, Dec 1967 (Descended).

9.31 Loves Last (South Face) Grade 4-

Take the central gully and then enjoy ice on rock.

Graham Love, Dave Carlyle, Sep 1985.

9.32 South East Ridge Grade 2-

From Classen Saddle climb snow slopes to arrive high on the Main Divide north of the summit, then continue to the summit.

First Ascent Unknown

9.33 Main Divide Grade 2-

From Classen Saddle traverse to the vicinity of Whataroa Saddle, then up south-eastern snow slopes (or rock depending on conditions) and then traverse the Main Divide to the summit.

Will Kennedy, Jack Lippe, Jan 1917.

For those peaks on the Main Divide, north-east of Brodrick, see the Godley Valley Section.

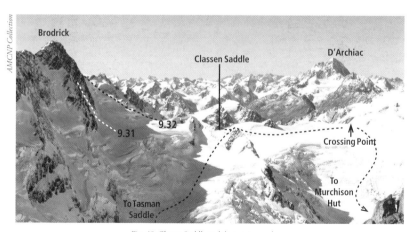

Fig. 45 Classen Saddle and the crossing used now.

Classen Saddle 2179m

Straightforward from the upper Murchison. Thomas Brodrick and his survey party were the first to climb to the saddle in December 1890.

9.34

To access the Classen Glacier do not cross Classen Saddle as this leads to an icefall (probably impassable). Instead, traverse south-east to the spot height 2178m (see map 260-I35, grid ref: 011-414) overlooking a tributary to the Classen Glacier. Descend this to gain the glacier below. Also see the Classen Glacier description in the Godley Valley section and see Fig. 44 and 45.

Liebig Range

The main climbs described here are those that ascend from the Murchison Valley. Several of the peaks have routes on their eastern sides, accessed from the Jollie, Cass and Godley Valley systems. Although these eastern climbs fall outside the coverage of this guide, they will be briefly noted. These valleys are seldom visited and offer excellent terrain for the novice and/or those looking for fantastic views of the major peaks of the Aoraki/Mount Cook region. Like the Murchison, the weather in these valleys is usually better than that experienced closer to the Main Divide.

It is of particular importance to note that the Jollie Valley is part of the Braemar and Mount Cook Stations and the Cass Valley is part of the Glenmore and Godley Peaks Stations. Neither valley is within the Aoraki/Mount Cook National Park. *Permission from the run-holders or farm managers is required and should be sought before accessing these valleys or the huts therein.*

Access to the Cass Valley is from Tekapo, past Lake Alexandrina and for the Jollie Valley, access is from the main road between Tekapo and Lake Pukaki.

Mt Phyllis 2444m

9.35

An easy climb along a snow ridge from Classen Saddle. Alternatively, from the Aida Glacier climb to the col east of the peak and then up to the summit.
(Probably) Otto Frind, Conrad Kain, Mar 1914.
(Possibly) Jack Stenhouse, Geoff Harrow, Rosemary Packer, Lyndsay Alston, Don Young, Rodney Hamilton, Aug, 1956.

Mt Sydney King 2521m

9.36

From the Aida Glacier climb north up a snow spur to the col then continue north-east along snow and rock 150m to the summit. Alternatively, climb to the col on the south-east ridge that leads from Acland, then up a rocky ridge to the summit. The Joie de Vivre Buttress, on the north-western side, has also been climbed - this can be accessed from Phyllis (see Route 11.5).
Otto Frind, Conrad Kain, Mar 1914.

Mt Acland 2562m

9.37

From the head of the Aida Glacier climb to the col between the peak and Sydney King, then ascend rocks to the top; or from the Aida Névé head directly up snow slopes to gain the ridge south of the summit. Alternatively, traverse from Richmond.

Otto Frind, Conrad Kain, Mar 1914 (from the Aida Glacier).

Coopers Mate 2280m

9.38 Grade 1

Gain the saddle east of the peak from either the Aida or Harper Glaciers. More direct routes from the Murchison Glacier exist.

S Drake, W F Crawshaw, David Hall, Jan 1947.

Mt Richmond 2509m

9.39

From the saddle east of Coopers Mate climb rock slabs on the west face to the summit. Alternatively, traverse from Acland.

Otto Frind, Conrad Kain, Mar 1914.

9.40   **North West Face**

From the Aida Glacier climb rock bands and snow slopes to the summit.

R Coombs, J Wild, Dec 1968.

9.41   **South West Face**

Use the saddle as for 9.39 and drop into the Harper Glacier. Then ascend the face.

C Morris, W Provan, M Clark, Dec 1980.

The Ant-hill 2517m

9.42

From Armadillo Saddle climb scree and snow slopes to the north-east of the peak. Alternatively, traverse the north ridge from Richmond.

Otto Frind, Conrad Kain, Mar 1914.

Armadillo Saddle 2180m

From the Murchison Glacier either follow easy scree and snow slopes to the pass or see the alternative route description in the Godley Valley section. The pass allows access to the east linking with the north branch of the Rutherford Stream, which descends into the Godley Valley. This is the easiest route to get from the upper Murchison to the Godley Valley.

Fig. 46 Mt Conrad, Liebig Range (from the west).

Mt Conrad 2598m

9.43   South Ridge

Climb the slopes of the Surprise Glacier to Godley Pass and then ascend the South Ridge. The South Ridge can be accessed nearer to Conrad by climbing the gully immediately north of Whispering Falls, and following a snow basin to the South Ridge. Alternatively, traverse from Armadillo Saddle or a point nearer the peak (two rock steps near the summit offer good quality climbing).

Conrad Kain, Otto Frind, Jan 1914.

9.44   North Ridge

Start on rock from the Harper Glacier under Armadillo Saddle. In good snow conditions sidle under the ridge to Conrad, gain access to the peak roughly 200m from the summit.

K Wade, I Dainis, Jan 1965 (Descended).

John Nankervis, Bob Gunn, Dec 1968.

Godley Pass 2254m

9.45

Straightforward on the Murchison side. The Godley side leads into the south branch of the Rutherford Stream. Armadillo Saddle is the more popular of the two passes, probably because it allows better access to the upper Murchison, when traversing from the Godley.

Otto Frind, Conrad Kain, Mar, 1914.

Olaf 2641m

9.46

As for Kenneth, gain the col and then climb the south ridge, again on poor rock. Alternatively traverse the Liebig Range from the north.

Alf Brustad, Kenneth Grinling, Adair Algie, Ronald Algie, Jan 1927.

Mt Kenneth 2638m

9.47

From the Murchison Glacier climb rock and snow to the col between the peak and Olaf. Continue up the north ridge on poor rock. Another option is to follow the Liebig Range from Ronald Adair.

Alf Brustad, Kenneth Grinling, Adair Algie, Ronald Algie, Jan 1927.

Mt Ronald Adair 2818m

9.48

Once above the Murchison Glacier climb grass and snow slopes to the north ridge, follow this across loose rock and the odd snow patch to the summit. An alternative is to traverse the Liebig Range from Hutton.

Alf Brustad, Kenneth Grinling, Adair Algie, Ronald Algie, Jan 1927

Mt Hutton 2822m

9.49

i Head up beside the waterfall, over grass and scree to the hanging valley west of the peak. Continue to the crest of the ridge and follow for 800m to the summit, traversing snow domes along the way.

Otto Frind, Conrad Kain, Jan 1914.

ii Scramble up grass and scree to the glacier north of the peak and then climb a snow gully to the north-east ridge. Traverse south-west over low peak to high peak.

iii From Rutherford Pass traverse north-east along a rock and snow ridge to the summit, over 3 km away! Alternatively, and no doubt easier, cross the pass and travel along the remnant Ridge Glacier and snow slopes on the south-east side of the Liebig Range.

iv *From the Cass Valley*. Gain the Ridge Glacier or Rutherford Pass then continue as for iii. This is a good route to ski tour.

Rutherford Pass 2272m

From near to the Murchison Glacier head up grass and scree slopes to a rock notch – this is the pass. If approaching from the west branch of the Cass River pass the moraine of the Faraday Glacier and continue up to the remnant Ridge Glacier. Then traverse to the rock notch.

Fig. 47 Mt Hutton, Liebig Range (from the west).

Mt Tamaki 2444m

9.50

i Easy scrambling from the Murchison.

Thomas Brodrick, Louis Sladden, 1892.

ii *From the Cass Valley*. Ascend easy snow slopes, at the head of the Ailsa Stream, to the south of the peak. From the north, traverse the ridge line from Rutherford Pass over spot height 2382m.

Mt Lucia 2617m

This peak is situated south-east of Tamaki and overlooks the Ailsa and Cass Valleys.

9.51 North East Ridge

Traverse Tamaki and Kehua Pass (2325m), continuing along the ridge line to Lucia (also, Kehua Pass is easily gained from the head of Ailsa Stream).

Nick von Tunzelman, Alex Parton, Dec 1963.

9.52 From Ailsa Stream

Starting from a shelf above the Ailsa Stream, climb up scree slopes into a snow couloir that leads to the north-west ridge and on to the summit.

C S Brockett, S J Harris, N D Dench, N Feierabend, Jan 1953.

An alternative lies up rotten but easy rock gained when $^2/_3$ up the couloir.

9.53   South East Ridge

Ascends from the confluence of Ailsa-Cass Valleys. Gained from Ailsa Stream.
J T Cruse, N J Mitchell, W Nixon, Dec 1956.

Ailsa Pass 2190m

Up valley of Liebig Hut, scramble up easy scree slopes that lead to a slight depression, which is the pass. Ailsa Pass provides access to the Cass Valley via Ailsa Stream.

Jollie Saddle 2084m

Gained by following the south-west side of the Ailsa Stream avoiding the waterfall under Mt Jukes. Continue up grass and scree into a hanging valley leading to the saddle. Alternatively, access it from the head of the Jollie River. First gained by Thomas Brodrick and Louis Sladden in February 1889, from the Jollie.

Mt Jukes 2526m

9.54

This peak is situated at the head of the Gammack Range and is separated from the Liebig Range by Jollie Saddle.
A D Jackson, S A Shrimpton, C A Reid, C W Don, Mar 1941 (North Ridge, descended North East face).
Neil Hamilton, C Cabelka, Apr 1952 (from the Jollie Valley).
Has been climbed in winter.

Jollie Peaks 2544m, 2454m

9.55

Again, easy scrambling from the Murchison to these ill-defined rock peaks.
C Denham, Jack Pattle, Jan 1936.

The Abbott 2630m

9.56

From the Murchison, easy grass and scree slopes lead to the ridge line, the summit is climbed easily from either direction.
Harold Porter, Jim Rose, J Milne, Jan 1925.
C S Brocket, S J Harris, N D Dench, N Feierabend, Jan 1953 (from Pinnacle Stream, a tributary to the Jollie River).

The Abbess 2607m

9.57

Gain Abbey Pass and descend to the Monk Glacier, towards Pinnacle Stream, then climb an easy couloir to the summit.
Harold Porter, Jim Rose, J Milne, Jan 1925.
C S Brocket, S J Harris, N D Dench, N Feierabend, Jan 1953 (from Pinnacle Stream, a tributary to the Jollie River).

Abbey Pass 2377m

Follow easy grass and scree slopes from the Murchison Valley floor or use the Monk Glacier if approaching from the Jollie side.

Monastery Peak 2580m

9.58

From the Murchison riverbed head up grass and scree slopes to a basin north east of the peak, then onto the summit.

Peter Graham, A Humphries, R B Seager, Mar 1918.

Mt Biretta (Priest's Cap) 2665m

9.59

From the vicinity of Monastery Peak or near Nun's Veil.

Tom Fyfe, Malcolm Ross, Samuel Turner, Dec 1905.

The peaks of the Liebig Range south of Biretta - Nun's Veil through to Mt Blackburn - are described in the Eastern Tasman section.

Marry Beare

Pat Deavoll on "Logan's Run".

Eastern Tasman

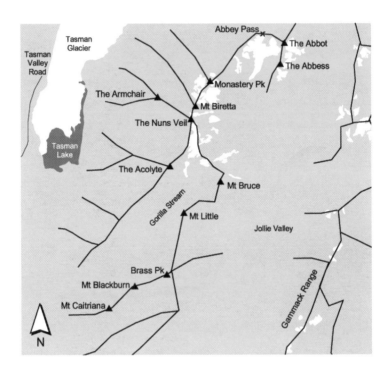

Eastern Tasman

In this small section the mountains from The Nun's Veil to Mt Blackburn are described. The peaks north of Nun's Veil, on the Liebig Range, are described in the Murchison Valley and Godley Valley sections. There are no huts in this area but some bivvy rocks can be found. Accessing this area usually involves crossing either the Tasman or Murchison rivers or the Tasman Lake. A boat, used for glacier sightseeing, can provide transport. Enquire at the Visitor Centre for more details.

Nun's Veil 2749m

10.0   Turner's Couloir   Grade 2-

Catch the boat up the lake and then cross the Murchison River. Alternatively, cross the Tasman Glacier and then deal with the Murchison River. Ascend an unnamed creek to the prominent couloir leading up between Nun's Veil and Mt Biretta. From the top of couloir climb a rock ridge to the summit.

George Bannister, Samuel Turner, Feb 1912 (Descended).

10.1   Unveiled   Grade 4+

Takes the central buttress on the West Face. Head up the groove on the left hand side of the face, continue past two rock bands (top one may be snow filled), then tend left into a gully leading to the top. The route involves 900m of climbing, compact pink slabs, chimneys, scrambling and one crux pitch of grade 20.

Sean Waters, Tim Balla, Mar 1996.

★ **10.2   Gorilla Stream Route**   Grade 1+

Catch the boat to the south-eastern side of the lake and travel south to Gorilla Stream, some parties have crossed the Tasman River near to Gorilla Stream – but this may not be possible in summer). Follow Gorilla Stream and ascend easily up the glacier to the summit. The last bit to the top is a bit exposed. The top offers a glorious viewpoint. At the head of Gorilla Stream a bivvy rock offers a small amount of protection (take a fly to add to it). From the lake to the bivvy rock allow ~6hrs.

Peter Graham, Mick Collett, Dr Mackay, 1905.

(Possibly) Andy Harris, Russell Braddock, Jun 1984.

10.3   Pinnacle Stream Route

Use the Jollie River, then Pinnacle Stream.

C S Brockett, S J Harris, N D Dench, Jan 1953.

Has received a winter ascent.

East Face

10.4   The Far Side   Grade 5

Takes the central buttress of the East Face, following 700m of quality rock (16 pitches) with a crux of 16. A route that requires commitment. The first ascent team descended Turners Couloir.

Kiersten Price, Dave Crow, Apr 1995.

AMCNP Collection

Monastery   Nun's Veil   Biretta   Blackburn

Armchair

10.0

Murchison Valley

Fig. 48 Liebig Range from Mt Chudleigh.

AMCNP Collection

Jollie Valley

10.2

Gorilla
Stream

Fig. 49 The upper section of the Nun's Veil, showing the Gorilla Stream Route.

The Acolyte 2290m

10.5

Can be climbed via Botanical Spur (as marked on map 260-H36) or from Irish Creek. Both can be accessed from south of the Tasman Lake.

Peter Graham, Miss Joachim, J Stout, Mar 1917.

Faye Kerr, John Herbison, Jun 1979.

Mt Bruce 2401m

10.6

Straightforward from the top of Gorilla Stream.

Peter Graham, Dorothy Holdsworth, Irene Chambers, R B Seager, Mar 1917.

Mt Little 2207m

An easy ascent from the top of Gorilla Stream.

First ascent unknown

Brass Peak 2343m

10.7

From the head of Gorilla Stream traverse the north ridge. Alternatively, climb from Chop Creek.

Peter Graham, Jack Lippe, Dorothy Theomin, Apr 1916.

Mt Blackburn (Rotten Tommy) 2490m

10.8

Climb Gorilla Stream to a scree slope and continue up to a col on the SW ridge via a right branch of scree. Follow the SW ridge to the summit. Gendarmes on the ridge can be turned on the NW side. An alternative route lies up the SW ridge from Tasman Point, traversing Mt Caitriana (1763m) and Cow Block Saddle (1821m) over poor rock.

Jack Clarke, C J Bainbridge, W G Tennant, 1903.

Dave Crow

10.4

Fig. 50 *Central Buttress on the East Face of the Nun's Veil.*

Alex Palman

Alison Grimsdell above Katie's Col. Le Receveur Peak and Big Mac behind.

Godley Valley

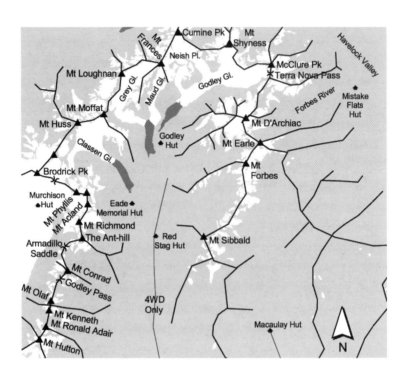

Godley Valley

The Godley offers distinct appeal for those looking for country less frequented than the adjoining Aoraki/Mount Cook region. Climbing is popular, especially on Mt D'Archiac - the highest peak in the area, but the Godley is probably best known for its world class ski touring country. For those looking specifically for information on ski touring a brief list of routes is provided. The Godley Valley and its tributaries are shown on the map opposite. Although Mt Sibbald is outside the coverage of this guide, routes on it are briefly described. The Godley is relatively untouched and provides not only remoteness but also a sense of timelessness - it's well worth a visit.

Glacial recession is evident throughout the valleys east of the Main Divide, but nowhere is it more striking than in the Godley region. The Godley glaciers continue to show the most dramatic retreat of all glaciers in the Aoraki/Mount Cook National Park. In 1862 when Julius Haast visited the area the Godley, Maud and Grey Glaciers joined to form one major valley glacier but they have each retreated to the point where they are now completely separate.

Access is more difficult than in other parts of the Aoraki/Mount Cook region and typically requires a 4WD vehicle to get well up the valleys. Also, there are no high huts. Glacial recession has made access to routes during summer more difficult. However, in winter, frozen lakes can sometimes provide easy and unique access. Due to the ongoing changes, some approach routes described here may not continue to be the best way to gain the upper valleys and glaciers – so check with park staff and the hut books in the area to gain the most up-to-date access information.

How to find what you are looking for
The Godley region is organised in the following order. To begin with the Godley side of the Liebig Range, north of Mt Hutton, is detailed followed by those peaks in the Classen, Grey, Maud, Neish and Godley Glacier areas. Those climbs accessed from Separation Stream are described next. A sub-section, Climbing Mt D'Archiac from the Havelock Valley follows and finally there is a short description of the climbs on Mt Sibbald, including those from the Macaulay Valley.

Access
The Godley region is most commonly accessed by vehicle from Tekapo via the Lilybank Road. However, the road on the west side of the Godley River, the Godley Peaks Road is also used to gain access to the peaks on the Liebig Range. The Havelock and Forbes valleys are used for 4WD and foot access from the east.

A number of high alpine passes and saddles also allow passage from valleys in the east, north and west. These include: the saddle north of The Ant-hill (from the Murchison) and Classen Saddle (from the upper Murchison), Terra Nova Pass (from the Havelock River), Stewart and Sealy Passes (both from the Perth River) and Grey Pass (from the Butler River).

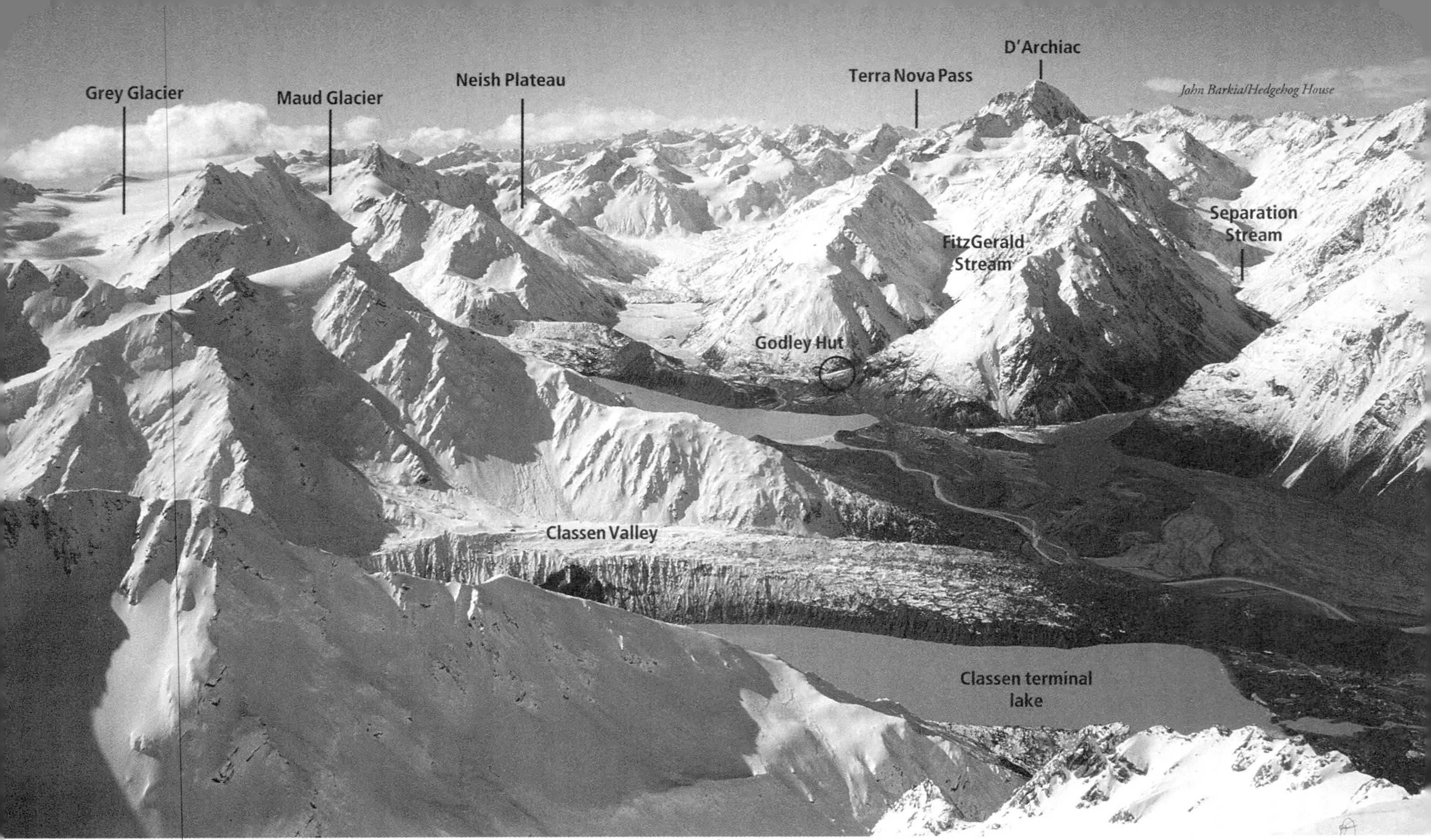

Grey Glacier

Maud Glacier

Neish Plateau

Terra Nova Pass

D'Archiac

Separation Stream

FitzGerald Stream

Godley Hut

Classen Valley

Classen terminal lake

John Barkla/Hedgehog House

Fig. 51 The Godley Valley and tributaries.

From Tekapo via Lilybank Road

On the eastern side of the Tekapo township, turn off Highway 8 onto the unsealed Lilybank Road and follow this for approximately 20 km to the Macaulay River. Although this stretch of road is navigable by 2WD vehicles the remaining 47 km is strictly 4WD only.

Crossing the Macaulay River, for example, is a serious proposition, even for proper 4WD vehicles (read: low clearance 4WD vehicles will not survive). Two 4WD's vehicles are recommended so you can pull out bogged vehicles.

Beyond the Macaulay River the road leads to Lilybank Station, to the left of the main buildings. Public access to the Godley Valley, and thus Aoraki/Mount Cook National Park, is both legal and permitted – so please don't call in to the station for permission.

However, please note that no legal access exists up Weka Stream or North Branch Stream. So don't venture up these streams or onto any pastoral land held by Lilybank Station without permission.

The road weaves between farm sheds and barns past pine trees to follow a fenceline. Leave gates as you find them. Past the station the 'road' becomes a route. It turns out onto the Godley River flats and proceeds up valley. The route, which is punctuated with sections of old road and cairns, remains on the eastern side of the valley. A sign welcoming you to AMCNP is situated about 5 km before **Red Stag Hut**, which in turn is located about 5 km from the road end and peters out near to Separation Stream. A vague foot track starts on the north side of Separation Stream and travels along the eastern edge of the lower Godley Lake for about 300m. **Godley Hut** is situated up on a moraine shelf, ten or so minutes past FitzGerald Stream.

On the western side of the Classen Lake outflow is the **Eade Memorial Hut**. The hut is situated about 700m downstream of the lake outlet and up on a high terrace. Access via the western side of the Godley Valley is also possible. The unsealed Godley Peaks Road turns off the main road between Tekapo and its airport. Godley Peaks Station, situated just past the Cass River, is about 18 km from the township. A 4WD road continues past the station. Permission from Godley Peak Station should be sought for access beyond this point.

The Macaulay Valley is situated east of the Godley Valley and can be accessed by 4WD (depending on river and snow conditions). Cross the Macaulay River as detailed above, turn right before Lilybank Station and continue up the true right of the valley. **Macaulay Hut** sits on the Lower Tindill Stream fan, 19 km up the valley. The Godley-Macaulay Conservation Area (the area contained between the Two Thumb Range, the Godley and Macaulay rivers and McKinnon Stream) and Mt Sibbald can be accessed from this hut. For more information about this amazing section of high country contact DoC at either Aoraki/Mount Cook or Twizel.

Although 4WD access is faster and easier, some parties have used mountain bikes to gain the upper reaches of the Godley and Macaulay valleys.

Shelter

Red Stag Hut. Owned by the New Zealand Deerstalkers Association (NZDA), has four bunks and some kitchen equipment (~950m, grid ref: 082-371).

Godley Hut. Owned by the NZAC, has eight bunks, a mountain radio (link to Christchurch) and some kitchen utensils (~1110m, grid ref: 086-445).

Eade Memorial Hut. Owned by the NZDA, has 4-6 bunks (~980m, grid ref: 065-401).

Macaulay Hut. Owned and operated by the Mackenzie Alpine Trust (Lake Tekapo), has 14 bunks, cooking facilities, a mountain radio (link to Christchurch) and solar lights. This hut was built for the wider community through generous community support and voluntary labour.

Times

Tekapo to Macaulay River, by 4WD vehicle ~ 45mins.
Macaulay River to Red Stag Hut by 4WD ~1.5hrs.
Red Stag Hut to Godley Hut, by foot 1.5 – 2hrs.
Separation Stream to Godley Hut, by foot ~ 35mins.
Separation Stream to Eade Memorial Hut ~ 1hr (the Godley and possibly Classen rivers will need to be crossed – this may not be possible in some conditions).
Tekapo to Macaulay Hut, by 4WD ~ 2.5hrs.

Ski Touring Routes

- Classen Glacier. Seldom visited due to difficulties of getting around the lake when not frozen.
- Maud Glacier. Superb ski run, one of the best in the AMCNP (B/C).
- Cumine Peak via Neish Glacier. Great care to be taken on the slope south of Sealy Pass (B).
- Terra Nova Pass. Easy skiing when lake is frozen (A).
- Pyramus Peak. From Saint Winifred Hut (B).
- FitzGerald Glacier. Good access to Mt D'Archiac without the troubles of the lake (B).
- Mt Forbes (B).
- Mt Sibbald, north peak, via Upper Tindill. Superb ski run in late spring (D).
- Nun's Veil via Gorilla Stream. Very steep skiing at the top (C/D).
- Nun's Veil via Jollie River (C/D).
- Abbey Pass - Monk Glacier (B).
- Jollie Saddle (A/B).
- William Grant Stream (A/B).
- Ailsa Stream -Jollie Saddle - Liebig Dome - Ailsa Pass. Very scenic round trip (B).
- Mt Lucia Shoulder (B/C).
- Mount Hutton via Ridge Glacier and descent via Huxley Glacier. Extreme skiing (D).

Route Grades

The Godley region has generally not received much climbing attention over the last 20 years and so information on the difficulty of routes, including grades, is lacking. The routes described here mostly do not have grades assigned. Climbers will need to use their best judgement at the time to estimate the difficulty of a given climb. To ensure that future editions of this guide do have grades - please email/send your suggestions and comments to the NZAC.

Fig. 52 Rutherford Valley and Liebig Range from the Godley.

Peaks of the Liebig Range – North of Mt Hutton

The eastern side of the peaks north of Mt Hutton are described here. The western approaches are detailed in the Murchison Valley section. The peaks south of and including Mt Hutton are described in the Eastern Tasman and Murchison Valley sections. Many of these peaks appear to have no recorded ascents from the Godley side.

Mt Ronald Adair 2818m

11.0   East Face
Access from Rankin Stream.
Rob Moffat, Steve Tulley, Gerry Essenberg, Jul 1993.

Mt Kenneth 2638m

11.1
From the head of the north branch of the Rankin Stream climb a narrow snow gut to gain the south-east ridge. Once on the crest continue over loose rock to final snow slopes and the summit.
A Baird, B S Charman, W E Limbrick, Jan 1959.

195

Olaf 2641m

See Route 9.46.

Godley Pass 2254m

See Route 9.45.

Mt Conrad 2598m

11.2   East Ridge

Climb from Rutherford Stream.

Philip Temple, Brian Turner, Jan 1977.

Armadillo Saddle 2180m

NB. The best crossing point is the saddle at ~2170m, between spot height 2220m and The Ant-hill (however Armadillo Saddle, as marked on maps, is fine).

Follow the north branch of the Rutherford Stream and then scree slopes to the saddle. Considerable avalanche danger may exist during winter and spring after new snowfall. This is regarded as the easiest and most convenient route from the Tekapo-Godley region to the upper Murchison Valley. It is also a popular crossing for ski tourers. Descending to Murchison Glacier: from the crossing point (~2170m, described above) traverse right (north) above bluffs without losing height at first, then follow a distinct ramp down to the Harper Valley floor. Follow the valley and descend the moraine wall to the Murchison Glacier on the true left of the stream.

The Ant-hill 2517m

11.3

From Armadillo Saddle (west of The Ant-hill) an easy scramble up scree and snow slopes.

Otto Frind, Conrad Kain, Mar 1914.

Ski touring option: From The Ant-hill ski north to the saddle south of spot height 2429m. Ski around the spur of this point on its eastern side to gain the glacier basin east of Mt Richmond. Then ascend towards Mt Acland and gain access to the Aida Glacier via the small notch at about 2400m.

Mt Richmond 2509m

See Route 9.39.

Mt Acland 2562m

See Route 9.37.

Mt Sydney King 2521m

11.4

From the head of the Joie de Vivre Glacier climb to the col south-east of Mt Phyllis then travel north-east along snow and rock to the summit. Also see Route 9.36.

11.5 Joie de Vivre Buttress

Climb the buttress directly to the summit from the Joie de Vivre Glacier.

G Vickers, D Launder, R Coombs, Dec 1968.

A NZMGA guides course put a number of routes on this buttress in March 1991.

Mt Phyllis 2444m

An easy climb from the col between Sydney King. From Classen Saddle follow the straightforward ridge to the summit.

Classen Saddle 2179m

This is the main route from the Godley to the Murchison Valley, however it is not generally crossed in summer due to glacier difficulties on the Godley side (Classen Glacier). Instead, access is via a crossing half way to Phyllis - described below.

First crossed by Peter Graham, George Rose, Apr 1906.

The Classen Glacier

Classen Glacier and Saddle. From Eade Memorial Hut follow the terrace up valley for about a kilometre before descending to the Classen Lake. Follow the true right of the lake to the moraine. A trough between the moraine wall and the Classen Glacier makes the travel a bit easier. Continue up the glacier around the bend keeping on the true right side. Pass the Joie de Vivre Glacier to the next glacier on the same side. Ascend this unnamed tributary glacier to a point roughly half way between Mt Phyllis and Classen Saddle. This point is marked as spot height 2178m (on map 260-I35, grid ref: 011-414). The icefall below Classen Saddle is generally not passable. An alternative route involves turning up the Joie de Vivre Glacier - the col at the head leads to the Aida Glacier, providing access to the head of the Murchison Valley.

Parties have also used the north side of the Classen Lake to gain the glacier: follow the Elizabeth Stream, which drains from its namesake glacier, until it turns north. Continue along the moraine shelf and then descend on to the Classen Glacier.

Descending to Murchison Hut. From the top of the tributary glacier (described above) descend in a south-west direction to join the Murchison Glacier. Continue across to the west side of the glacier until the Murchison Hut becomes obvious on a rocky shelf 150m above the glacier, situated under Mt Cooper.

Traversing to Tasman Saddle. Traverse on the Murchison side to Classen Saddle and then travel south-west toward a rock buttress (2225m) in the centre of the glacier. Turning to the north side of the buttress, pick the best line down into the Murchison Glacier before angling toward Tasman Saddle.

Fig. 53 Classen Glacier overview.

Huss

Mannering

Brodrick

Whataroa Saddle

Sydney King

Tasman Saddle

Murchison Glacier

Acland

11.14

Classen Glacier

Godley Valley →

Don Bogie

Brodrick Peak 2669m

See Routes 9.29 – 9.33.

11.6

From Whataroa Saddle follow the rock and snow ridge of the Main Divide. Alternatively, turn to the western side and climb snow slopes that lead to a point north-east of the summit.

West Face

11.7   Original Route

Drop into the névé from a point west of Whataroa Saddle. Climb the prominent rib on the face, gaining the north ridge, then continue to the summit.

Dave Bamford, John Nankervis, Feb 1978.

11.8   Slab Route   Grade 3

Six pitches of excellent red rock. Start just left of the major left facing corner and finish 100m below, and to the south of the summit (crux 15/16). The slabs can be seen from the Main Divide between Hochstetter Dome and Aylmer. Climbed from the upper Whymper (see the back cover photo).

John McCartney, Sam Bosshard, Feb 1995.

11.9   North Buttress   Grade 3+

Climb the buttress at the head of the true right branch of the Whymper Glacier.

Dave McNulty, Ray Button and four NZMGA course participants, Mar 1986.

Whataroa Saddle 2400m

From Classen Saddle or near to, traverse north-west over the upper slopes of the Classen Glacier to arrive on Whataroa Saddle. The saddle was first gained by Otto Frind and Conrad Kain in 1914 but not used as a crossing until 1953.

Mt Mannering 2669m

11.10

From Whataroa Saddle ascend snow and rock on the Main Divide, passing an overhang near the summit by using a gut nearby or turning to the north-west side. An alternative route from the saddle lies up the slopes on the western side, approaching the summit from the south-west.

Otto Frind, Conrad Kain, Mar 1914.

11.12   West Face

From the Whataroa. Interesting rock slabs and snow patches.

Dave Bamford, John Nankervis, Grant Stotter, Richard Hancock, Feb 1977.

11.13   East Rib

Gained from the Classen Glacier.

Keith McNaughton, John Gamlen, Jan 1967.

Mt Huss 2502m

11.14   North Ridge (Main Divide)

Ascend a rock buttress, west of a snow couloir between the Sustins and Easter Glaciers, from the Classen Glacier. At the head of the couloir use snow and ice slopes to gain the Main Divide north-east of the peak, as close to the summit as possible.

David Hall, Gordon (Snow) Mace, Dec 1935.

11.15   South Ridge (Main Divide)

A steep rock climb. The ridge has three steps, the first can be turned on the left and the second on the right, with an exposed traverse on rock dropping straight to the glacier below. The third step involves easy scrambling.

Noel Sissons, Mary Atkinson, Mar 1979.

11.16   West Ridge

From the Whataroa. A mixed route with good rock.

Dave Bamford, John Nankervis, Grant Stotter, Richard Hancock, Feb 1977.

11.17   West Face

Ian Jowett, Noel Sissons, Mary Atkinson, Dec 1980.

Mt Moffat 2638m

11.18

The peak can be climbed from the south-east ridge via Upton, Bruce Murray and Panorama. Upton can be turned on the north-east side. The south-east snow ridge involves a narrow section of loose black rock that leads onto the southern flanks then onto the summit. Alternatively, the rock face can be climbed directly, leading to the summit.

A J Scott, Alf Brustad, Russell Fraser, Jan 1933.

11.19   From the West

Climb from the Gino Watkins Glacier.

Laurie Osborne, Bruce Waterhouse, John Harrison, B H (Snow) Williams, Jan 1954.

11.20   South Ridge

From the Gino Watkins climb the west face of an unnamed peak (2543m) to access the ridge of Moffat. Descend the north ridge.

John Nankervis, Phil Castle, Grant Stotter, Pat Thorn, Dec 1978.

Mt Livingstone 2561m

11.21

From the col east of Moffat climb snow and ice slopes.

A J Scott, Russell Fraser, Alf Brustad, Jan 1933.

11.22   From the West (then South Ridge)

John Nankervis, Phil Castle, Grant Stotter, Pat Thorn, Dec 1978.

Upton Peak 2328m

11.23

Can be climbed from either Bruce Murray or Panorama (avoiding Bruce Murray).

Will Kennedy, Jack Lippe, Feb 1925 (from Panorama).

Bruce Murray 2120m

11.24

The peak can be climbed from Panorama, from Elizabeth Glacier (gaining the col between the summit and Panorama) and from Easter Glacier.

A J Scott, R H Booth, David Hall, Apr 1931.

Panorama Peak 2117m

11.25

Traverse from Bruce Murray or climb the South East Arête. The north-east approach is described in the Grey Valley section.

T A Fletcher, J Butcher, Feb 1923 (via the South East Arête).

The Grey Glacier

The Grey and Maud Glaciers are no longer joined at their snouts. Both have receded to the point where the terminal lake now separates them (NB map 260-I35, 1996, shows the Grey and Maud glaciers joined). The recession of these glaciers has made access more difficult – but not impossible.

Access

If travelling from Eade Memorial Hut, traverse the west side of the terminal lake, west of Godley Hut, to the Grey Glacier. The icefall mid way up the Grey may prove to be impassable during summer. An alternative route could lie over Gordon Peak.

If travelling from Godley Hut two options are possible. 1) Follow the route described from Eade Memorial Hut. This will initially involve crossing the Godley River - beware - this may not be possible. 2) Cross the river that joins the two lakes below Godley Hut. Follow the isthmus to the Maud Glacier and then traverse over the toe of the ridge descending from Gordon Peak.

Panorama 2117m

11.25

From the North East scramble up scree from the lower Grey Glacier. At bluffs near the head of the ridge, traverse out on to rock faces to the north, then continue to the summit by snow slopes on the western side.

Edgar Williams, Will Kennedy, T A Fletcher, Dec 1917.

Fig. 54 Main Divide peaks (horizon) and the Grey Glacier.

Fig. 55 Peaks of the Grey Glacier.

Frances

Fletcher

Grey Pass

Gordon

11.34

11.32

11.36

Loughnan

Takrouna

Alamein

Grey Glacier

Panorama

11.27

Cassino

Upton Peak 2328m

11.26

Climb directly from the Grey Glacier.

Will Kennedy, Jack Lippe, Jan 1919.

Cassino Peak 2450m

Cassino, Alamein and Takrouna were known as the Grey Virgins, and resisted attempts for many years. Alamein and Takrouna remain unclimbed directly from the Grey.

11.27 South Ridge

Climb from the Grey Névé above the icefall to the hanging glacier. Then follow steep snow and rock to the Main Divide onto the low summit. Traverse under rock pinnacles between the summits and up the right hand face to the summit proper.

John Harrison, Ian Baine, B H (Snow) Williams, Dec 1952.

11.28 From the West

Laurie Osborne, Bruce Waterhouse, John Harrison, B H (Snow) Williams, Jan 1954.

11.29 North Ridge (Main Divide)

Climbed from the Nansen Névé on the Westland side. Descend via a couloir back to the Nansen.

John Nankervis, Phil Castle, Grant Stotter, Pat Thorn, Dec 1978.

Alamein Peak 2361m

11.30

From the Nansen Névé.

Stan Conway, Matt Fowlds, John Sampson, Laurie Ryan, Jan 1949.

Takrouna Peak 2357m

11.31

Climbed from the Nansen Glacier.

John Harrison, B H (Snow) Williams, Laurie Osborne, Bruce Waterhouse, Jan 1954.

Mt Loughnan 2590m

11.32

At the head of the Grey Glacier climb up to two detached rocks at the base of the third buttress east of the peak, then ascend the rock rib to the Main Divide. As an alternative, head up snow slopes west of the detached rocks to the Main Divide, then traverse the serrated ridge turning gendarmes on the south. The first peak is considered the summit.

J Shanks, D A Carty, H Smith, L Dumbleton, Dec 1935.

John Harrison, B H (Snow) Williams, Laurie Osborne, Bruce Waterhouse, Jan 1954 (from the west, then by way of the south ridge).

Mt Alack and the TV Slab as seen from the Cleves Glacier, Fox Névé.

11.32i North West Flank
From the north branch of the Butler.
Don French, Paul Richardson, Jan 1982.

Grey Pass 2253m
From the head of the Grey Glacier climb easy slopes. The Grey icefall is usually negotiable at either edge. Grey Pass should be crossed at its lowest point. Alternatively, climb Seymour to within 50m of the summit and then descend a short couloir which provides access to the west ridge of Seymour.

Seymour Peak 2400m
11.33
Easily climbed from the head of the Grey Glacier.
Will Kennedy, Jack Lippe, Feb, 1925.

11.33i North Ridge from the North Butler Lake
Rob Rowlands, Clive & Wilma Rubens, Wilf Dickerson, Jan, 1983

Mt Frances 2479m
11.34
Climb easy snow slopes from the head of the Grey Glacier.
Will Kennedy, Jack Lippe, Feb, 1925.

Mt Fletcher 2467m
11.35
Traverse from the summit of Gordon. From the col between the two peaks ascend the south ridge to gain the low peak. From the summit of Frances use the north-west ridge. Watch for loose rock - in 1992 a large rock avalanche fell down the east face, crossed the Maud Glacier and continued some way up the other side of the valley.
A J Scott, Alf Brustad, Russell Fraser, Jan 1933 (High Peak).
Will Kennedy, Jack Lippe, Jan 1918 (Low Peak).

Gordon Peak 2090m
11.36
Climb to the col above of the Grey Glacier and then up snow slopes to the summit. Alternatively, climb directly from below the Grey Glacier icefall. The peak has also been climbed from the Maud Glacier, using the south-east ridge (first ascent).

The Maud Glacier
From the Godley Hut cross the river that joins the two lakes. Follow the isthmus to the Maud Glacier (there are some faded red painted circles on the odd rock). From Eade Memorial Hut either follow the route described for the Grey Glacier or head to the Godley Hut (crossing the Godley River) and continue from there.

Alamein Peak
Takrouna
Loughnan
Gordon Peak
Grey Glacier
Fletcher
Grey Pass
Seymour Peak
Frances
Jacqueline Col
Wolseley
Maud Pass
Neish Plateau
Maud Glacier
Ruth Glacier
Godley Glacier →

Lloyd Homer/IGNS

Fig. 56 The Grey and Maud glaciers (looking NW from above the Godley Valley).

Gordon Peak 2090m

11.37

Starting from near the junction of the Maud and Grey Glaciers ascend tussock slopes and a south-east rock face.

Edgar Williams, Will Kennedy, T A Fletcher, Dec 1917.

Mt Sutton-Turner 2437m

11.38

From Jacqueline Col.

David Hall, Gordon (Snow) Mace, Nov 1935.

Jacqueline Col 2314m

This is not a recommended pass to Westland. See Grey or Sealy Passes.

Mt Walton 2403m

11.39

From either Maud Pass or Jacqueline Col.

First ascent from Neish Plateau.

Maud Pass 2370m

Straightforward from either the Maud Glacier or Neish Plateau.

Ski Touring Option: The Maud Glacier is an excellent ski tour, particularly when combined with a round trip: Neish Plateau – Cumine Peak – Maud Pass – Maud Glacier. Best when the glacier lake is frozen.

Mt Kennedy 2492m

11.40

Climb sound rock from Maud Glacier to low peak and then traverse poor rock to high peak.

Edgar Williams, A J Scott, R H Booth, Jan 1932.

Mt Wolseley 2558m

11.41   South Ridge

From the Maud Glacier gain the ridge just short of the summit.

B R Young, I R Wood, H Elder, J Porter, Jan 1951 (full ridge)

Neish Plateau and the Godley Glacier

Access

From Godley Hut

Continued recession of the Godley Glacier and fluctuating lake levels has affected the access around the terminal lake significantly. Conditions change constantly and so a variety of routes should be kept in mind when planning a visit the Godley Glacier. There are three possible routes.

1) Travel up the true left side of the terminal lake using a shelf near to the waterline. Check the lake level first. Some parties have become bluffed. Also, significant rockfall hazards exist.

2) Use the true right side of the terminal lake, but this involves crossing the lake outflow.

3) Climb up behind the hut to a flatter part of the slope at about 1600m elevation. Traverse at this level, following the valley side all the way to the tarn west of the Trident Glacier. Continue past the tarn to the stream that drains from the Trident. Descend this stream to the Godley Glacier.

Currently route 1) is considered impassable. Route 3) has been used successfully by a number of parties. During winter access is much improved as the glacier lake is typically frozen.

The Neish Glacier is the largest tributary to the Godley Glacier and joins about three kilometres up-valley of the terminal lake. The Neish Plateau area is popular with ski touring parties and climbers alike. Those visiting the plateau may need to use tents or snowcaves for accommodation or access the plateau from Godley Hut in winter when the lake is frozen. A number of peaks, with superb views of Westland, can be climbed from the Neish Plateau.

Once on the Godley Glacier travel up valley turn up the Neish Glacier to negotiate the icefall. The Neish Icefall is often impassable. Instead climb a steep slope to the SW of Sealy Pass and traverse to the middle section of the Neish Glacier. (This traverse is often prone to slab avalanche hazard!). The plateau can also be reached from the Maud Glacier via Maud Pass. Sealy Pass, accessed from the Neish Glacier, allows passage to the West Coast via Scone Creek.

The following peaks can be climbed from the Neish Plateau.

Mt Wolseley 2558m

11.42 East Ridge

Follow the long rocky east ridge from the junction of the Godley and Ruth glaciers, or from nearer to the Neish Glacier. A long and interesting route with good rock on the section between the Neish and Ruth Glaciers.

Richard Tornquist, Noel Strack, Jan 1953.

Wolseley
White Pyramid
Kennedy
Vitoire
Gorrie Peak
Cumine Peak
McKinnon Peak
Neish Plateau
Ruth Glacier
Sealy Pass
Scone Creek
Petermann
Amherst Glacier

Lloyd Homer/IGNS

Fig. 57 The Neish Plateau.

11.43

Climb to the col north of the peak from the Neish Glacier. Then head up a sound rock ridge to the summit.

Will Kennedy, Jack Lippe, Dec 1920.

Mt Kennedy 2492m

Described in the Maud Valley section.

Mt Walton 2403m

11.44

From Maud Pass or the col between White Pyramid.

Will Kennedy, Jack Lippe, Feb 1925.

Frank Barta, K Hall, J Richards, S Maffey, R Bradshaw and one other, Aug 1939.

White Pyramid 2412m

11.45

From the Neish Plateau ascend to the col north of Walton, then follow the Main Divide to the summit.

Edgar Williams, A J Scott, R H Booth, Jan 1932.

Mt Victoire 2517m

11.46

Ascend snow slopes to the north of White Pyramid from the Neish Plateau and climb the snow and rock ridge south of the peak.

David Hall, Gordon (Snow) Mace, Nov 1935.

11.47

From the Neish Plateau, climb to the col north-east of low peak, then follow the Main Divide (loose rock when not snowclad).

11.48 From the North Butler Lake.

John Nankervis, Phil Grover, Phil Castle, Dean Stotter, Oct 1980.

Gorrie Peak 2425m

11.49

Gain the col to the south-west and then traverse along the Main Divide.

S A Wiren, E C A Ferrier, G Lockwood, Dec 1934.

Cumine Peak 2484m

11.50

Traverse along the Main Divide from Gorrie. Alternatively, climb from McKinnon or the col west of, along the Main Divide. Access via the south-west shoulder, from the Neish Plateau, is easy and is also an excellent ski tour.

Johannes Anderson, A Sutton-Turner, Jack Lippe, Will Kennedy, Dec 1920.

McKinnon Peak 2504m

11.51

Traverse from Cumine or climb snow slopes from the Neish Plateau.

Johannes Anderson, A Sutton-Turner, Jack Lippe, Will Kennedy, Dec 1920.

Sealy Pass 1722m

Ascend easy snow slopes to the pass. This is the best route from the Godley Valley to Westland. E.P. Sealy first crossed this pass in 1869 descending to Scone Creek.

Mt Petermann 2346m

11.52

Traverse from Sealy Pass along the rock of the Main Divide, then climb snow slopes west of the summit. Alternatively, cross Sealy Pass to snow slopes on the western side of the peak.

T A Fletcher, A Sutton-Turner, Jack Lippe, Jan 1922.

The following peaks can be climbed from the Godley Glacier.

Mt Shyness 2355m

11.53

Climb from Stewart Saddle or Amherst Glacier. Head up snow slopes onto a snow ridge that leads past a prominent rock pinnacle toward the summit. Alternatively, climb the snow face of Petermann from the Amherst, then over the ridge to easy snow slopes on the Sealy Pass side.

V R McGregor, J Dampier-Crossley, Jan 1961.

Elaine Norton and J Shanks climbed a virgin peak in this area in Jan 1941, which may have been the pinnacle described above.

Stewart Saddle 1905m

Use easy snow slopes of the Amherst Galcier from the Godley Glacier to access the saddle. The saddle can be used to access Westland via the Bettison Stream.

Malthus Peak 2210m

11.54

From the vicinity of Stewart Saddle climb snow slopes to gain the Main Divide slightly west of the peak.

11.55

Climb to the plateau south-west of the peak by any number of routes from the Godley Glacier. From the plateau join the Main Divide or use the rock face to the south.

T A Fletcher, Will Kennedy, A Sutton-Turner, Jack Lippe, Dec 1920.

11.56   South Rib
From the Godley Glacier climb the rock and snow rib which leads onto the peak.
Gary Ball, P Gill, W Hewson, D Henson, P Bennett, Mike Andrews, Dec 1972.

Dennistoun Peak 2315m

11.57
Traverse from the summit of Malthus. Descend the east ridge to the Main Divide col and then climb the west ridge.
T A Fletcher, Will Kennedy, A Sutton-Turner, Jack Lippe, Dec 1920.

11.58
From the plateau to the south-west of Malthus traverse the south-eastern slopes to the Main Divide col between Malthus and the peak. Continue up the ridge to the summit or use the slopes on the Westland side.

11.59
As for 11.58 but continue to and climb the south ridge rather than the Main Divide col.

11.60
Gain the plateau east of the peak by the best route possible from the upper Godley Glacier. Then use steep snow slopes to access a rock ridge that descends to the south from the summit.
G P Raywood, R C Bradshaw, R Freeman, J H Christie, Dec 1938.

McClure Peak 2486m

11.61
From Terra Nova Pass climb the snow and rock south ridge, avoiding large rock buttresses on the eastern side, regaining the ridge about 200m from the summit. This is more difficult than it looks.
Will Kennedy, Jack Lippe, Feb 1925.

11.62
Climb directly from the head of the Godley using a tributary glacier to access the Main Divide west of the summit.
First Ascent Unknown

11.63   North Ridge
Gain the ridge from Hidden Col.
Emma de Lacey, R Pearce, G Watson, Feb 1966.

Terra Nova Pass 2066m
Easy slopes on the Godley side lead to the pass but may be complicated by crevasses late in the season, in which case traverse the rock ledges on the lower slopes of Pyramus. This is a popular route for parties travelling to the Godley from the Havelock Valley via the Saint Winifred Stream or vice versa.
First crossed by Jim & George Dennistoun, Sydney King, Jock Richmond, Jan 1914.

Fig. 58 The peaks of the upper Godley Glacier, including Mt D'Archiac.

Lloyd Homer/IGNS

Pyramus Peak 2253m

11.64

Climb from the head of the Godley to a col south-west of the peak and then up to the summit. Alternatively, climb the northern rock ridge from Terra Nova Pass

Edgar Williams, A J Scott, R H Booth, Jan 1932 (from the Godley).

The Commander 2337m

11.65

Either climb Pyramus from Terra Nova Pass and then follow the north-east rock ridge or gain the ridge directly from the Godley.

Edgar Williams, A J Scott, R H Booth, Dec 1931.

The Onlooker 2449m

11.66

Ascend the western rock ridge directly to the summit from Revelation Col.

Edgar Williams, S H Barnett, Bruce N Turner, Jan 1933.

Revelation Col 2338m

Use the Dennistoun Glacier for access. However, if glacial conditions in the lower reaches are not favourable then use its eastern fringe and traverse the lower slopes of The Commander.

Mt D'Archiac 2875m

This mountain is the highest peak between the rest of the Aoraki/Mt Cook region and the Kaikoura Range. Its size and location allows it to be seen from as far as Ashburton.

11.67   East Ridge

From Revelation Col climb the eastern rock ridge to a sharply defined snow-crest which abuts onto the mountain. Traverse up to the right, over good rock, to a final snow and rock ridge, to the summit. Alternatively, where the snow-crest joins the mountain, a short traverse leads to a couloir, which in turn joins the summit ridge. Another option, suitable in winter/spring involves a rising traverse from Revelation Col, across the north-east face, onto the North Ridge (possibly easier than the East Ridge). Also see route 11.77 from the Forbes River.

Jim Dennistoun, Laurence Earle, Jack Clarke, Mar 1910 (climbed from the Forbes).
Vic Walsh, Keith Curry, Bruce Naylor, Aug 1961.

11.68   North Ridge

At the junction of the Godley and Dennistoun Glaciers ascend the broad based north ridge and a northern snow slope that follows. From here climb to the junction of two rock spurs that border either side of the northern snow slope. Ascend either a rocky couloir or a spur to the east. Traverse along good rock on the narrow north ridge. A large tower can be turned on the east. An interesting rock climb.

Neville Johnson, H J Newberry, Ian Powell, Dec 1934.

The North Face was skiied by Mark Seddon and Kane Henderson in 1999.

Don Bogie

Fig. 59 Mt D'Archiac from the west.

11.69 Trident Glacier Route (then West Ridge)   Grade 3+

From Godley Hut follow the Godley Glacier to Marjorie Falls. Then climb scree slopes north-east of the falls to the Trident Glacier. Snow slopes then lead to the rocky West Ridge. Climb this, enjoying steep and interesting climbing to the summit.

W H Scott, P F Scully, A Thompson, Betty Lorimer, 1935.

Bryan Sissons, Ian Jowett, Aug 1974.

11.70 FitzGerald Stream Route

From Godley Hut travel up the FitzGerald Stream to join the West Ridge at about 2100m. To avoid a steep pitch on the ridge - cross the ridge onto the northern side and traverse the upper slopes of the Trident Glacier. Continue as for route 11.69.

Possible first ascent: Bob Unwin, Jack Stanton, Hallam Smith, 1940

11.71 South West Ridge   Grade 3

Climb up the FitzGerald Glacier to about 2400m and gain the ridge. The ridge up to the junction with the north-west ridge involves some steep snow and the occasional section of poor rock punctuated with gendarmes.

Graeme Fyfe, Alf & Hunter Dowell, Peter Berry, Margaret Jeffereys, Dec 1953 (from the FitzGerald)

Separation Stream

The Separation Stream drains from the southern side of Mt D'Archiac and joins the Godley Valley about 1.5 km from the lower Godley Lake. It is at this point, the southern side of the stream, that most parties leave their 4WD vehicles before walking to Godley Hut or venturing up Separation Stream itself.

The walk up Separation Stream to Separation Col is enjoyable but a little deceptive. For those heading to the col, after having driven in late in the day, there is a 1100m climb from the Godley Valley. In winter this travel can be slowed considerably by deep snow.

Follow the stream mostly on the true right to the Separation Glacier. Depending on conditions, ascend the glacier on the true right and continue up to Separation Col (2256m). Most parties bivvy or tent near to the col or slightly toward Mt Coates. Superb views of Aoraki/Mt Cook are possible on a good day from Coates, not to mention Mt D'Archiac.

The South West Ridge, South Face and South East Ridge of Mt D'Archiac can all be accessed from either the Separation Glacier or Col.

Ski tour option: Separation Stream to Ballium Snowfield.

Mt D'Archiac 2875m

South Face

11.72   The Bandaid Route   Grade 4-
The face has a prominent snow gully just right of a central rock buttress. Move up to and follow the left edge of the gully – climb a short distance to an obvious block, from here move up a left trending corner-groove (crux). Continue up and left to gain the crest of a central rib. Follow the rib to the summit. (McLeod's crampon was held together by elastoplast).
Bill McLeod, Peter Dickson, Nov 1992.

★11.73   South East Ridge   Grade 3
This classic 600m ridge can be climbed from either Separation Col or from the Forbes side. The ridge includes three rock steps the first of which can be turned on the eastern side. The latter two buttresses present more difficult climbing. Above the buttresses the climbing on the ridge becomes more straightforward and beyond the intersection with the East Ridge it usually entails a snow ridge (possibly corniced). In late summer the ridge may involve easy rock scrambling. The easiest descent is via the East Ridge (via a snow couloir first then down the ridge to Revelation Col).
Jack Pattle, Trevor James, Bernie McClelland, Stan Conway, John Sampson, Feb 1951.
Rob Rainsbury, Eric Saggers, Jul 1979.

Separation Col 2256m

Gained from Separation Stream and Glacier on the Godley side and from the Forbes River on the eastern side.

Fig. 60 South West Ridge and South Face of Mt D'Archiac.

Don Bogie

Mt Coates 2400m

11.74

A straightforward climb from Separation Col. Alternatively, ascend snow slopes from the confluence of the Separation and Butcher Glaciers to join the south-east ridge close to the summit. Coates can also be climbed from Twilight Col.

Edgar Williams, A J Scott, R H Booth, Jan 1932.

Twilight Col 2094m

Mt Earle 2410m

11.75

Climb the rock ridge directly from Twilight Col.

Jim Murphy, Hugh Wright, Feb 1912.

Mt Forbes 2583m

11.76

From the Ballium Snowfield.

Edgar Williams, Jan 1932

Climbing Mt D'Archiac from the Havelock Valley

Those intending to climb Mt D'Archiac and/or neighbouring peaks or planning to cross Separation Col into the Godley region will need to use the Havelock Valley for access. Terra Nova Pass can also be used to access the Godley from the Havelock.

Four wheel drive vehicle access beyond Erewhon Station, at the head of the Rangitata River system, and some way up the Havelock, is possible, but access is dependent on the state of the rivers. For those on foot, cross the Clyde River after Erewhon Station and follow the north bank of the Havelock River to Freezing Point. Cross the Havelock River and continue to **Mistake Flats Hut** at the confluence of the Forbes and Havelock Rivers. This is an eight bunk DoC hut (~800m, grid ref: 233-484) and is situated at the back of the flats near the beech forest. From Mistake Flats Hut to Separation Col allow 6-8hrs.

11.77

To get to Separation Col tramp up the Forbes River to gain the South Forbes Glacier. Use the rock buttress half way up and on the south side of the glacier to access the upper slopes and then Separation Col (2256m). From the Col a number of options can be considered:

i) Traverse to Revelation Col and then continue up the East Ridge of Mt D'Archiac (Route 11.67). This is the easiest route from the Forbes.

ii) It is also possible to climb the steep couloir at the head of the South Forbes Glacier.

Also see the South East Ridge and South Face route descriptions (11.72 & 11.73) as these can be climbed from Separation Col.

Shaun Barnett/Black Robin Photography

Fig. 61 The Forbes Valley and Mt D'Archiac. Circle denotes Mistake Flats Hut.

Mt Sibbald 2811m

Although outside the AMCNP boundary, Mt Sibbald is a prominent peak and a popular climb. The usual approach is from the Macaulay Valley. Macaulay Hut, described at the beginning of the Godley Valley section, provides a good base. However, a high bivvy could be useful.

11.78   North Ridge

From the upper reaches of the Macaulay Valley follow the Upper Tindill Stream to gain the saddle north of the peak. Then follow steep glacier slopes south to the north summit - the traverse from the north to the main peak (south) is mostly rock now and has one or two difficult spots.

J Howie, R Wills, Jan 1948.

Ski option: Ski from the South Summit all the way to the Macaulay Valley floor.

11.79

From McKinnon Stream in the Godley, then onto the North Ridge.

Neville Johnson, H J Newberry, Ian Powell, Dec 1934.

A variation: use McKinnon Stream and then scree slopes directly to the North Ridge.

Ross Cullen, Peter Fowler, Pip Lynch, Jeremy McMahon, Dec 1981.

11.80

From Lucifer Flat in the Godley.

Edgar Williams, Will Kennedy, Dec 1917.

11.81 South East Ridge

First climbed as part of a traverse, from the north branch of the Macaulay, using the south-west ridge as a descent.

G D T Hall, A H Hines, L Whitworth, Jan 1936.

Spencer Glacier Area

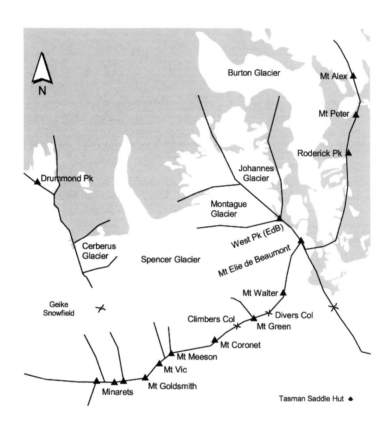

Spencer Glacier Area

This region is relatively inaccessible. It includes the Burton and Spencer glacier systems. Approaches from the West Coast are long and wild. The upper Tasman Glacier provides the quickest approach.

Access

From the Tasman Glacier, Divers Col (Route 7.24)) or the Walter-Elie Col provides the best access to the upper Spencer Glacier. From Centennial Hut travel to the Geikie Snowfield on the Franz Josef Névé, the most popular route is via the Cerberus Glacier, all the way to the Spencer. Alternatively, follow the Styx Glacier then down a rotten ridge and moraine wall onto the Spencer Glacier. There is no air access allowed into the Spencer; the nearest landing sites are the Geikie Snowfield and Centennial Hut.

To reach the Burton Glacier, descend the Spencer Glacier and climb over the toe of the Burton Ridge of Mt Elie de Beaumont. Alternative routes lie via the Whataroa Valley and Callery Saddle, or up the Callery River onto the Burster Range and via Tatare Saddle. These routes are serious, demanding, and long, requiring some information before they are tackled. If you do go into the Spencer Glacier make sure you take a map and compass as all access routes to the Spencer Glacier are committing.

Shelter

A number of large bivouac rocks are found on the terraces beside the Callery River just above where it joins the outflow of the Burton Glacier. Searching in the high basins or glacial and river terraces may reveal more bivouac rocks.

Times

From Tasman Saddle Hut over Divers Col to the upper Spencer Glacier takes about 5 hours. From Centennial Hut or the Geikie Snowfield allow 4-6 hours, down the Styx or Cerberus glaciers. The other routes into the Spencer region take a number of days.

Mt Elie de Beaumont 3109m

12.0   Whymper Spur   Grade 4

This route is situated in the Whataroa Valley and is therefore fairly inaccessible from the Aoraki/Mt Cook side. The Whataroa side of Lendenfeld Saddle provides the quickest access to the route, but is very broken and potentially dangerous. Commencing from the floor of the Whymper Glacier, ascend the prominent spur leading onto the upper part of the Maximilian Ridge. The spur becomes more difficult at the top. The rock is not particularly good. See Fig. 33.

George Harris, K Nannery, Nov 1970.

★ **12.1   Maximilian Ridge**   Grade 4+

From the Burton Glacier gain the ridge via a couloir south of Roderick Peak. Then follow the pinnacled ridge (the lower part of the ridge may be

Fig. 62 The Spencer Face of Elie de Beaumont.

224

avoided by using the névé of the Burton Glacier) up over a prominent step, along a level section, and up 190m of mixed ground to the Anna Plateau under the summit of Mt Elie de Beaumont.

Ed Cotter, Ed Hillary, George Lowe, Earle Riddiford, Jan 1951.

12.2   Burton Spur   Grade 4+

From the upper névé of the Burton Glacier (reached via the lower part of Route 12.1) ascend left onto the crest of the rib. Mixed climbing leads onto a snow arête and snow slopes leading to the summit.

Dave Bamford, Kevin Boekholt, Russell Braddock, John Nankervis, Feb 1984.

West Peak 3054m

12.3   North Ridge and West Ridge   Grade 3+

Climbs on these two ridges are complex. Both have usually been gained via the Johannes Glacier, which is best reached from the lower Burton via a stream bed and couloir on the true left of the tip of the Johannes Glacier. The North Ridge has been climbed from above the upper Johannes Glacier icefall. The ridge consists of steep but pleasant rock climbing.

Dave Bamford, Peter Fullerton, George Kendall, John Nankervis, Feb 1978.

A more intricate route begins on the upper North Ridge, crosses the prominent spur between the North and West Ridges into a couloir, and up the last 200m of the North Ridge.

D A Carty, Jack Cox, G Somerville, Dec 1936.

12.4   The West Ridge   Grade 3

This ridge is gained from the southern edge of the Johannes Glacier. On the last 500m the route leaves the ridge and follows snow leads out onto the great slab above the Montague Glacier, until the upper part of the spur between the Montague and Spencer glaciers is reached. It is a further l00m to the summit.

D E Cooper, D R Lowe, J H Leonard, M Lucas, R Watts, Dec 1959.

P Duncan, H Fairburn, H Gifford, J H Leonard, D Medland, Bev Price, I Simpson, in January of 1963, used the Montague Glacier to gain the upper Johannes Glacier and then repeated the upper West Ridge.

12.5   Montague Spur   Grade 3+

Gain the ridge separating the upper Spencer and Montague Glaciers (good bivouac sites here), head up the edge of the Montague Névé, and onto the large schist slab dropping from the West Peak. Continue up steepening snow to the left of the rib before moving right again onto the rib, which is followed to the West Peak.

Peter Coradine, Ian Jowett, Dec 1970.

Spencer Face

12.6   Carroll-Strong Route   Grade 4

Head up the avalanche chute to the left of the Central Spur, then move left onto a snow and rock rib, which turns into an ice arête before reaching the crux icecliffs. These may vary from season to season. Finish on the ridge connecting the West and East Peaks. An avalanche prone route.

Kevin Carroll, Dick Strong, Dec 1971.

★ 12.7   Central Spur   Grade 4+

An elegant and classic route. Gain the foot of the spur from the left and follow this beautiful line up a snow and ice arête until icecliffs are reached. Later in the summer the arête may involve some technical rock climbing. Depending on the season the icecliffs provide a difficult crux. Then on to the main summit.

Bryan Pooley, Rob Rainsbury, John Stanton, John Visser, Dec 1972.
Steve Elder, Mike Headifen, Aug 1983.

12.8   Right Flank   Grade 3+

Climb up the broad snowface onto the lower shoulder of Mt Elie de Beaumont on the ridge to Mt Walter.

Warrick Anderson, Wilfrid Lammerink, Paul Scaife, Jun 1974.

Mt Walter 2905m

12.9

From the col between Mts Walter and Elie de Beaumont.

Earle Riddiford, Ed Cotter, Jan 1951 (Descended).

West Face

12.10   The Assessor   Grade 4

Starting at the lowermost rocks on the face, ascend very good rock for twelve pitches, crossing two overlaps, en route to the summit (crux 15).

Bill Atkinson, Nigel Shepherd, Feb 1983.

12.11   The Assessed   Grade 4-

100m higher and to the right of The Assessor, follow the left slanting corner. (crux 13).

Stu Allan, Eric Saxby, Feb 1983.

Mt Green 2837m

North West Face

12.12   The Pink Route   Grade 4

From the slopes leading down from Divers Col to the Spencer Glacier, ascend the rock face leading directly to the summit. Ten pitches (crux 17).

Phil Pitham, Mark Whetu, Feb 1983.

12.13   West Ridge   Grade 3

From the Spencer Glacier climb up onto the Edwards Glacier névé below Climbers Col and head left onto the ridge. Follow the snowslopes and rock ribs to the summit. The ridge could also be gained from the slopes below Divers Col.

D A Carty, L J Dumbleton, J D Willis, D J Stanton, Jan 1938.

Mt Coronet 2651m

12.14   Grade 2+

Climb onto the Edwards Glacier névé from the Spencer Glacier. From the névé follow a prominent couloir onto the Divide to reach a small rock peak well south of Climbers Col. Follow the Divide south to Coronet.

Dave Bamford, Peter Fullerton, George Kendall, John Nankervis, Jan 1978.

Mt Meeson 2716m

12.15   West Rib   Grade 3+

From the glacier to the left of the rib, traverse into a narrow couloir breaching the length of the lower rib. Ascend the couloir to a snowslope and then up the final rock arête on good rock (crux).

Dave Bamford, Peter Fullerton, George Kendall, John Nankervis, Jan 1978.

Mt Vic 2807m

12.16   West Rib   Grade 4

From the Spencer Glacier, the lower rib involves climbing in gullies on the right of the icefall (watch out for ice blocks). The gullies may be snow-filled. The route emerges onto a rock arête that continues in a series of buttresses and arêtes before the final snow and rock ridge to the summit. Crux grade 15 in the lower section. The route could have a number of variations.

Mike Andrews, Bill King, Pete Swanson, Jan 1981.

Mt Goldsmith 2909m

12.17   Grade 2+

From the Geikie Snowfield traverse the slopes, below the Minarets, from Mt Matenga to a snow basin across two rock spurs running down from the Minarets. Ascend the basin and onto the Main Divide, then up the summit ridge.

Miss I Corry, Mark Lysons, Jan 1933.

Franz Josef Glacier

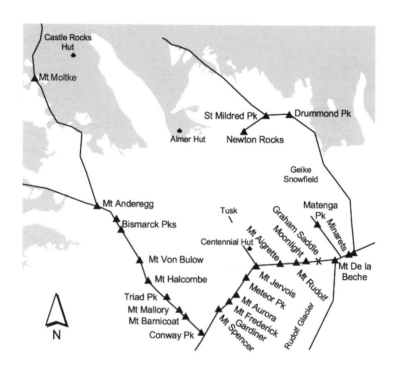

Franz Josef Glacier
Ka Roimata o Hine Hukatere

The extensive névés of the Franz Josef Glacier are bordered in the east by a series of peaks along the Main Divide. To the south, the Fox Glacier and its névés can be reached easily via a number of passes across the Fritz Range and to the north the remote Spencer Glacier Region provides rugged access to the western flanks of Elie De Beaumont and other peaks. The peaks along the Divide offer both short rock routes in summer and ice climbs in spring and winter.

Centennial Hut was built by the New Zealand Alpine Club in 1993 and provides an excellent base for the climbs on the Main Divide. Centennial also provides a much-needed link between the east and west for those traveling from the Tasman Valley, Pioneer and Almer Huts. And, the Franz Josef Névé is a superb ski touring area.

Access
From the east, Graham Saddle (Route 7.11) provides a good route. From the West Coast, routes up the Franz Josef Glacier can often be troublesome. Travel directly up the glacier usually depends on the state of the second icefall below the Almer Ridge and **Almer Hut**. Check with Westland National Park staff or Franz Josef guides about the state of the icefall. A route along the Baird Range to Almer Hut, known as the "Goatpath", exists, but is difficult and not recommended.

A much longer alternative lies via the Fritz Range, which separates the Franz Josef and Fox Glacier watersheds. This route is an excellent ski tour and in winter a fast way from Pioneer Hut (see the Fox Glacier section), provided the weather is fine. From the terminal of the Franz Josef Glacier, commence by crossing the glacier above the first icefall and ascending to **Castle Rocks Hut**. From the hut climb to the saddle above and traverse Mt Moltke, continuing along the undulating Fritz Range, crossing the Sollas Ridge. Further along, Halcombe Col provides quick access to the Fox Glacier. To access the Franz Josef Névé, continue further along and angle up to the Pench Ridge, west of Von Bulow, and follow around the Davis Snowfield to **Centennial Hut**. Centennial Hut is situated on the ridge which extends north-west below Mt Jervois. If using this route, take a map, as route finding can sometimes be difficult - beware of mist later in the day.

If the above routes do not appeal, then good access to the Franz Josef Glacier can be found via the Fox Glacier and West Hoe or Newton passes. It is also possible to fly into the Geikie and Davis snowfields by ski plane or into Almer and Centennial huts by helicopter, from the West Coast, or the Aoraki/Mt Cook side.

Shelter
Almer Hut. Owned and operated by the Westland National Park, the hut has cooking utensils, blankets, radio and 12 bunks (~1680m, grid ref: 841-443).

Castle Rocks Hut. A WNP hut with four bunks – *but no radio* (~1160m, grid ref: 808-466).

*Fig. 63 Upper Franz Josef Névé including the Minarets and Mt De la Beche (winter conditions). Circle denotes Centennial Hut. * Denotes butres with crag routes.*

Centennial Hut. An NZAC hut, it has a radio, cell phone coverage, solar powered lights (including a 12v cell phone re-charging jack!) and 12 bunks. There is also a vestibule including a warden's bunkroom (~2400m, grid ref: 864-406).

Times

Franz Josef Glacier Road to Castle Rocks Hut 4-5 hours (check glacier conditions).
Franz Josef Glacier Road to Almer Hut 1 day (depending on icefall).
The "Goatpath" Route 8-14 hours (local knowledge necessary).
Almer Hut to Centennial Hut 3-4 hours.
Almer Hut to Pioneer Hut 5-7 hours.
Almer Hut to Graham Saddle 4-8 hours.
Centennial Hut to Graham Saddle ~1 hour.
Centennial Hut to Pioneer Hut 2-3 hours.

Ski Touring Routes

- Franz Josef Glacier/Centennial - Castle Rocks Hut (Fritz Range) (B).
- West Hoe Pass and Newton Pass (B, B).
- Mt Von Bulow. Superb view point and easy skiing from Centennial Hut.
- Drummond Peak and St Mildred Peak (A). Easy skiing from Centennial Hut (A).
- Minarets from the west. Very steep. Subject to icefall, avalanches and dangerous crevasses (B/C).
- Rudolf Glacier and Graham Saddle. Best east-west (B). For west-east (D) or carry skis and use crampons.

Newton Rocks 2287m, 2291m

An easy climb from the col leading to St Mildred Peak.

Henry Newton, Ebenezer Teichelmann, William Batson, Jan 1902.

St Mildred Peak 2395m

An easy ascent from either Drummond Peak or Newton Rocks.

First ascent unknown.

Drummond Peak 2514m

13.0   Grade 2-

From Centennial Hut a straightforward climb. The glacier ramp east of the Newton Rocks and St Mildred Peak allows access to the west ridge. A final 30m rock headwall before the summit needs to be negotiated. Stunning views of all the Main Divide peaks including the Spencer Face of Elie de Beaumont can be enjoyed from the summit. In winter, on skis, this is an excellent half-day jaunt.

Alex Graham, Miss Marsden, Mar 1916.

Matenga Peak 2665m

13.1

This is the highest peak on the Lindon Ridge which extends westward from the Minarets. Probably first climbed via its west ridge.

Alex Graham, Miss Marsden, May, 1916.

Minarets 3031m (West), 3040m (East)

13.2   North West Face   Grade 4

From the Geikie Snowfield, traverse round onto one of the feeder arms of the Spencer Glacier and ascend the prominent rock face onto the West Minaret via a series of interconnecting snow ramps that start at the centre of the face. The ramps steepen towards the top and finish three to four easy rope lengths west of the summit.

Dave Bamford, Jim Strang, Mar 1979.

★ **13.3**   Grade 2+

From north of Graham Saddle ascend the prominent snowslopes to the saddle between De la Beche and the Minarets. The rock spurs nearer De la Beche have also been used. It is also possible to traverse the steep slopes under De la Beche, above the Rudolph Glacier, arriving high on the De la Beche Ridge.

Hugh Chambers, Jack Clarke, Feb 1912 (Descended).

Peter Graham, Charles Buchanan, C J Thornton, Feb 1922.

The following peaks at head of the Franz Josef Névé are generally short and easy climbs and so have not been graded. Since the addition of Centennial Hut a number of these peaks and features have received ascents via short and in some cases difficult routes, during summer and particularly in winter – and so an attempt to grade these has been made.

Moonlight Peak 2700m

An easy ascent from Graham Saddle.

Katie Gardiner, Jack Pope, Mar 1929.

Mt Rudolf 2743m

Both Main Divide ridges provide relatively easy scrambling.

Peter Graham, M Graham, Jan 1914.

West Face

13.4   Dawes-McInnes Buttress   Grade 3

From the Franz Josef Névé follow directly up the centre of the face to the summit.

Hamish MacInnes, D Dawe, May 1955.

13.5   **A Nice Affair**   Grade 3

Ascend ice right of the Dawes-McInnes buttress. Using a small corner just right of the direct line to the summit (not the big corner on the right of the face). When the small corner, offering 70° ice, runs out, break left through a short step. Continue up snowfield to summit. Descend to the north via two steep rappels to the névé.

Don French, Sep 1994.

13.6   **Big Day Out**   Grade 3

A line right of Route 13.5 Descend the NE ridge.

First ascent party unknown, Jun 1997.

13.7   Grade 3+

An obvious gully to the right of Rudolf provides an enjoyable ice climb in spring/winter. It joins the Main Divide approximately 200m south of the summit. A cruisy half-day option.

First ascent unknown

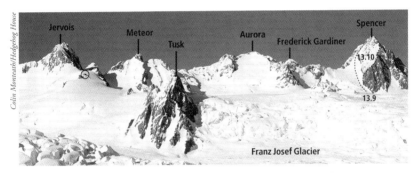

Fig. 64 Mts Jervois – Spencer, Franz Josef Glacier. Circle denotes Centennial Hut.

Aigrette Peak 2665m

An easy climb from the Divide or from the Franz Josef Névé.

Frank Alack, Katie Gardiner, Mar 1937.

Jervois 2630m

Easy scrambling on the northern Divide ridge. The southern Divide ridge is steeper and has good rock.

Alex Graham, B Marsden, Apr 1916.

★ **13.8**   **North West Ridge**   Grade 2+

Follow the ridge above Centennial Hut over two distinct gendarmes and onto the summit. Good rock. An excellent warm-up before breakfast.

Miss I Corry, Mark Lysons, Jan 1933.

When iced up the south-west face of Jervois looks to have plenty of new route potential. Some short crag-style routes have been developed on the rock buttresses near Centennial Hut by Peter Taw and John Entwisle. The first route (crux 18) is situated south-west of the hut, on the third buttress from the left as you face it. The second route (crux 20) is on the distinctive red buttress north-east of the hut, and north of Jervois. This route takes a groove.

Meteor Peak 2624m

The ridge from Jervois traverses a small peak and descends a short steep section before easy scrambling leads to the summit. The southern Divide ridge is steepish and rotten.

Katie Gardiner, Jack Pope, Mar 1929.

Mt Aurora 2663m

A small snow peak easily climbed via the north Divide ridge, or via the north-west snowslopes from Franz Josef Névé.

Alex Graham, B Marsden, Apr 1916.

Mt Frederick Gardiner 2680m

Usually traversed along the Divide. See Route 7.10.

Katie Gardiner, Jack Pope (probably in the early 1930s)

Colin Monteath/Hedgehog House

13.16
13.14
13.15
13.10   13.12   13.13   Davis Snowfield

Fig. 65 Western and south-western aspects of Mt Spencer.

Mt Spencer 2788m

The main Divide ridges of Spencer, especially the south ridge, are notoriously rotten. The western aspects are comprised of excellent rock, however, and the South West Face offers plenty of scope for winter/spring ice routes.

13.9   North Ridge   Grade 1+

Ascend a mixture of good and bad rock just west of the northern Divide ridge. It is usually covered by snow through to mid-summer and serves as a good descent route (but watch the schrund).

Ebenezer Teichelmann, Alex Graham, Mar 1914.

13.10   North West Ridge   Grade 2+

The ridge rises steeply from the Franz Josef Névé with good rock and then eases back and leads up to the summit.

Frank Alack, H K Douglas, Jan 1936.

13.11

A variation to the North West Ridge: climb the face to the right. The first pitch and a half is straightforward and is followed by five pitches of 14-15 on good rock, to where it meets the NW Ridge. Some small roofs provide the cruxes.

Carol Nash, K Longhurst, Feb 1986.

(B McKerrow and S Drake also climbed another variant in the general area in Apr 1991.)

13.12   North West Pinnacle   Grade 4-

Between the North West Ridge and the West Buttress is a steep rib of excellent rock ending in a small pinnacle.

Carol McDermott, Craig Stobo, Jan 1985.

★ 13.13   West Buttress   Grade 4-

A relatively long but not especially difficult route, on excellent quality and steep rock, which leads directly to the summit (crux 15).

Phil Castle, Phil Grover, Jan 1981.

South West Face

13.14   Acid Punch   Grade 4+

An ice route that follows the gully immediately to the right of the West Buttress. It arrives on the summit ridge 10m west of the summit. Roughly four pitches (the first two can be thin, depending on ice coverage). Best in winter/spring.

Anjali Pande, Alex Palman, Sep 2000.

★ 13.15   Jungle Drums (South West Buttress)   Grade 4

This route is situated just right of the West Buttress and follows nine pitches (crux 16) of excellent rock. Claimed by many but first climbed by:

Peter Taw, Alistair Byron, Feb 1989.

★ 13.16   Pitch Black   Grade 4+

Takes the second narrow ice gully about 30m right of the Jungle Drums Buttress. The climb arrives on a col 20m east of the summit. Descend gullies to the north (Route 13.9). Again, good in winter/spring.

James Wright, Alex Palman, Sep 2000.

Fig. 66 South West Face of Mt Spencer.

Conway Peak 2899m

13.17   Grade 2-

From the Franz Josef Névé ascend to Frenchay Col (2685m) and up the Main Divide ridge before turning west and up to the summit.

Miss I Corry, Mark Lysons, Jan 1933.

The first ascent of Barnicoat (and so presumably Triad and Mallory) was by Peter Graham, Julian Grande, J Milne, Mar 1923.

Triad can be climbed on the Franz side from West Hoe Pass.

Alex Palman

Centennial Hut overlooking thre Franz Jsef Glacier and the West Coast.

Fox Glacier

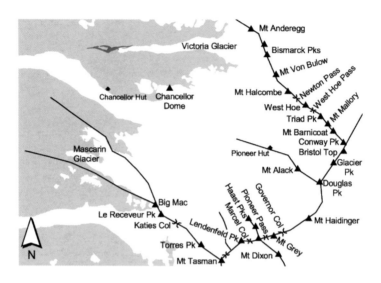

Fox Glacier

Te Moeka o Tuawe

This is the most popular high climbing area on the West Coast. Pioneer Hut provides an excellent climbing base with access to numerous recommended climbs on the 3000m peaks surrounding the head of the Fox Glacier. The routes are generally demanding but by starting from a high base their seriousness is reduced. The whole area is an excellent winter and spring ski touring region. As access is not easy most parties elect to fly in by ski-plane or helicopter.

Access

From the east the best route is via Governor Col (see Route 6.48) from Haast Ridge or Plateau Hut (crossing the East Ridge of Dixon). Other routes from Plateau Hut, such as Marcel Col, are considerably more difficult but can be quick in hard conditions. The route via Graham Saddle is circuitous, involving crossing the Franz Josef Glacier névé and West Hoe Pass, but it provides a beautiful and reasonably safe high alpine journey.

From the West Coast the best route is up the Fox Glacier. From the glacier terminus head up the left side (north) of the glacier to get onto the glacier proper. Cross over the white ice to the south side and drop into a rocky gully between the glacier margin and the scree/moraine. Follow this gully until opposite the Victoria Falls. Cross the glacier again to the north side and follow rocks beside the glacier until a prominent bluff, next to a creekbed, is reached. Continue past this, moving off the ice to gain a vegetated shelf. Continue for another 150m and then turn left up a creekbed/track that weaves up through the vegetation to the western end of the Chancellor Shelf. The historic **Chancellor Hut** is situated at the upper end of the shelf. Conditions on the Fox Glacier, more specifically where parties need to get on and off it, change quickly. Check current conditions with Alpine Guides Westland or DoC.

Beyond Chancellor Hut, continue to the top of the shelf and then drop onto the "the trough", a flat section near the edge of the Fox Glacier. Then follow the edge of the glacier keeping hard under Chancellor Dome. Crevasses at this point can present problems late in the season. From here, head up the left side of the glacier, toward Von Bulow, and then swing around, to travel up the Fox Glacier parallel to the Fritz Range before finally angling across to the prominent depression known as the Pioneer Gap between the upper and lower Pioneer Ridge. Ascend the snow slopes close to the toe of the upper Pioneer Ridge (but beware of slab avalanches in winter and spring). **Pioneer Hut** is situated on the west side of the gap.

A popular descent route from Pioneer Hut, especially on skis in winter, is along the Fritz Range described under the Franz Josef Glacier section. This route can be accessed either from West Hoe or Newton passes (and traversing above the Franz Josef Névé) or via Halcombe Col.

Other access and/or descent routes lie along the Victoria Range starting from Rocky Creek or along the southern side of the Fox Névé via the Paschendale Ridge and Boyd Creek. The former is not recommended because of its length and the latter because of rockfall danger in Boyd Creek.

Air access is also possible. Ski-planes land under the South Face of Douglas, about 30 minutes from Pioneer Hut. Helicopters and ski-planes also land on the south side of the Fox Névé, on the Big Mac landing strip, below Katies Col. Chancellor and Pioneer huts can also be accessed by helicopter.

Shelter

Chancellor Hut. A classic hut from a bygone era situated in a spectacular spot on the Chancellor Shelf. Westland National Park staff are doing a superb job restoring this old hut to its former glory. It has friendly keas and a radio. The toilet has one of the best views in New Zealand. There are 12 bunks (~1250m, grid ref: 762-401).

Pioneer Hut. Owned by NZAC and managed by WNP. The hut is serviced with cooking utensils and a radio. This 15 bunk hut is also a popular ski-mountaineering base (~2380m, grid ref: 822-380).

Ski touring routes

- Marcel Col. Provides access to Lendenfeld Peak (and Mt Tasman) (B).
- Katies Col. Subject to crevasses (A/B).
- Pioneer Hut - Chancellor Hut (C). Superb ski run. Upper névé (B), lower névé (C).
- Fritz Range. Superb exit from the Franz and Fox Glaciers. Recommend overnight at Castle Rocks Hut (4 bunks only), although one day is fine (B/C).
- Access from the Fox Glacier (B).

Times

Fox Glacier Road to Chancellor Hut 5-7 hours.
Chancellor Hut to Pioneer Hut 5-6 hours.
Pioneer Hut via the Paschendale Ridge to the Fox Glacier Road 9-10 hour.
(Don't forget this time is going downhill. It's slower coming in.)
Pioneer Hut to Castle Rocks Hut, via the Fritz Range, 6-9 hours.
(This is a walking time. Skiers will make faster time.)
Pioneer Hut to Centennial Hut 1.5-2.5 hours.
(Also refer to the Franz Josef Glacier section for times.)

Halcombe 2659m

14.0   North Couloir   Grade 3-

A popular half-day outing rewarded with fantastic views of the Main Divide peaks and the Franz Josef Névé. There are a number of routes. The easiest appears to be the narrow gully on the north side, accessed from the flat col west of the peak.

Alex Graham, Ebenezer Teichelmann, Henry Newton, Feb 1907 (Possibly via a different route).

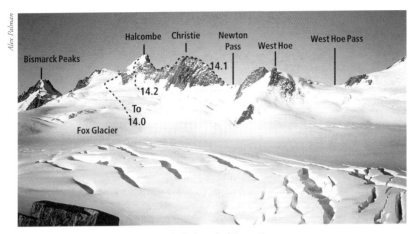

Fig. 67 Peaks north of Pioneer Hut.

Fig. 68 Halcombe Peak from the north.

241

Fig. 69 Peaks north-east of Pioneer Hut.

14.1   **East-West Traverse**   Grade 3-
From Christie follow the ridge to Halcombe.
Frank Alack, H K Douglas, Dec 1935 (Traversed both Christie and Halcombe).

14.2   **Pioneer Face**   Grade 2+
The broad snow face that can be seen from Pioneer Hut.
Anne Stocker, Franz Barta, Feb 1941.

14.2i
A short loose rock band to the west followed by snowslopes to the summit. Climbed from near the same col as Route 14.0.

14.2ii   Grade 3
A good quality rock buttress on the Franz side of Halcombe offers a worthwhile three pitch route. The last pitch is desperately loose however, so rapping off is recommended.
Peter Taw, Alistair Byron, 1988.

Christie 2636m

14.3
From Newton Pass traverse the ridge to the summit.
Frank Alack, H K Douglas, Dec 1935.

Newton Pass 2492m

This pass can be used to access the Franz Josef Névé, and is especially useful for those parties travelling from Centennial to Chancellor Hut.

West Hoe 2574m

Straightforward from the Franz Josef side.

Peter Graham, Frank Alack, Katie Gardiner, Mar 1929.

A J Rycroft, H Pfrunder, Franz Barta, Sep 1941 (on skis).

West Hoe Pass 2501m

This is the most commonly used pass on the upper Fritz Range for travel to and from the Franz Josef. Late in the summer a schrund can present difficulties, in which case Newton is a good alternative.

Triad Peak 2649m

Relatively straightforward from West Hoe Pass, on the Franz side.

First ascent unknown.

Mallory 2756m

14.4   Grade 2

The snow ramp from the Franz Josef side, involves some rock near the summit.

E Sealy, I Johnson, David Lewis, J T Holloway, Jan 1937.

South Face

14.5   Grade 4

A seven pitch mixed route on the left side of the face.

John Entwisle, Ross Clapcott, Gerry Kennedy, Fiona Mackenzie, Trevor Streat, Nick Cradock, Dec 1990.

★ **14.6   The Thing**   Grade 4+

Direct to the left summit. Similar in difficulty to Douglas Peak (L. Couloir), but with more continuous steepness and less slogging. A five star route according to the first ascent team. Seven pitches. (Alpine Ice 4).

Nick Cradock, Matt Wilkinson, S Hall, Dec 1990.

14.7   Irvine   Grade 5-

A deep five pitch chimney left of centre. At the top sneak around to the left to avoid the overhang. Descend the gully left of the face (one rap at the bottom). (Alpine Ice 4+).

Nick Cradock, Dave Vass, Oct 1996.

14.8   The Balcony Line   Grade 4+

Immediately right of the main rock buttress. The route lies directly under the summit. The first few pitches are relatively straightforward but steeper ground (up to 80°), including chandeliers, above provides the crux. Continue up the obvious line to the crest of the west ridge below the summit. Rappel down the Franz side on good rock bollards to a snow slope (beware of snow conditions in spring). Seven pitches.

Bruce Hasler, Dean Staples, Tarn Pilkington, Oct 1996.

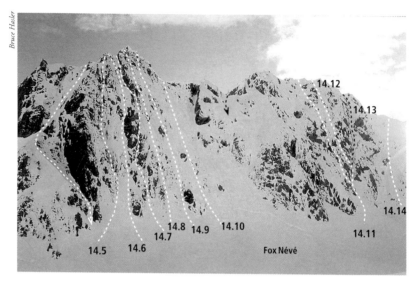

Fig. 70 South Face of Mts Mallory and Barnicoat.

14.9 Grade 5-

Seven pitches of ice up to 85° (descended north gully).
M Ruth, E Breitinger, Nov 1993.

14.10   Right Side Grade 3+

Seven pitches. Descend into the Franz (one rap) or rap the route. (Alpine Ice 3).
Nick Cradock and others from a guides course, 1993.

Barnicoat 2800m

The route by which the first ascent of this peak was made is not clear.
Peter Graham, J Milne, Julian Grande, Mar 1923 (possibly from the Franz side).

South Face

14.11   Rope Boy Grade 4+

Start up the obvious corner-ramp, directly under the high peak, moving left a quarter of the way up. Join ice patches by zig zagging, finishing between the east (high) and west peaks. About half way up there is a rock band (crux) with a chimney that connects the upper and lower snowfields. Descent: head over the west peak to a low point before Mallory (may involve an abseil), then a short steep rappel onto a snowfield to the south-west, then backclimb or rappel to the néve. A very pleasant 6 pitch mixed climb.
Don French, Mar 1993.

14.12   Lust for Life   Grade 5+

Similar to Rope Boy. Climb the corner-ramp to the summit. In a good ice year you could continue directly up after the third pitch. Steep and sustained. Seven pitches.

Craig Jefferies, Allan Uren, Sep 1999.

14.13   Tigger   Grade 4+

Ascend the obvious right leaning ramp (as for Route 14.12), finishing right of the summit. About six pitches of sustained 70-80° mixed climbing involving vertical bulges. First ascensionists rapped into the Franz.

David Kneen, Marcel Geelen, Dec 1999.

14.14   East Shoulder   Grade 3+

Right of the South Face of Barnicoat, just right of the dominant bluff. The top half sports ice up to 55°. A good climb for those not looking for a big day out. First ascent party descended the route.

Stu Gray, Brian Williamson, Jan 1987.

Conway Peak 2899m

★ **14.15   Moonshine Buttress**   Grade 4

Climb the south-west rib from the névé for about nine rope lengths on good rock. Sustained grade 14/15 climbing with a crux of 17. The route weaves its way up the pinkest rock to the right of the broad flat buttress. Although descending into the Franz is possible it is not recommended. Abseil the route, using a range of fixed gear. A superb route – put this one on the list.

Greg & Deanne Landreth, Apr 1984.

Previously on Barnicoat, the Moonshine Buttress has been moved on to Conway, as it marginally closer to that massif and summit.

14.16   Grade 4-

A couloir to the left of the peak contains one steep pitch (65-70°). Arriving on the ridge west of the peak, traverse the summit and descend to Frenchay Col.

Stu Gray, Brian Williamson, Jan 1988.

14.17   Grade 2+

Ascend a couloir to the right of Conway onto the Main Divide and traverse to the summit.

R Bates, E McMahon, Nov 1976.

14.18   Grade 2+

From Bristol Top head along the pinnacled Main Divide and onto the summit just off the Divide.

Alex Graham, Henry Newton, Feb 1907.

Bristol Top 2891m

14.19   Grade 2+

From the névé of the Explorer Glacier climb mixed ground (with rotten rock) to just south of the summit.

Alex Graham, Henry Newton, Feb 1907.

14.20   Grade 3

The Divide ridge from Glacier Peak is a pinnacled, enjoyable climb. Also refer to Upper Tasman Glacier Section.

Harold Porter, Vic Williams, Dec 1930 (from the east).

Glacier Peak 3002m

★ **14.21   West Ridge**   Grade 3+

Rises in a series of rock towers inter-connected by snow ridges. Possibly a safer and more enjoyable alternative to the West Face, offering a view onto the face for descent purposes. Deceptively good.

First ascent unknown.

14.22   West Face   Grade 2+

From the Explorer Néve ascend the snowface directly to the summit, avoiding icecliffs and schrunds where necessary. This route is subject to avalanches, particularly in the afternoon. Late in summer the route can become cut off due to crevasses and schrunds. The rock rib on the right, below the Glacier-Douglas col, can provide alternative access to the snowslopes. The summit of Glacier Peak and the ridge near, can become dangerously corniced. Otherwise a straightforward climb, providing good access to and from Douglas.

Alex Graham, Henry Newton, Ebenezer Teichelmann, Jan 1907.

John Glasgow, George Harris, J Andrews, A Banks, Aug 1967.

Douglas Peak 3077m

14.23   North Divide Ridge   Grade 3-

Ascend either Glacier Peak or to the Glacier-Douglas col. Follow the snow ridge to a short 30m ice/rock step to the summit ridge. This is the best way off Douglas and usually involves one abseil. Descend Route 14.22.

Frank Alack, F Gardiner, T Sheehan, Apr 1931.

14.24   North Face   Grade 4

Ascend the snow slopes under the West Ridge and up in to a narrow couloir to the right of a prominent rock buttress. Where the couloir ends, climb the mixed rock and snowface to the summit. (Routes have been descended on the left of the face, but this is not a good idea.)

Bill Denz, Ian Ross, Nov 1972.

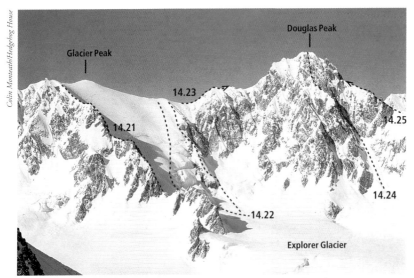

Fig. 71 West Ridge of Glacier Peak and the North Face of Douglas Peak.

★ **14.25   Pioneer Ridge**   Grade 3+

Usually gained from the Explorer Glacier. An exhilaratingly exposed route which follows an arête, a rock step, another arête and then leads up to the final rock wall which provides the crux. If the top rocks are iced turn this rock step on the South Face.

Alex Graham, Henry Newton, Ebenezer Teichelmann, Jan 1907.

There are a series of gullies on the south side of the Pioneer Ridge, 200m east of Pioneer Hut and adjacent to the Cleves Glacier. When in condition (spring, winter) these gullies provide good short ice climbs. Descend on to the Explorer Névé. First ascents are unknown.

South Face

Although the main routes on the face are described below, some variations exist, including a line west of the Left Couloir, arriving on the Pioneer Ridge between Alack and Douglas. Descend a loose gully to the Explorer Névé.

(Possibly) John & Malcolm McNamee, Jun 1982.

★ **14.26   Left Couloir**   Grade 5-

Follow the narrow couloir that gradually widens and meets the central arête. Continue up and traverse into the upper Central Couloir and up to the summit. A classic and highly recommended climb.

George Harris, Murray Jones, Dec 1968.

Bill Denz, Chris Timms, Aug 1971.

247

Fig. 72 South Face of Douglas Peak.

★ **14.27   Central Couloir**   Grade 5+

Follow the lower right couloir to near the foot of the obvious narrow notch (at 2/3 height), then traverse leftwards into the Central Couloir. Ascend steep ice, for a couple of pitches, which gradually relent, leading to the summit. Superb.

Nick Cradock, John Davie, Colin Dodge, Rolland Logan, William Trengrove, Aug 1977.

14.28   Right Couloir   Grade 5

Climb the couloir to an obvious deep notch, which can be ascended or else avoided using a ramp on the left. Then exit via a wide couloir onto the Ayres Ridge.

Bill Denz, Ian Ross, Nov 1972.

Colin Dodge, Andrew Smith, Aug 1973.

14.29   Far Right Rib   Grade 4+

Follow the rock rib, right of the Right Couloir, which joins the Ayres Ridge.

Geoff Bartram, Ben Read, Jan 1979.

14.30   Ayres Ridge   Grade 4

An unrelenting ridge between Mt Haidinger and Douglas Peak with many rock towers, varying in soundness. The final rise to the summit of Douglas is probably the hardest section and can be avoided on the east.

Harry Ayres, Bruce Gillies, Feb 1953.

Mt Alack 2759m   Grade 2+

All the ridges, except the North Ridge, which is reportedly very loose, provide pleasant short climbs from Pioneer Hut.

Frank Alack, H K Douglas, W E Wilson, Dec 1934

George Harris, G Hasler, T Choate, Ian McGregor, Aug 1966.

★ The TV Slab

14.31

A steep slab of rock, west of Alack, above the Cleves Glacier, offers good crag climbing. It gained notoriety and a name when Graeme Dingle and others climbed it for a TV crew during the 70's (one pitch; crux 15/16).

South Face

Over the years several short ice routes have been climbed. Who actually climbed – and recorded them – first, is somewhat unclear. Here are a couple:

14.32   Southern Gully

Six pitches of 50-60° ice.

Paul Wopereis, A Taylor, Feb 1985.

14.33   Alack Attack   Grade 4+

A direct seven pitch line to the summit. The first three pitches are on the icefields and the next four are on the upper wall. A good short technical climb that involves some mixed ground. (Alpine Ice 4).

Nick Cradock, A Marquis, Dec 1996.

Colin Monteath/Hedgehog House

Fig. 73 West Face of Haidinger.

Mt Haidinger 3070m

14.34   Haidinger-Douglas Col   Grade 3
From the Albert Névé, beyond the ski-plane landing strip, ascend the snowslopes left of the West Face routes.

Joe Fluerty, Mark Lysons, M H Williams, Feb 1934 (Descended).

West Face
Classic climbs. Many variations exist on the face. The far left buttress, the gully between the buttresses, and a narrow gully right of the Right Buttress have all been climbed. The most prominent routes are:

★ 14.35   Left Buttress   Grade 3+

From the névé, 200m of pleasant scrambling on good rock (crux 10) is followed by 40° snowslopes and final exit gullies onto the South Summit. Superb climbing.

Jim Jolly, John Stanton, Dec 1969.

★ 14.36   Right Buttress   Grade 4-

Excellent rock climbing, best followed up a weakness on the right side (crux 12), although the centre of the buttress has been used (crux 15). Follow the snowslope to exit onto the South Summit.

Graeme Dingle, Peter Gough, George Harris, Murray Jones, J Andrews, Dec 1967.

14.37   West Ridge   Grade 3

From the névé gain the rounded rib beside the West Face, heading up easy mixed ground and tending out left to finish up the same summit gullies as the West Face routes.

First ascent party unknown.

Keith Woodford, Bruce Nowell, John Perrin, Aug 1971 (taking a line right of *the Right Buttress*).

14.38   Albino Merino   Grade 4

The couloir between the West and South Ridges.

Dave Crow, Lyn Bowering, Sep 1985.

★ 14.39   South Ridge   Grade 3-

If climbed from Governor Col, a step halfway along the ridge must be ascended, otherwise the ridge is fairly straightforward (beware of cornices) until the last 100m of rock, which if iced, can be tackled either by traversing out slightly on the East Face or up the couloir to the west.

Jack Clarke, Edward FitzGerald, Mattias Zurbriggen, Feb 1895.

(Possibly) T Choate, G Hasler, Aug 1966.

14.40   Grade 3-

The ridge can be gained at many points. The most elegant way lies up the arête which reaches the ridge 400m before the summit.

Joe Fluerty, Mark Lysons, M H Williams, Feb 1934.

Grey Peak 2882m

A short easy ascent from either Governor Col or Pioneer Pass.

Harold Porter, J Milne, A Ritchie, Feb 1923.

Mt Humdinger 2796m

From the col with Grey Peak it is an easy ascent.

★ 14.41   Grade 3

The North West Rib provides 150m of sound rock climbing on red rock (crux 14).

Ian Whitehouse, Brin Williman, Dec 1971.

14.54ii

Haast Corner

14.54i

14.53

14.52

14.51

14.50

14.49

West

Middle Pk

14.47

14.46

High Pk

14.44

14.43

14.42

Humdinger

To Pioneer Hut

Pioneer Pass

Dixon

Grey

Governors Col

Grand Plateau

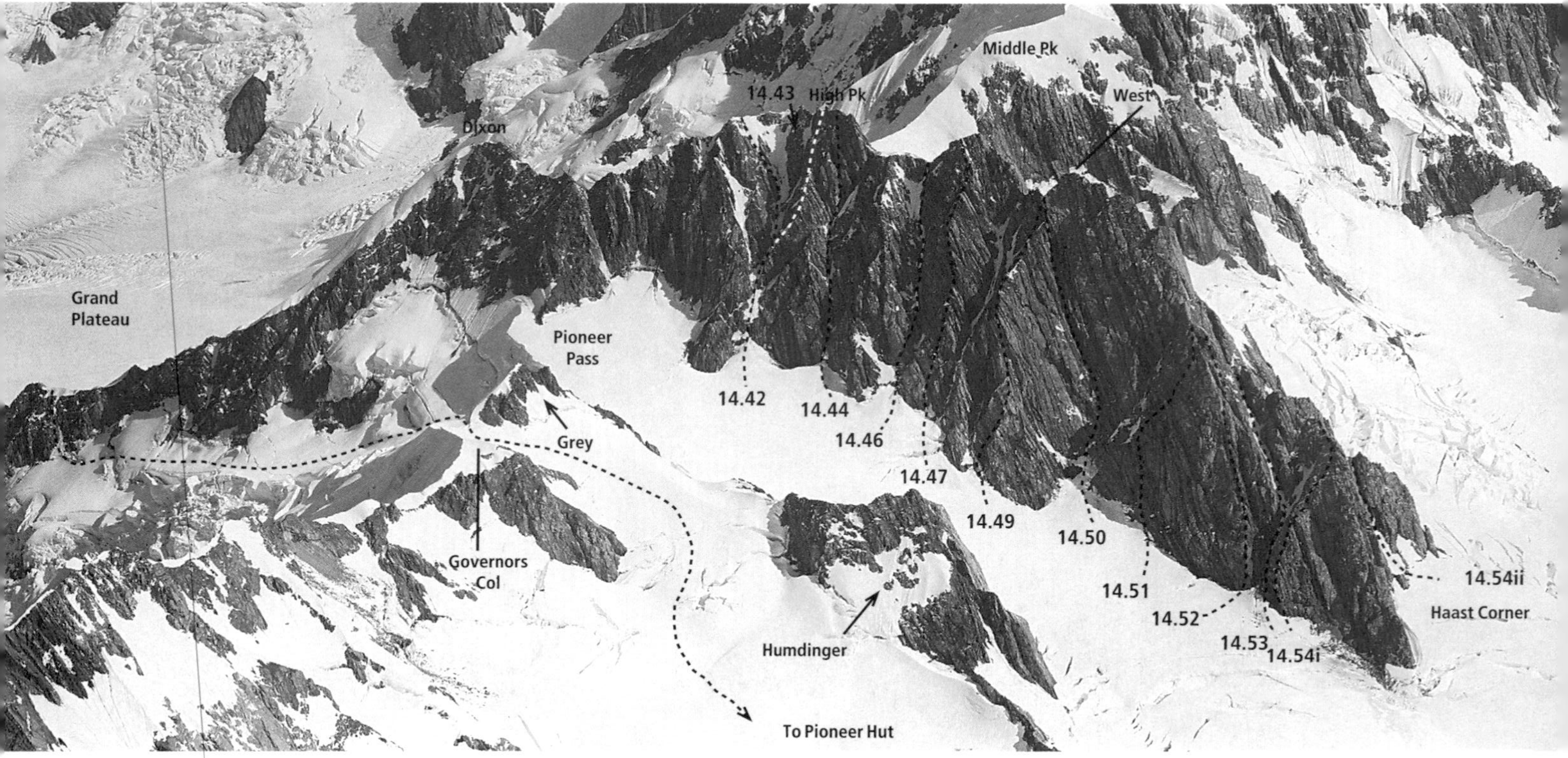

Fig. 74 The three peaks of Mt Haast from the north.

The rock on the western slopes offers pleasant climbing. The first ascent from this direction was by Frank Alack, H K Douglas, W E Wilson, Dec 1934.

Mt Haast 3114m

High Peak

14.42   **From Pioneer Pass**   Grade 3-

Ascend the prominent couloir 150m west of the crest of Pioneer Pass, reaching the Main Divide about 100m east of where the Haast massif abuts the Divide.
Mavis Davidson, Rod Hewitt, A F Reid, Jan 1955.

14.43   **North Spur**   Grade 3

Gained from a quarter of the way up Route 14.42. Climbing is steepish without being technical. The rock is fairly sound to begin with and very shattered towards the top.
Jack Murrell, Bev Noble, Jan 1973.

14.44   Grade 4+

Ascend the next obvious gully right of Route 14.42, then up mixed ground, the rock being the more difficult.
John Goulstone, Mike Rockell, Aug 1982.

Middle Peak 3099m

14.45   **From High Peak**   Grade 3+

An exposed scramble over loose rock that can be complicated by icy conditions.
Frank Alack, H K Douglas, Jan 1936.

14.46   Grade 3-

The prominent couloir to the left of the North East Rib has been used for ascent and descent. The route comes out 80m east of the Middle Peak.
Mike Rockell, Michael Venz, plus party of three, Aug 1979.

14.47   **North East Rib**   Grade 4-

A direct climb up a series of steps on the rib, the lower and middle sections of which are somewhat loose. Crux pitches of grade 12 but nowhere very difficult, unless iced up.
Austin Brookes, Peter Moore, John Trotter, Jan 1973.

14.48   **Middle-High Peak Col**   Grade 3-

Ascend from the upper Marcel Glacier via a snow couloir.
Harold Porter, Jack Pope, Mar 1933. A variant was added by M Radajewski and A Slater in Jan 1994.

West Peak 3065m

A predominantly rock peak with plenty of scope for new variations, especially on its south-west face.

14.49 North East Rib Grade 4-

500m of climbing consisting of four rock buttresses with linking snow ridges. The lower buttress is comprised of good rock, the second is steep rotten rock, and the remainder good rock.

Austin Brookes, Bruce Farmer, Ralph Miller, Jan 1978.

14.50 Atkinson-Hall Route Grade 4+

Ascend the face right of the North East Rib via an ice gully with a rock crux (15/16) at $^2/_3$ height. The top section is on generally poor rock.

Bill Atkinson, Rob Hall, Nov 1981.

14.51 Nash-Aimer Route Grade 4

A face route that starts between the Atkinson-Hall and North Spur routes. From the bottom move gradually left until the North Spur route is visible, move right over chossy ground then straight up to join the North Spur route, climbing 20m of superb exposed slab. This route meets the North Spur route where it flattens then continues to the summit. Good red rock provides cruxes of 16/17 and allows good pro.

Carol Nash, Greg Aimer, Jan 1986.

14.52 North Spur Grade 3+

Starting just right of Route 14.51. Traverse right across a ledge low on the spur and then ascend the rib until the large gully on the right meets the top of the rib. Then ascend the face above on excellent rock. Higher up the ridge flattens out before rising again to the summit.

Harry Ayres, G Harrow, A C Rattray, Apr 1952.

14.53 Couloir Route Grade 3

Ascend the prominent couloir between the North Spur and the West Ridge. The couloir turns left higher up and the route follows the rock face described in Route 14.52.

First ascent party unknown.

14.54 West Ridge Grade 3+

The ridge drops from the summit to Haast Corner. There are a number of variations on the lower section.

i) Bohny-Sidler Spur Grade 3+

Ascend the rib to the right of Route 14.53 to gain the ridge proper, ascend to a prominent gendarme, which can be turned on the north or traversed, and then up the face, where the North Spur joins the ridge, to the summit.

H Bohny, T Sidler, Jan 1955.

ii) Couloir Grade 3+

A small couloir separating the north-west extremities of the ridge was used by E R B Graham and D J Heraud, Feb 1957 and a route 150m further west was climbed by Ron Dickie and Gordon Hasell in 1958.

★ iii) Traverse of the three peaks   Grade 4

This route involves one of the West Peak ascent routes and then traverses the Middle and High Peaks. A pleasant climb made quite committing because of its length. The rock near the Middle and High Peaks is loose. A classic.

H Bohny, T Sidler, Jan 1955.

Marcel Face

The south-western aspect of Haast offers a good range of gullies that are usually well iced through to December. There have been several harder routes put up on the Marcel side since the 1970s, however only some have been recorded.

14.55   West-Middle Peak Col   Grade 3

Ascend from the Marcel Glacier up steep snow into the righthand of two narrow couloirs leading to the col. Then on up the main ridge to the summit.

Phil Houghton, D G Herron, A R Page, Richard Tornquist, Jan 1959.

14.56   Grade 4-

Start below high peak but trend right arriving about 50m east of the High Peak summit. Involves several short but steep steps. Five pitches.

(Possibly) Dave Chowdhury, Brendan Kane, Dec 1999.

14.57   Valentine Gully   Grade 5-

This five pitch route takes a prominent narrow gully almost directly below the high peak. It tops out between high peak and the next obvious prominence to the east (crux at the bottom). Descend to Marcel col.

Dave Langrish, Lyn Bowering, 14 Feb 1987.

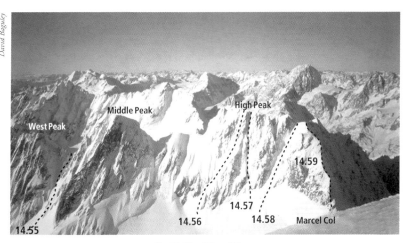

David Baguley

Fig. 75 Marcel Face of Haast.

14.58   Grade 3+

Gully between high peak and divide peak.
Mike Andrews, D Warren, Colin Dodge, Dec 1972.
Variation: A Smith, Wilfrid Lammerink, Jan 1973.
Don Bogie, Peter Sommerville, Jun 1979.

14.59 High Peak from Marcel Col   Grade 2+

Follow an easy snow ridge and turn west off the Main Divide, along a rock
ridge to the summit. A regular descent route. Despite the easy access, watch
for loose rock late in summer (also see Route 6.35).
Alex Graham, Henry Newton, Feb 1907.
Frank Alack, G Mitchell, R Macklow, Aug 1934.

Marcel Col 2987m

From Pioneer Hut a route around Haast Corner is usually viable early in the
season but may require careful route finding through crevasses. If this option
is cut off an alternative can be found under Lendenfeld Peak – continue
from under Haast further up the Heemskirk Glacier. Beware of cornices on
the col - scene of a few falls! The route is not difficult but can require some
crevasse navigation.

Lendenfeld Peak 3194m

14.60 From Marcel Col   Grade 2

From Marcel Col the route is straightforward (however, hard ice can form
easily here, especially in winter). This is also the most common way Engineer
Col and the North Shoulder of Tasman are gained. An easy descent route,
but beware of the cornice that sometimes forms on the summit of Lendenfeld.
Alex Graham, Henry Newton, Feb 1907.

14.61 Aurora Australis   Grade 3

Gain the large snow shelf left of Hamilton-Berry rib by a short rock/mixed
step. Ascend to the top left end of the snow shelf through a mixed gully to
the summit ice-cap.
Andrew McAuley, Andrew Corvini, Feb 1992.

14.62 Hamilton-Berry Rib   Grade 3+

The bottom 200m provides steep sound climbing and the rib then slowly
relents to form a "Giant's Staircase".
Alan Berry, Neil Hamilton, Dec 1955.

14.63 North West Couloir   Grade 3

Up the snow and ice gully between the two rock buttresses. This route may
lack ice later in summer.
Merv English, Peter Hillary, Nena Ritchie, Jul 1978.

★ **14.64   North West Rib**   Grade 3+

Parallels the Hamilton-Berry Rib, with good climbing on slabs and ribs of excellent rock.

Dave Bamford, John Nankervis, Feb 1977.

★ **14.65   West Face**   Grade 4

A short hard climb on excellent rock, commencing on the right side of the face (crux 16).

Lindsay Bell, Don Bogie and Ken Hyslop climbed the face more directly, whereas John Allen and Zane Williams climbed a line commencing from the gully on the right, Nov 1978.

14.66   From Engineer Col   Grade 2

Straightforward, but slightly threatened by avalanches off Mt Tasman. Glacier access can sometimes become cut off.

Alex Graham, Henry Newton, Feb 1907 (Descended).

Mt Tasman/Rarakiroa 3497m

★ **14.67   North Shoulder**   Grade 3+

This route starts from Engineer Col and is best gained from Lendenfeld Peak (via Route 14.60). The col can be accessed directly from the Heemskirk Glacier but is sometimes cut off or threatened by icecliffs/avalanches off Tasman. Above Engineer Col, the route usually follows steeper ice gullies to where Syme Ridge joins the North Shoulder. Although the section above the col has changed markedly over the last 15 years it still provides a relatively straightforward route onto the shoulder. The broad North Shoulder eventually narrows into an exhilarating ridge, which leads to the summit. Also used as a descent route.

Marcel Kurz, Harold Porter, Jan 1927 (Descended).

14.68   Heemskirk Face   Grade 3+

Start up a broad gully on the right of the face until above the prominent central icecliff. Then move up left towards the North Shoulder. The icecliff is currently threatening the route.

Maurice Conway, Wayne McIlwraith, Dec 1972.

Pete Robertson, John Webby, Aug 1977.

14.69   Arapiles oh Arapiles   Grade 3+

Follow the ridge between the Heemskirk Face and North Buttress. Poor rock. First ascent team descended a couloir into the Abel Janszoon after reaching the top of the North Buttress.

M Roberts, A Slater, Jan 1994.

14.70   North Buttress   Grade 4+

Ascend snowslopes towards Witches Col at the foot of the buttress, and head up the northern side of the rib. After 200m cut back onto the rib and follow it to the prominent notch (may require an abseil). Above here cut left and find the best and safest route through the icecliffs.

Alan Berry, Neil Hamilton, Dec 1955.

Dave Vass, Nick Cradock, July 1998.

Fig. 76 *Mt Tasman and its lieutenants Mt Haast (L), Lendenfeld Peak and Torres Peak (R).*

Witches Col 2860m

A snow col situated the top end of The Buttress, at the base of the North Buttress (Route 14.70). Witches Col allows access to the Able Janszoon Face.

The Buttress 2801m, 2776m

This is a large ridge that extends north from the foot of Tasman's North Shoulder separating the Heemskirk and Abel Janszoon Glaciers.

14.71 COMAC   Grade 3-

A seven pitch route up an arête on the North Face, climbed from the lower Heemskirk Glacier.

Nick Cradock, D Owen, Susan McNair, Feb 1987.

★ 14.72 Centurion   Grade 5

The major zigzag buttress right of the North Buttress, in the centre of the face is capped by steep ice onto the North Shoulder. 19 rope lengths of excellent mixed climbing involves three major steps, the third can be avoided to the right. First ascent team bivvied twice en route (a good site is at 2/3 height). Direct variation. Climb the third buttress directly (crux 18).

Dave Crow, Andy MacFarlane, Jon Taylor, Jun 1994 (Direct variation).

David Hiddleston, Dave Vass, Spring 2000.

14.73 White Jasmine   Grade 5

Start up the same gully as Route 14.74 to gain the broad rock buttress on the left. Follow the buttress tending left to exit via a hidden couloir that leads through the final rock curtain below the icecliffs. Ascend through the icecliffs onto the North Shoulder.

Dave Bamford, John Nankervis, Mar 1983.

14.74 Abel Janszoon Face   Grade 5

Ascend a gully line to the left of the prominent icecliffs in the middle of the face, moving right onto the central snowfields. Finish up steep sastrugied ice to the left of the summit.

Merv English, Murray Jones, Dec 1977.

14.75   Grade 5

Ascend the gully start of Route 14.74 and instead of moving right on the large snowfields continue straight up the gully systems onto the North Ridge of Mt Tasman.

Steve Elder, Jun 1986.

★ 14.76 Nipple Rib   Grade 5

Starting on the left side of the Stevenson-Dick Couloir, head up steep snow to the foot of a major rib leading to the West Ridge. Ascend rock of reasonable quality for 15 pitches to emerge onto a prominent rock tower known as the Nipple, 130m below the summit of Tasman.

Phil Grover, John Nankervis, Jan 1982.

14.77   Harris-Jones Rib   Grade 4+

The route ascends the lower Stevenson-Dick Couloir and then moves left onto a subsidiary rib beside the couloir. The rib's rock is of variable quality, but nowhere severe.

George Harris, Murray Jones, Jan 1969.

14.78   Stevenson-Dick Couloir   Grade 3+

A continuous 800m slope descending from the West Ridge, averaging 40-50°. Beware soft snow avalanches and rockfall. Has been skied!

Doug Dick, Harry Stevenson, Dec 1941 (Descended).

★ 14.79   West Ridge   Grade 4

A classic climb. Remoteness, lack of escape routes, and the need usually to traverse Torres Peak make this a long route. Above the Torres-Tasman Col use the rock ribs on the Balfour Glacier side and then follow the narrow arête upward. The arête gradually broadens out towards the summit of Tasman.

Les Cleveland, Neil Hamilton, John Lange, Jan 1951. (Descended during the first Tasman-Torres Traverse).

Torres Peak 3160m

14.80   Torres-Tasman Col   Grade 4

A short route of steep snow and ice, which unfortunately tends to act as a funnel for any rubbish falling from the surrounding slopes.

Rob Rainsbury, John Visser, Jan 1971 (Descended).

14.81   North East Face   Grade 5

From the Abel Janszoon Glacier ascend steep, loose rock and steep snowfields (which may not exist later in summer) reaching the ridge 200m west of the summit.

Bill Denz, Geoff Gabites, Mike Perry, Aug 1977.

14.82   North East Couloir   Grade 3+

A steep, but relatively straightforward route involving 200m of snow, a 70m leftward traverse, and then a couloir to the summit ridge.

Alan Berry, J M Davie, Hugh Tyndale-Biscoe, I R Wood, Jan 1954 (Descended).

North Face

14.83   Red Rib   Grade 4-

The obvious rib, next to the North East Couloir consisting of a buttress of good rock, with a 20m gendarme $^1/_3$ of the way up.

A Abrahams, J Hough, M Kirby, C Schaap, Mar 1968.

14.84   Coberger Route   Grade 3+

Further west another route ascends the bluffs from the snowfields above the Abel Janszoon Glacier.

Oscar & A Coberger, Jan 1950.

★ **14.85   West Ridge**   Grade 4

Access onto the ridge varies. Starting from Katies Col ascents have been made on the northern side of the lower buttress (the first ascent in 1907) and up the ridge itself from the col. The best routes, though, involve skirting round onto the snowfields above the Balfour Glacier and either ascending a snowslope onto the ridge above the first step or ascending the first prominent rib falling south-west from the ridge. Then follow the winding arête and rock steps to the summit.

Alex Graham, Henry Newton, Ebenezer Teichelmann, Feb 1907.

Le Receveur 2609m

★ **14.86**   Grade 2-

A classic easy snow arête from Katies Col, however schrunds may prove difficult late in the season.

Harold Porter, Marcel Kurz, Feb 1927.
Frank Alack, G Mitchell, R Macklow, Aug 1934.

Big Mac 2565m

14.87   Grade 2-

Gain the Castries Glacier to the west of the peak, then to the summit.

Frank Alack, G C Arras, D Mackie, Feb 1932.

14.88   Grade 2

From the col between Big Mac and Le Receveur.

Frank Alack, H K Douglas, W E Wilson, Dec 1934.

14.89   Mistaken Identity   Grade 2+

Climb the buttress overlooking the Fox Névé. An abseil may be required to get off.

Dave McLeod, Tim Morrison, Rob Hughes, Mar 1983.

Balfour Glacier

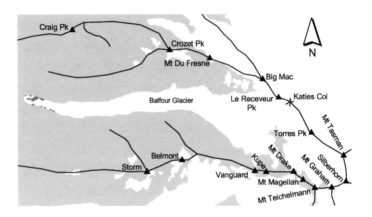

Balfour Glacier

The upper névé of the Balfour Glacier is remote and access is not easy. It is cut off from the lower glacier by a 700m cliff, over which the glacier plunges, not to mention the infamous Balfour Gorge. The peaks surrounding the upper névé are spectacularly steep. On the northern side there are demanding ice climbs and classic rock spurs on Torres Peak and Mt Tasman. On the southern side are a series of rock buttresses on Mts Magellan and Drake. These buttresses are comprised of arguably the best quality rock in the region and can only be described as outstanding. The area's remoteness and lack of huts, however, makes climbing a more demanding undertaking. In the Lower Balfour, Kupe (name pending approval) is situated between Drake and Vanguard on the Balfour Range.

Access

From the east the best route is from the Grand Plateau over Silberhorn or Graham (see Routes 6.23, 6.24 and 6.25). An alternative route from Empress Hut is also possible. This involves traversing the La Perouse Glacier, climbing the South Face of either Drake or Magellan and then descending in to the Balfour (possibly using the abseil routes on either of these mountains), not a suitable option for those with big packs. A traverse of Clarke Saddle and Teichelmann from the La Perouse also allows access to the head of the Balfour. From the summit of Silberhorn the route is straightforward, but sometimes complicated by crevasses.

From the Fox Névé, Katies Col provides the best access: sidle round snow slopes below the first subsidiary spur of the West Ridge of Torres, moving across to an obvious small col/notch on the Left Rib of the South Face of Torres. Descend a steep gully on the south side of the col to the Balfour Glacier. The right hand side (looking down) of this gully is now equipped with two double bolt belays that allow the slope and schrund below to be abseiled safely. Under some conditions, when crevasses are closed, it may be possible to cut around under the toe of the rib. It is possible to fly to the Big Mac landing strip, north-west of Katies Col.

Shelter

The Balfour Glacier is narrow and prone to avalanches, especially off Mt Tasman and under Mts Graham and Teichelmann. Shelter usually involves bivvying, snowcaving or tenting. Remember to site your abode away from any avalanche danger. A ledge on the Satellite Buttress, under Mt Drake, provides a good-weather perch for those climbing on Drake or Magellan.

Times

Pioneer Hut - Katies Col 2-3 hours.
Katies Col - Balfour Névé 2-3 hours.
Grand Plateau - Balfour Névé via Graham Spur or Silberhorn 6-7 hours.

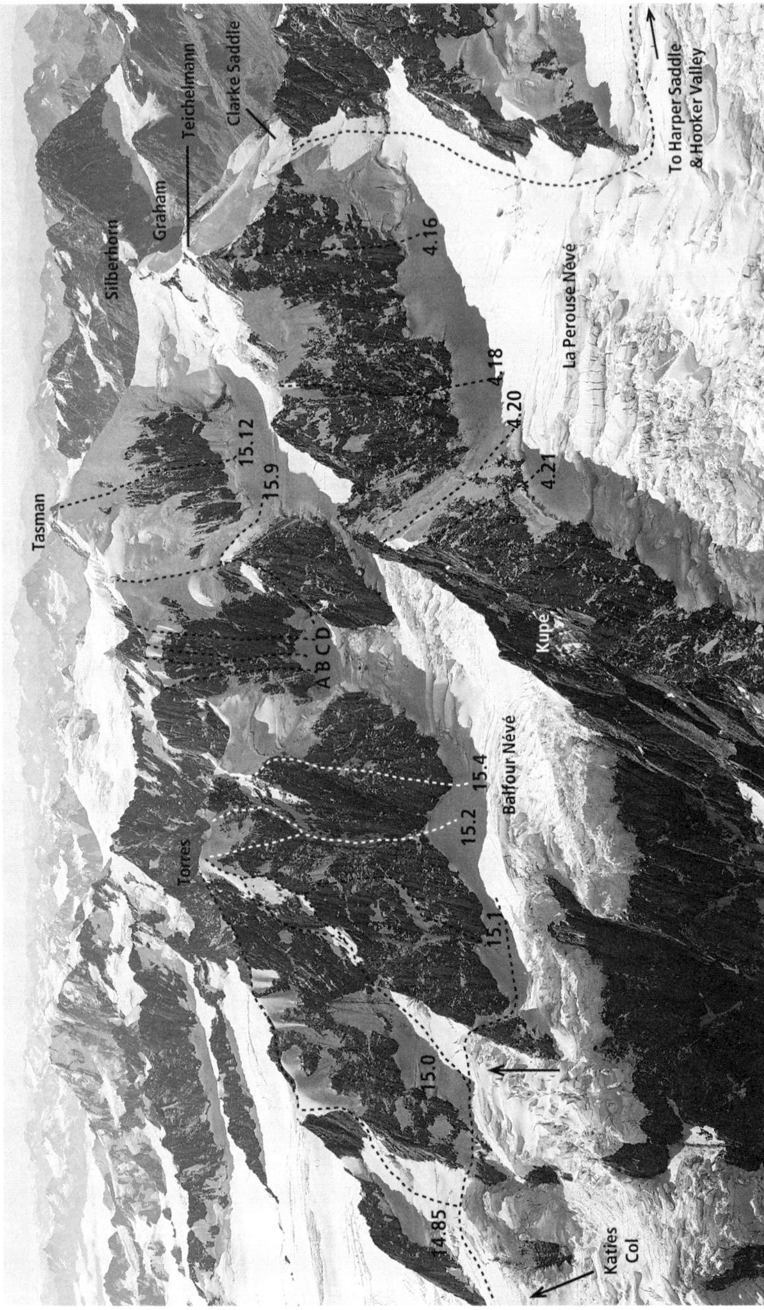

Lloyd Homer/IGNS

Fig. 77 Balfour and La Perouse glaciers. For the Hidden Face: A = Route 15.5, B = Route 15.6, C = 15.7 and D = 15.8.

Alpine Rock

The nature of alpine rock routes means the climber generally needs more route information to ensure s/he is on route. The descriptions that follow are brief, so for those intending to visit this area *Balfour Rock* is recommended. This is a separate and more detailed guidebook that provides pitch-by-pitch descriptions, topos and equipment requirements (for more details see the back section of this guide).

Many of the routes on Mts Magellan and Drake have been established using rockshoes and these peaks have been equipped for abseil descent. Other descents involving snow may be possible but only with mountaineering boots and equipment. It is therefore advisable for those parties wearing only rockshoes to carry one ice axe, in case snow is encountered on summit ridges etc.

Torres Peak 3165m

Left Rib

15.0 Grade 3+

Ascend the glacier on the Katies Col side of the rib until confronted by a 200m rock step. Climb the step near the crest (crux) and follow the snow arête to the summit.

Alan Berry, J M H Davie, I R Wood, Hugh Tyndale-Biscoe, Jan 1954.

A variant, *Torres Forres,* follows the same general line but takes an ice gully above and left of the suspended snowfield, rejoining the main route above.

G McKinnon, J Taylor, M Scott, Feb 1997.

South Face

15.1 Grade 4

From the Balfour Névé, snowslopes and gullies on the lower half of the buttress lead up through rotten rock. Cut left through the rotten rock band onto the ice crest leading to the summit.

Dave Bamford, John Nankervis, Ian Whitehouse, Brin Williman, Jan 1980.

15.2 The Man From Head Office Who Found It Harder To Get Off Than To Get Up (formerly Central Gully) Grade 4

Ascend the major gully that separates the Left and Right ribs. A series of ice steps in the lower part of the gully are followed by snow and ice slopes leading right onto the Torres-Tasman Ridge near the summit of Torres.

Dave Bamford, Russell Braddock, Andy Harris, John Nankervis, Oct 1983.

15.3 The Direct Harder To Get Off Than Get Up (formerly Central Gully Variation) Grade 5

Ascend the gully as for Route 15.2 and then break left and climb steep ice directly to the summit.

Russell Braddock, Andy Harris, Sep 1984.

15.4   Right Rib   Grade 4

From the Balfour Névé, start up steep rock in the centre of the rib, which after three rope lengths eases back and leads on to a snow and ice rib curving up to the Tasman-Torres ridge.

Dave Bamford, Keith Woodford, Dec 1978.

Mt Tasman/Rarakiroa 3497m

Hidden Face

A very big icefall crevasse may present difficulties when accessing the routes on this face. (See mid section colour shot.)

15.5   Hippo Takes A Holiday   Grade 6

Ascend a corner system 50 metres left of the Direct route. Exit onto the Torres-Tasman ridge just above the buttress, above the col.

Brian Alder, Dave Vass, Sep 1989.

15.6   Direct   Grade 6

Begin up the gully left of the Sissons Buttress, then ascend a narrow gully and rock pitch to gain the ridge edge of a prominent snowfield. Head up a pitch of steep bulging ice (crux), and then follow the broad gully out right. A fierce climb.

Guy Halliburton, Alan Woods, Jan 1982.

15.7   Mortimer-Sissons Gully   Grade 5+

The route heads up a deep gully left of the Sissons Buttress. The gully widens out, and the route tends right and leads to an amphitheatre. Move right again and up to the ridge.

Greg Mortimer, Noel Sissons, Nov 1979.

★ 15.8   Sissons Buttress   Grade 5

Ascend the prominent rib just right of centre of the face. The rock is comparatively solid and the climbing sustained. The rib peters out and is followed by 200m of snow and ice.

John Fantini, Noel Sissons, Jan 1975.

15.9   Balfour Rib   Grade 4

The bottom section of buttress is avoided by snowslopes beside the Balfour Face (although the first ascent climbed the buttress). Then it is up, around, and through ice bulges to the Tasman-Torres ridge.

John Harrison, Brian Hearfield, Wally Romanes, Jim Wilson, Dec 1959.

Balfour Face

★ 15.10   Mists of Avalon   Grade 6

Ascend steep ice left of the buttress followed by Route 15.11. Thirteen pitches (first four are the crux). Reportedly harder than the original line.

John Fantini, Tony Dignan, Jan 1986.

Alex Palman

Fig. 78 Balfour Face of Mt Tasman.

15.11   **Left Buttress**   Grade 6

Ascend the rock buttress on the left side of the face, but right of the prominent icecliffs. Steep climbing on rock gives way to mixed ground and then steep ice onto the summit icefields.

Marty Beare, John Entwisle, Feb 1983.

★ 15.12   Rattus Balfourus   Grade 6

Just right of the Left Buttress is a narrow couloir leading up to the headwall ice shared with Route 15.13. From here it is possible to either ascend the icewalls out left or tend right towards the Tasman-Silberhorn ridge.

Russell Braddock, Kim Logan, Nov 1982.

15.13   Original Route   Grade 6

The route that started it all. Ascend the gully (or the rib on its right) in the centre of the face before being confronted by rising icewalls. Climb these tending left and finish up 45° ice slopes to the summit. Some parties have climbed the ice walls direct and finished on the Tasman-Silberhorn ridge.

Bill Denz, Bryan Pooley, Dec 1971.
Bill Denz, Phil Herron, Jun 1975.

A few lines have been added to the right side of the face, including a route by Lionel Clay and Adrian Daly, who worked on it in the late 1980s (a right hand gully variation). Dave Andrews and Neil Harding-Roberts completed a buttress route in winter 1984, but it is not clear where this goes. The following routes exit onto the Tasman-Silberhorn ridge.

15.14   Grade 6-

Gully right of the Original Route. Steep, with hard ice in winter.

Athol Whimp, Andrew Lindblade, Jul 1993.

15.14i   Mr Curly's Big Adventure   Grade 5

Climb the Right Buttress involving 200m of rock. The first pitch is solid, but the rest is more exciting (crux 16). 200m of ice follows the rock, starting at 70° and kicking back, as the route joins the Silberhorn-Tasman ridge at mid height.

Jonathan Chapman, Joe Stock, Jan 1995.

15.15   A Right Buttress Variant

100m right of the Original Route.

Jeff Sandifort, T Vervonsi, Jan 1997.

Silberhorn 3309m

15.16   Grade 2

An easy, but remote snow climb from the Balfour Glacier.

Bill Beaven, Norman Hardie, Jim MacFarlane, Earle Riddiford, Dec 1948.

Mt Graham 3203m

Like Silberhorn, an easy snow climb.

Mt Teichelmann/Rakirua 3144m

15.17   Grade 2+

Either via Silberhorn or Mt Graham, there is little difficulty apart from the final rock cone (choss). Also see Routes 6.21 and 6.22. First ascent from the Balfour Glacier:

Alan Berry, A Clough, R C Western, Dec 1955.

15.18   Couloir Route   Grade 3

A snow gully leads up onto the north-western side of Mt Teichelmann. This has also been used as a descent route, but beware of rockfall.

Nick Von Tunzelmann, A Bowden, Bob Cunninghame, Alex Parton, Jan 1967.

Mt Magellan 3065m

15.19   Grade 3

Traverse a sharp arête west from Mt Teichelmann to a prominent rock tower (this is not the summit), then down and along another sharp arête. Other than abseiling Route 15.23 into the Balfour, this is the easiest way off Magellan. Also see Route 4.17.

Erica Beuzenberg, Gottlieb Braun-Elwert, Jun 1989.

15.20   Outlier Buttress   Grade 4

A prominent rib leading onto the knob between Mts Teichelmann and Magellan is climbed by way of a crack system up the centre (crux 14).

Merv English, Peter Hillary, Nov 1976.

Lionel Clay, Adrian Daly, winter 1986.

★ 15.21   Balfour Buttress   Grade 4+

Start at the toe of the buttress, beside an icefall, or from ramps to the right (which lead from the Magellan-Drake snow apron). Sustained climbing on excellent rock leads up with the climb slowly relenting (crux grade 15). Descend by either abseiling Route 15.23 or traverse to Teichelmann.

Stu Allan, Jim Jolly, Feb 1976.

West Face

The following three routes start from the Magellan-Drake snow apron. The large schrund is usually best dealt with at the Magellan end. The routes are described left to right. Once on the snow apron, follow the base of the West Face.

15.22   Ménage à trois   Grade 6+

Climb the distinctive ascending buttresses that scar the centre of the face. This route starts off the snow at a point about half-way along the base of the face. There are three bolts on the route, which arrives on the Balfour Buttress about 70m from the summit. Descend by rapping Route 15.23. This is a sustained route (crux 20).

Alex Palman, Peter Dickson, Nick Flyvbjerg, Jan 1996.

The route following the obvious corner, where the West Face meets the Drake-Magellan ridge, is Pooh Corner. Starting from a small ledge just left of Pooh Corner is:

Fig. 79 *Mts Magellan and Drake, from the Balfour Névé.*

Outlier Buttress

Magellan

West Face

Drake

West Wall

Satellite Buttress

15.20
15.21
15.22
15.23 15.24
15.25
15.26
15.27
15.28
15.30
15.33
15.36
15.38
15.40

★ 15.23 Anyone Can Play Guitar   Grade 6-

This route follows the steepest and cleanest rock on the face, directly to the summit. The steep 'punch–in-the-guts' first pitch is the crux and thereafter the route relents. There are bolt belays on every pitch, allowing this route to serve as an abseil descent - two 50m ropes are mandatory (crux 19).

Alex Palman, Nick Flyvbjerg, Jan 1995.

★ 15.24 Pooh Corner   Grade 5+

From the snow, climb up blocky ledges to a small orange belay ledge (bolt) about 5m left of the base of the corner. This belay also serves Route 15.23, to the left, on the face proper, and is a good spot to leave ice tools and plastic boots. Climb the three-star sweeping corner for eight pitches. The route arrives high on the Drake-Magellan ridge, about two pitches from the summit. There are single bolt belays on the first 8 pitches (mostly 13-16, crux of 19 may be avoidable). Descend by rapping Route 15.23.

Alex Palman, Peter Dickson, Nick Flyvbjerg, Jan 1996.

15.25 Magellan-Drake Col   Grade 4

A thin edge of rock leads up on the Magellan side of the dark gut. Once on the col, the ridge up to Magellan has better rock.

Dave Bamford, John Nankervis, Ian Whitehouse, Brin Williman, Feb 1980.

Mt Drake 2974m

Also refer to Routes 4.16 - 4.18.

North Face

15.26 Bonaventure   Grade 4+

The half-size outlier buttress on the left side of Drake. A superb quarter-day climb. From the névé climb the central weakness midway between the black rock band on the right and the left hand margin of the buttress. The route is comprised of deceptively good rock. A small roof 3/4 of the way up (crux 19), is probably avoidable. Four pitches equipped with double bolt belays – abseil off.

Alex Palman, James Wright, Feb 1998.

★ 15.27 Shogun   Grade 5+

This is the largest and most distinctive buttress on Mt Drake. The climbing is both superb and sustained, however after the Crows Nest Ledge it relents somewhat and becomes more broken. The toe of the buttress fell away in 1998 and so access onto the buttress now looks harder (was 14). A snow ramp to the left of the buttress might offer a way.   A classic and sustained route (crux 16).

Paul Aubrey, Richard Pears, Jan 1981.

15.28 Samurai   Grade 7-

A wild ride. The thin buttress right of Shogun. An awesome line with a sting in the tail. Occasional bolt belays and runners (crux 23).

Peter Dickson, Alex Palman, Feb 1989

15.29   Golden Hind   Grade 6+
Ascends the left side of the Central Buttress. Starts on a slabby buttress (that Samurai shares for access) and climbs the line of least resistance up corners and cracks on the left of the central buttress crest (crux 19).
Carol McDermott, Peter Dickson, Mar 1988.

★ 15.30   Pelican   Grade 7
Ascends the clean red rock of the Central Buttress all the way to the summit, never deviating more than six metres. A technical start is followed by an arête capped by an intimidating roof (crux 22). The Pelican takes the left side of the roof and continues up a series of towers to the summit. Occasional bolt belays and runners. Very sustained. There are two first pitch options: follow the obvious crack system to the wave and traverse to the edge of the buttress (20) or continue up the crack to join the buttress higher (22).
Peter Dickson, Alex Palman, Feb 1989.
Superconnected: A one pitch direct start to the Pelican. Desperate moves up the angular buttress lead to easier ground above. Three bolts (crux 27).
Alex Palman, Feb 1996.

15.31   URGA Memorial Route   Grade 6+
This follows a classic corner, between the Pelican and the Right Hand Buttress, which sweeps up to the large roof, shared with the Pelican. Take the right hand side of the roof via a detached plate (crux 19). The climb finishes at the Crows Nest Ledge.
Alex Palman, Peter Dickson, Feb 1989.

15.32   Red Scorpion   Grade 7-
Climb the centre of the Right Hand Buttress, taking the right pillar at the top. Start as for Astrolabe but traverse left along a break to gain the buttress proper. Continue up through great rock involving cracks, roofs, slabs and a headwall (crux 23). All pitches are equipped with double bolt belays and some have bolt runners. Mostly 17-20. Stunning.
Alex Palman, Peter Dickson, Mar 2000.

★ 15.33   Astrolabe   Grade 6-
A classic route. An almost perfect buttress of red rock forming the junction of the North Face and the West Wall. Once on the Satellite Buttress, scramble up the next 30m rock step to the base of the buttress. Astrolabe starts in the obvious right facing corner at the toe of the buttress (there are two corners – the left one being easier). Superb climbing leads to the Crows Nest Ledge and continues directly up the arête to the top of the West Wall. Two easy pitches lead to the summit. The seventh pitch involves under-clinging a small roof (crux 17) however most of the climbing is 14-16.
Carol McDermott, Mark Defourneaux, Peter Dickson, Mar 1988.

A third pitch variant involves climbing the arête directly rather than moving left, grade 18.
Alex Palman, James Wright, Mary Butler, Feb 1998.

West Wall

The rock making up this 300m wall is again nothing short of sensational by local standards, offering overlapping plates and finger cracks. The *Corsair* also serves as an abseil descent route for all other routes on Mt Drake. To access the West Wall, follow the Astrolabe description and then continue up the scree/snow gully at the base of the wall, passing a bivvy sized rock, All the West Wall routes share the same scramble to the summit. The following routes are described from left to right.

15.34   Physical Graffiti   Grade 6+

Takes the first obvious recessed corner at the base of the face (bolt belay at ground level). The route keeps a constant distance from Astrolabe. Occasional bolt belays and runners. Balancy and technical climbing (crux 19).

Alex Palman, Peter Dickson, Feb 1989.

15.35   Buccaneer   Grade 6+

This route starts on a ledge ~20m right of Physical Graffiti. The ledge houses two large flakes behind which plastic boots and tools can be stashed. Climb through the initial overhanging fist crack to the shelf above and continue up. At the Crows Nest Ledge, traverse 10m right to a corner and crack system, which trends back left. Follow this to the top of the wall (the Corsair route crosses at the top of the fifth pitch and finishes right). Occasional bolt belays and runners (crux 20).

Alex Palman, Peter Dickson, Feb 1989.

★ 15.36   Corsair   Grade 6+

This route also serves as an abseil descent. Start on the same ledge as for the Buccaneer but climb up flakes through the overhang to the right. Move right to a crack and follow to a double bolt belay. Climb the headwall to the Crows Nest Ledge and then up to a belay shared with the Buccaneer. Climb the face left of the belay and past a bolt runner to a double bolt belay. Head through the crux (22): two bulging overlaps (bolt & wire) to another DB belay (crux can be avoided by traversing into the Buccaneer). Finally, move up a finger crack right of the Buccaneer off-width. Technical and sustained.

Peter Dickson, Alex Palman, Feb 1989.

15.37   No Push, No Baby

A good two-pitch route that ends at the Crows Nest Ledge. Take the large crack system right of the Corsair. The second pitch trends left up a steep layback crack (17, 20).

Alex Palman, Peter Dickson, Mar 2000.

15.38   Spanish Armada   Grade 5+

A buttress to the right of the West Wall. The line runs up just left of the crest. The route has good rock and is 5-6 pitches long to the ridge line. From here one can traverse to the summit of Drake (and descend via the Corsair route) or descend the Bamaphone route (crux 17/18).

Carol McDermott, Steve Moore, Mar 1988.

15.39   Bamaphone Route   Grade 4-

Starts from the highest point of the snow slope. Up the corner and edge right of the Spanish Armada. Rappel the route or continue to the summit (see 'Getting off Mt Drake'). About 5 pitches, crux 13.

Dave Bamford, John Nankervis, Feb 1980.

15.40   Original Route   Grade 4-

Ascends the rock face between the Bamaphone route and the rightmost limit of Drakes West and North West Ridges. The rock is good, but there is a dodgy argillite band at the start. The route arrives on the West Ridge 4-5 pitches from the summit (easy scrambling). Unique views of Kupe and the Lower Balfour as well as the La Perouse Glaciers can be gained. A short and easy rock climb.

Nick Von Tunzelmann, A Bowden, Bob Cunninghame, Alex Parton, Jan 1967.

Getting off Mt Drake

Abseiling the *Corsair.* This is probably the easiest and quickest way off – provided you have two 50m ropes. From the summit of Drake scramble west along the summit ridge for 55m to a large (~3m) rock, shaped as though it has a cap (it also has a cairn atop). Turn right and descend north for 50m of easy scrambling, following cairns. Turn west and drop down a gully/corner to a double bolt belay. From here rappel to the top of the West Wall and continue abseiling down the equipped *Corsair* route to the base of the wall (5 full pitches). Continue abseiling to the Satellite Buttress and the névé, as required.

Abseiling the Bamaphone: This could be a useful alternative to the Corsair descent if you only have one rope. From the summit of Drake continue past the large rock (cairn atop) until the top of the Spanish Armada route can be seen. The next gully is the Bamaphone route, abseil down it. From the foot of the route cross the snow slope to the base of the West Wall and continue abseiling (~3 more pitches to the névé).

Kupe 2510m

A distinctive peak with a 600m triangular north face visible from Katies Col. Kupe was first climbed (by accident) by the Wopereis brothers in 1980 during a traverse from Drake to Vanguard. The peak was not visited again until Bryan Moore and others added three new routes to the North Face in 1992 and named the peak Kupe, in keeping with the explorer theme of the area. Access to Kupe is not easy. Options include travelling up the Cook and Balfour valley systems or arriving from the lower Fox Glacier via the Paschendale range. It appears that more new route potential exists.

15.41   Drake-Kupe-Vanguard Ridge   Grade 4+

Makes Malte's "cheval" look like a footpath.

Anton & Paul Woperis, 1980.

Fig. 80 Fox, Balfour and La Perouse névés.

Lloyd Homer/IGNS

275

North Face

15.42 Captain Incredible & The Naked Dancing Girls Grade 5+

From the avalanche cone on the left of the face, gain the edge of the headwall and continue to the summit (crux 16). Descend by abseiling the route.

Bryan Moore, Tony Ward-Holmes, Eric Bradshaw, Dec 1992.

15.43 Kupe Direct Grade 6

This is the central line on the headwall. Balancy climbing on solid red greywacke leads to an overhang (crux 19) two pitches below the summit. Descend by rappelling the route.

Bryan Moore, Tony Ward-Holmes, Eric Bradshaw, Dec 1992.

15.44 The Sinusoidal Ridge

Takes the right hand ridgeline to a gendarme at 2/3rd height where it joints the headwall. An abseil is needed to pass the gendarme. The climb was abandoned somewhere on the headwall due to a difficulty that couldn't be passed. The climb remains uncompleted. A crux of 16 was encountered before the headwall.

Bryan Moore, Tony Ward-Holmes, Eric Bradshaw, Dec 1992.

Vanguard 2331m

15.45 From the Balfour Glacier

D H Lewis, R D Dick, Jan 1938.

Guiding companies

Steve Schreiber
- NZMGA Ski Guide
  Mt Hutt Heliguides Ltd.
  42 Spaxton Street, Methven
  Ph/Fax: +64-3-302 8119
  Email: mthuttheliguides@xtra.co.nz

Brede Arkless
- A fully qualified guide who climbs in
  the mountains of New Zealand and
  many other countries.

  Ph: +64-3-435 0006 and
  mobile 025 2265579 or
  Home address: 3A North West Arch,
  Twizel, South Canterbury
  Email: Bredearkless@hotmail.com

Adventure Consultants Ltd
- Guided Ascents • Instruction Courses
- Ski Touring • Film Locations
- International Expeditions

  PO Box 97, 58 McDougall Street,
  Lake Wanaka 9192, Central Otago
  Ph: +64-3-443 8711
  Fax: +64-3-443 8733
  Email: info@adventure.co.nz
  www.adventure.co.nz

Alpine Guides (Aoraki) Ltd
- Guided Ascents • Heliskiing
- Climbing Instruction Courses
- Backcountry Courses

  PO Box 20, Mount Cook 8770
  Ph: +64-3-435 1834
  Fax: +64-3-435 1898
  Email: mtcook@alpineguides.co.nz
  www.alpineguides.co.nz
  www.heliskiing.co.nz

New Zealand Outside
PO Box 17-673, Christchurch
Ph: +64-3-326 7516
Fax: +64-3-326 7518
Email: charles@outside.co.nz
www.outside.co.nz

Southern Alps Guiding
PO Box 15, Twizel,
Mt Cook Region 8773
Ph: +64-3-435 0890
Fax: +64-3-326 7518
mobile: 025 342 277
Email: charles@outside.co.nz
www.mtcook.com

Alpine Recreation Ltd
- Tramping • Climbing • Ski Touring

  PO Box 75, Lake Tekapo,
  South Canterbury
  Ph: +64-3-680 6736
  Fax: +64-3-680 6765
  Email: alprec@voyager.co.nz
  www.alpinerecreation.co.nz

Alpine Guides Fox Glacier
- Glacier Walks • Ice Climbing
- Spring Ski Touring • Mountain Trips
- Instruction Courses

  Main Road (SH6), PO Box 38,
  Fox Glacier
  Ph: +64-3-751 0825
  Fax: +64-3-3 751 0857
  Email: foxguides@minidata.co.nz
  www.foxguides.co.nz

**Mount Aspiring Guides & Alpine
Instruction NZ**
- NZMGA and UIAGM Team of
  Specialists • Ascents • Ski Touring
- Ski Mountaineering
- Mountaineering Courses

  PO Box 345, Wanaka, Central Otago
  Ph: +64-3-443 9422
  Fax: +64-3-443 9540
  Email: aspguide@xtra.co.nz
  www.mtaspiringguides.co.nz

Information sources for this book

New Zealand Alpine Club: *Alpine Journals, Bulletins, The Climber* magazine and the *NZAC Handbook*. Also, Unwin and Godley hut books.

Canterbury Mountaineering Club: *The Canterbury Mountaineer* and *News*.

Hut books from Aoraki/Mt Cook National Park and Westland National Park; i) *in situ* books, ii) those sourced from the National Archives (Christchurch and Wellington) and the Hocken Library (Dunedin).

Ascents Books from Aoraki/Mt Cook National Park Visitor Centre (1962-1978, 1979-1983, 1983 – 2000).

Aoraki/Mt Cook National Park information brochures: *Working around helicopters* (1999) and *Aoraki/Mount Cook National Park – the ancestor of Ngai Tahu* (1999), among others.

The Conquest of Mount Cook. By Freda du Faur. George Allen & Unwin, 1915.

Peter Graham: Mountain Guide. An Autobiography. Reed, George Allen & Unwin, 1965.

The Hermitage Years of Mannering & Dixon. By Guy Mannering. GM Publications, 2000.

Balfour Rock - A guide to alpine rock climbs, Balfour Region, Westland National Park. By Alex Palman. Axel Publishing, 1998.

Bergschrunds of the upper Hooker Glacier, Mount Cook National Park. By Alex Palman, M.Sc. Thesis. University of Canterbury University, 1994.

Great Peaks of New Zealand - History and description of classic routes on 16 major peaks. By Hugh Logan. NZAC/McIndoe, 1991.

South Island Rock – A guide to the best rockclimbing areas in the South Island. By Ivan Vostinar. Tim Wethey, 2000.

Mt Cook Alpine Regions. Mavis Davidson & Rod Hewitt. NZAC, (2nd Ed, revised) 1972.

Additions to the Barron Saddle – Mt Brewster Guidebook. By Ross Cullen. NZAC, 1997.

4WD South Island – 107 Off Road Adventures. By Ken Sibly & Mark Wilson. Volume 1 (revised). Shoal Bay Press, 2000.

Other publications that might be useful

Arthur's Pass National Park Mountaineering Guide. By Graeme Kates (4th Ed 1998).

Available from DoC HQ, Arthur's Pass. Also check out: http://members.tripod.com/~Gra_NZ/mg/Mghome.htm

Queenstown Rock & Ice Guide – Summer/Winter. Rock and ice climbing, including Wye Creek. Mountain Works (3rd Ed 1996). Available from Mountain Works, 45 Camp St, Queenstown.

Tramping in the South Island - Arthur's Pass to Mt Cook. By Sven Brabyn & Elise Bryant (revised), 1997.

Wanaka Rock - a climber's guide. Crags up Matukituki Valley - from Hospital Flat to Phoebe Creek & Raspberry Flat roadend. By Wanaka Rockclimbing Club Inc. Available from PO Box 101, Wanaka or The Adventure Centre, 99 Ardmore St, Wanaka.

The following publications are available through the NZAC and in most cases, main libraries. A full list of publications and prices published regularly in *The Climber.* Most titles can be ordered through the Club Headquarters Office in Christchurch.

The Climber. A quarterly magazine covering New Zealand rock and alpine climbing. NZAC. Also available from some bookshops.

Alpine Journal. A yearly publication of the NZAC, covering both rock and alpine climbing. NZAC.

The Mt Aspiring Region. By Allan Uren and Mark Watson. NZAC, 2001.

The Darrans Guide - The Darran and Wick Mountains near Milford Sound. By Murray Judge & Hugh Widdowson. NZAC (1st Ed 1990).

Barron Saddle - Mt Brewster - Haast Pass north to the southern boundary of Mt Cook National Park. By Ross Cullen. NZAC (1st Ed 1993). An update can be found on the NZAC website: www.nzalpine.org.nz/climbing/brew.htm.

Climbing Guide for the Nelson Lakes Region. By Simon Noble. NZAC (1st Ed 1995).

Dunedin Rock - Long Beach, Mihiwaka, Osborne. By Dave Brash. Dave Brash (1998).

Moirs Guide Book (Southern Region) - Trampers guide to Fiordland National Park. By Robin McNeil. Great Southern Lakes Press (6th Ed 1995).

Moirs Guide Book (Northern Section) - Trampers guide from southern Mt Aspiring National Park to the Landsborough River. By Geoff Spearpoint. NZAC (6th Ed 1998).

Port Hills Guide. By Lindsay Main, Published 1998

Contact information, websites & emails

New Zealand Alpine Club: level 6, Manchester Courts, Cnr Manchester and Hereford Sts, PO Box 786, Christchurch. Ph/Fax: +64 3 377 7595. Email: nzac@alpineclub.org.nz.

Just about every link you could possibly want can be found on the New Zealand Alpine Club site: www.nzalpine.org.nz. From this site you can access information about weather, gear, climbing guides, other organizations etc. The NZAC also publishes a quarterly magazine - *The Climber*. To submit material or to subscribe, email: climber@alpineclub.org.nz.

Women Climbing. Was formed to encourage women's participation in climbing and includes beginners, experienced climbers and professional guides and instructors. There are regional branches in Dunedin, Christchurch, Wellington and Auckland. www.nzalpine.org.nz/womenclimbing/index.htm

Canterbury Mountaineering Club: PO Box 2415, Christchurch. www.cmc.net.nz .

NZ Mountain Guides Association: Box 10, Aoraki/Mt Cook or www.nzmga.co.nz

Mapworld: www.mapworld.co.nz

Powerband – a NZ bouldering site: www.powerband.org.nz

The Arthur's Pass Webscape: www.softrock.co.nz/apis/infoind.htm

NZ Area Climbing Guides: www.geocities.com/~nzclimbing/guides/

Weather & conditions

Metphone (pay per minute):
Mountain Forecast General Ph: 0900 99966.
Canterbury High Country Ph: 0900 99926.
Metfax Ph: 0900 77999.
New Zealand Metservice: www.met.co.nz

NZ satellite images: www.oneweather.nzoom.com/index.html

NZ brief mountain forecast: www.met.co.nz/wxbin/mountain

Radio: National Programme. Mountain Forecast: after 4pm News daily. Long Range Forecast (6 day): 12:30pm daily.

Victoria University MetVUW: www.rses.vuw.ac.nz/meteorology

Australian/NZ Situation Maps: www.bom.gov.au/weather/national/charts

Also: www.geog.canterbury.ac.nz

South Island snow stability information: www.avalanche.net.nz

Transport

Intercity Bus services: www.intercitycoach.co.nz
Interisland Ferry and Tranzrail train services: Ph: 0800 802 802
Atomic Shuttles (Chch): www.atomictravel.co.nz. Ph: 03 322 8883

Rock grade comparison table

French	UIAA	USA	Australasian
3	iv/iv+	5.5	10
3+	iv+/v	5.6	12
4	v	5.7	13/14
4+	v+	5.8	15
5	vi-	5.9	16/17
5+	vi	5.10a	18
6a	vi+	5.10b	19
6a+	vii-	5.10c	20
6b	vii	5.10d	20/21
6b+	vii/vii+	5.11a	21
6c	vii+	5.11b	22
6c+	viii-	5.11c	23
7a	viii	5.11d	23/24
7a+	viii+	5.12a	24
7b	viii+/ix-	5.12b	25
7b+	ix-/ix	5.12c	26
7c	ix	5.12d	27
7c+	ix+	5.13a	28
8a	x-	5.13b	29
8a+	x	5.13c	30
8b	x/x+	5.13d	31
8b+	x+	5.14a	32
8c	xi-	5.14b	33
8c+	xi	5.14c	34
9a	xi/xi+	5.14d	35
9a+	xi+	5.15a	36

(source: rockfax.com)

Route Index

Sections are marked in bold. Please note this index lists named routes only, it is not intended to be a complete list of climbing routes in the Aoraki/Mount Cook region.

283